Deducibility and Decidability

Geoffrey —
For amusement only.
Rorty.

Deducibility and Decidability

R. R. Rockingham Gill

ROUTLEDGE
London and New York

First published 1990
by Routledge
11 New Fetter Lane, London EC4P 4EE

Simultaneously published in the USA and Canada
by Routledge
a division of Routledge, Chapman and Hall, Inc.
29 West 35th Street, New York, NY 10001

Typeset by Stephen Ashworth Typesetting, Oxford
Typeset at Oxford University Computing Service
Printed in Great Britain by
TJ Press (Padstow) Ltd, Padstow, Cornwall

British Library Cataloguing in Publication Data

Gill, R. R. Rockingham
Deducibility and decidability.
1. Mathematical logic
I. Title
511.3
ISBN 0-415-00033-5

Library of Congress Cataloging in Publication Data

Gill, R. R. Rockingham,
Deducibility and dedicability / R. R. Rockingham Gill.
p. cm.
Includes bibliographical references.
ISBN 0-415-00033-5
1. Logic, Symbolic and mathematical. 2. Decidability (Mathematical logic) I. Title.
BC135.G495 1990 89-27524
160–dc20

Table of Contents

Preface

This little book would have borne the sub-title 'An Exposition of the Theory of Kurt Gödel', had I thought of it before Mostowski did. Exposition is, by Locke's description, the regular and methodical disposition of truths, and laying them in a clear and fit order, to make their connexion and force be plainly and easily perceived; and so demands, each time it is freshly done, small departures from the 'order of truths' that has prevailed.

In this case, the main expository innovation is the unification, provided by the notion of Σ-provability, of the theory of effectiveness and the theory of truth: here we find an immediate and satisfying grounding of effectiveness in the semantics of the existential quantifier, and so are enabled to bypass entirely the graceless aridities associated with recursive functions, Turing machines, Markov algorithms, etc. I have taken the space vacated to deal more expansively than is ordinarily done with recursive definitions and the standard techniques for converting them into 'explicit'—curious word!—ones: the central role that these ideas play in the drama is not often expressly recognized. It has also seemed sensible to expand on diagonalization: usually nipped over in a few lines, the gesticulating at ancient paradoxes, the breathless retailing of decorative *curiosa* concerning liars, barbers and hangmen, only contribute to the overwhelming suspicion that the wool is being pulled over one's eyes.

Otherwise, the book is conceived in a spirit of conceptual minimalism. It is the deposit of some years' teaching a third-level course in mathematical logic to students of philosophy who are at home in the predicate calculus (i.e. the material surveyed in the terminological appendix). I have shortened it by substituting allusions to other people's writings for certain explanations and discussions that seem tangential: things that would be explicated verbally in the classroom, as necessary to prevent misunderstandings or reveal un-noticed connexions. I have also not put in any problems: this is I think on the whole a bad idea, but mine seemed banal and derivative, and the discipline involved in doing other people's problems, translating from one terminology to another, is in any case very valuable.

Mathematical logic does not have the cachet it once enjoyed amongst philosophers; yet the work of Gödel and Tarski, undoubtedly its finest flower, has actually attained *cultural* significance; that is why it is still necessary to give as clear and straightforward an account as possible of the complex argument grounding the startling phenomena. To mathematicians, of course, it needs no defence: it is more mathematics.

I am deeply indebted to Stephen Ashworth for his meticulous setting of a complex document. For partially defraying clerical and typesetting costs I am grateful to the Pantyfedwen Fund and the Research Committee of my college.

Lampeter, Dyfed
June, 1989

R. R. R. G.

I
The Natural Numbers and their Conventional Ordering

I.1 The system of natural numbers, as ordered by the predicate[1] '*mn.m* is less than *n*', has the following properties (amongst others):
—the ordering is *transitive*: for any natural numbers *k*, *l*, *m*, if *k* is less than *l*, and *l* than *m*, then *k* is less than *m*;
—the ordering is *connected*: for any natural numbers *m*, *n*, either *m* is less than *n*, or *m* is the same as *n*, or *n* is less than *m*;
—the ordering is *irreflexive*: no natural number is less than itself;
—there is a *least* natural number—that is, a natural number than which none is less;
—every natural number has a *successor*: for every natural number *m*, there is a natural number *n* such that *m* is less than *n* but there is no natural number between *m* and *n*.

We shall now consider a set of sentence-forms that these five sentences standardly fit: we have assumed (see A.5) that x, y, z are distinct variables, and that L is the first binary predicate-letter; for any expressions *e*, *f* of the formal language, we write $\ulcorner e < f \urcorner$ instead of $\ulcorner \mathrm{L}ef \urcorner$.[2] Then **S** is the set whose members are the following five sentence-forms

$$\forall x.\forall y.\forall z.(x < y \supset y < z \supset x < z)$$
$$\forall x.\forall y.(x < y \vee x = y \vee y < x)$$
$$\sim \exists x.x < x$$
$$\exists x.\sim \exists y.y < x$$
$$\forall x.\exists y.(x < y \wedge \sim \exists z.(x < z \wedge z < y))$$

[1] Unexplained technical words, and ordinary words in technical use, are normally defined elsewhere in the book, usually in the appendix; consult the index first.

[2] The 'corners' are explained in *Quine 1951*, §6.

Before going on, we need some standard abbreviations. First, we write 'σ' for '$x.\iota y.(x<y \wedge \sim\exists z.(x<z \wedge z<y))$', so that σ is a singulary descriptor-form; and, for any expression e, we write $\ulcorner e' \urcorner$ in place of $\ulcorner \sigma[e] \urcorner$. Next, we introduce the concept of a *formal numeral*, as follows:

—the *formal numeral for* 0 is the subject-form $\iota x.\sim\exists y.y<x$;
—if the *formal numeral for* a natural number n is the subject-form s, then the *formal numeral for* $n+1$ is s'.

And, for any number n, we write $\ulcorner \bar{n} \urcorner$ in place of $\ulcorner$the formal numeral for $n\urcorner$. (Thus, for any number n, $\overline{n+1}$ is $\bar{n}'$, which is $\sigma[\bar{n}]$, which is the subject-form $\iota y.(\bar{n}<y \wedge \sim\exists z.(\bar{n}<z \wedge z<y))$.) Finally, we shall make incessant use of the notion of *bounded quantification*: for any variable α and expressions s and M, we write

$\ulcorner \forall\alpha<s.M \urcorner$ for $\ulcorner \forall\alpha.(\alpha<s \supset M) \urcorner$,
$\ulcorner \exists\alpha<s.M \urcorner$ for $\ulcorner \exists\alpha.(\alpha<s \wedge M) \urcorner$,
$\ulcorner \exists_1\alpha<s.M \urcorner$ for $\ulcorner \exists\beta<s.(M^{\alpha}_{\beta} \wedge \sim\exists\alpha<s.(M \wedge \alpha\neq\beta)) \urcorner$, and
$\ulcorner \iota\alpha<s.M \urcorner$ for $\ulcorner \iota\alpha.((\exists_1\alpha<s.M \wedge \alpha<s \wedge M) \vee (\sim\exists_1\alpha<s.M \wedge \alpha=\bar{0})) \urcorner$,

β being the first variable different from α that doesn't occur in M or s.

It is now simple to establish

THEOREM I.1.1. *If s is a subject-form and P a singulary predicate-form, then*

$$\vdash (\forall x<s.P[x] \equiv \forall x.(x<s \supset P[x]))$$
$$\vdash (\exists x<s.P[x] \equiv \exists x.(x<s \wedge P[x]))$$
$$\vdash (\exists_1 x<s.P[x] \equiv \exists_1 x.(x<s \wedge P[x]))$$
$$\exists_1 x<s.P[x] \vdash \iota x<s.P[x] = \iota x.(x<s \wedge P[x])$$
$$\sim\exists_1 x<s.P[x] \vdash \iota x<s.P[x] = \bar{0}.$$

I.2 Amongst the sentence-forms that are formally deducible from **S** are the following:

$$\exists_1 x.\sim\exists y.y<x$$
$$\forall x.\exists_1 y.(x<y \wedge \sim\exists z<y.x<z)$$
$$\forall x.(x=\bar{0} \vee \bar{0}<x)$$
$$\forall x.\forall y.(x=y \equiv \sim(x<y \vee y<x))$$
$$\forall x.\forall y.(x<y \equiv \sim(x=y \vee y<x))$$
$$\forall x.\forall y.(x<y' \equiv \sim y<x)$$
$$\forall x.\forall y.(x'<y \equiv \exists z<y.x<z).$$

Less easy to prove is the following result:

THEOREM I.2.1 *If S is an extension of* **S**, *P a singulary predicate-form, and m a natural number, then*
— $S \vdash \exists x < \bar{m}.P[x]$ *if, for some number n less than m,* $S \vdash P[\bar{n}]$;
— $S \vdash \forall x < \bar{m}.P[x]$ *if, for every number n less than m,* $S \vdash P[\bar{n}]$.

PROOF. We shall only prove the first, using mathematical induction. To this end, let θ be the following English predicate

⌜m.m is a number such that $S \vdash \exists x < \bar{m}.P[x]$ if, for some number n less than m, $S \vdash P[\bar{n}]$⌝.

We shall show that θ is true of the least natural number 0, and is true of the successor of any number of which it is true; as θ is 'determinate', it follows that it is true of every number.

Lemma 1. θ is true of 0

Proof. Were it not, it would be the case that $\exists x < \bar{0}.P[x]$ is not formally deducible from S although, for some number n less than 0, $P[\bar{n}]$ is; that is impossible, as there is no number less than 0.

Lemma 2. θ is true of the successor of any number of which it is true

Proof. Suppose θ is true of a number m. First, if n is less than m and $S \vdash P[\bar{n}]$, then—as θ is true of m—$S \vdash \exists x < \bar{m}.P[x]$, and so $S \vdash \exists x.(x < \bar{m} \wedge P[x])$. Second, if n is the same as m and $S \vdash P[\bar{n}]$, then—as $\bar{n}$ is in this case the same formal numeral as $\bar{m}$—$S \vdash \exists x.(x = \bar{m} \wedge P[x])$. Consequently, if n is less than $m+1$ and $S \vdash P[\bar{n}]$, then $S \vdash (\exists x.(x < \bar{m} \wedge P[x]) \vee \exists x.(x = \bar{m} \wedge P[x]))$, and so $S \vdash \exists x.((x < \bar{m} \vee x = \bar{m}) \wedge P[x])$, whence $S \vdash \exists x < \overline{m+1}.P[x]$ (as $S \vdash \forall x.((x < \bar{m} \vee x = \bar{m}) \supset x < \overline{m+1}))$.

Thus $S \vdash \exists x < \overline{m+1}.P[x]$ if, for some number n less than $m+1$, $S \vdash P[\bar{n}]$; and so θ is true of $m+1$.

It follows from the two lemmata—θ being 'determinate'—that θ is true of every number, and consequently that for every number m $S \vdash \exists x < \bar{m}.P[x]$ if, for some number n less than m, $S \vdash P[\bar{n}]$.

Q.E.D.

Mathematical induction, as a 'method of proof', is ubiquitous in both elementary arithmetic and metamathematics and *a fortiori* in the metamathematics of formal elementary arithmetic. We use it in the following form: *a 'determinate' predicate that is true of 0 and is true of the successor of every number of which it is true, is true of every number.*

Suppose, for example, one wishes to show that every number is either even (divisible by 2 with remainder 0) or odd (divisible by 2 with remainder 1); one considers the predicate

'm.m is a number that is either even or odd'

observes that it is true of 0 (because 0 is even) and is true of the successor of any number of which it is true (because $m+1$ is odd if m is even and even if m is odd), and concludes—since it is 'determinate'—that it is true of every number.

The use of predicates that are not 'determinate' leads to well-known paradoxes: one such is the predicate '$m.m$ is a small number', which is certainly true of the first few numbers, apparently true of the successor of any number of which it is true, yet certainly not true of large numbers; another is Berry's predicate, '$m.m$ is an integer nameable in fewer than nineteen syllables', for which see *Russell 1908*, p. 60. An 'extensional' formulation of induction—perhaps in the form: *a set that contains 0 and contains the successor of every number that it contains, contains every number*—merely disguises the reliance upon 'determinacy': and the best comment on such a manoeuvre is that of Uncle Remus—'Youk'n hide de fier, but w'at you gwine do wid de smoke?'. Dedekind thus avoids the issue when he says that "a system S ... is completely determined when with respect to every thing it is determined whether it is an element of S or not" in §2 of *The Nature and Meaning of Numbers*; Frege is bolder in §27 of *Conceptual Notation*. For contemporary discussion, see *Dummett 1975* and *Wright 1982*.

Using Theorem I.2.1 and the results preceding it, we deduce the next theorem, which tells us that, for example, the sentence-forms $\overline{17}<\overline{50}$ and $\overline{13}\neq\overline{144}$ are formally deducible from **S**:

THEOREM I.2.2. *Suppose m and n are natural numbers; then*

— $\mathbf{S} \vdash \bar{m}=\bar{n}$ *if m is the same as n;*
— $\mathbf{S} \vdash \bar{m}<\bar{n}$ *if m is less than n;*
— $\mathbf{S} \vdash \bar{m}\neq\bar{n}$ *if m is not the same as n;*
— $\mathbf{S} \vdash \sim\bar{m}<\bar{n}$ *if m is not less than n.*

PROOF. 1) If m is the same as n, $\bar{m}$ is the same formal numeral as $\bar{n}$, and so $\vdash \bar{m}=\bar{n}$, whence $\mathbf{S} \vdash \bar{m}=\bar{n}$; 2) If m is less than n, then for some natural number k less than n m is the same as k, whence (by 1) $\mathbf{S} \vdash \bar{m}=\bar{k}$; hence (by Theorem I.2.1) $\mathbf{S} \vdash \exists x<\bar{n}.\bar{m}=x$ and so $\mathbf{S} \vdash \exists x.(\bar{m}=x \wedge x<\bar{n})$, whence $\mathbf{S} \vdash \bar{m}<\bar{n}$; 3) If m is not the same as n, then m is less than n or *vice versa* and so (by 2) $\mathbf{S} \vdash (\bar{m}<\bar{n} \vee \bar{n}<\bar{m})$, whence $\mathbf{S} \vdash \bar{m}\neq\bar{n}$; 4) If m is not less than n, then n is less than $m+1$ and so (by 2) $\mathbf{S} \vdash \bar{n}<\overline{m+1}$ whence $\mathbf{S} \vdash \sim\bar{m}<\bar{n}$.

Q.E.D.

The past few pages have given some impression of the strength of **S**, but we must not run away with the idea that *every* relevant form that is standardly assigned 𝕋 is formally deducible from it: $\sim\exists x.(x \neq \bar{0} \wedge \forall y < x. y' < x)$ is an example of one that isn't.

That this form is standardly assigned 𝕋 is obvious since there is no number, different from the least number, the successor of any number less than which is also less than it. To see that the form is not formally deducible from **S** we consider a non-standard assignment that is a model of **S** but not of it—that is, the forms in **S** are all 'non-standardly' assigned 𝕋, but it itself is not: the conclusion then follows using well-known properties of formal deducibility (cf. Theorem A.10.3). This model of **S**—*A*, say—is to differ from the standard ones only in that it assigns to L the extension of

'*mn*. either *m* and *n* are both odd, and *m* is less than *n*; or *m* is odd and *n* is even; or *m* and *n* are both even, and *m* is less than *n*'.

The members of the universe are therefore ordered as follows

$$1, 3, 5, 7, 9, \ldots \quad \ldots \quad 0, 2, 4, 6, 8, \ldots$$

and that *A is* a model of **S** follows from the fact that the ordering is transitive, connected and irreflexive, there is a 'least' member (viz. 1), and each member has a 'successor' (that of *m* being $m+2$); but *A* is not a model of the form under discussion, because there *is* a member, different from the 'least' member, the 'successor' of any member 'less' than which is also 'less' than it—viz. 0.

I.3 What we had hoped, of course, was that **S** would be strong enough for all relevant forms that are standardly assigned 𝕋 to be formally deducible from it. That it is not *too* strong, not strong enough for any such form that is *not* standardly assigned 𝕋 to be formally deducible from it, follows from Theorem A.10.3 and the fact that all five forms in it are standardly assigned 𝕋. So, in the terminology of A.10, **S** is sound but not complete—and the question naturally arises whether *any* set (of forms relevant to **S**) is both sound and complete.

The positive answer to this question is exemplified by the set $\mathbf{S}^+$, whose members are the five forms in **S** plus the rogue form $\sim\exists x.(x \neq \bar{0} \wedge \forall y < x. y' < x)$. That it is sound is obvious and that it is complete was proved by Langford (*Langford*; cf. *Tarski 1936a*, §5).

S is incomplete because it has a model that is radically non-standard; by contrast, $\mathbf{S}^+$ is complete *despite* having such a model. For an example, consider *B*, which is to differ from the standard ones only in that it assigns to L the extension of

'*mn*. either $m \simeq 2$ and $n \simeq 1$; or $m \simeq 2$ and $n \simeq 2$ and $m < n$;
or $m \simeq 2$ and $n \simeq 0$; or $m \simeq 1$ and $n \simeq 1$ and $m > n$;
or $m \simeq 1$ and $n \simeq 0$; or $m \simeq 0$ and $n \simeq 0$ and $m < n$'

(we are writing $\ulcorner m \simeq n \urcorner$ in place of $\ulcorner m$ is divisible by 3 with remainder $n \urcorner$). The members of its universe are ordered as follows

$$2, 5, 8, 11, \ldots \quad \ldots \quad \ldots 10, 7, 4, 1, 0, 3, 6, 9, \ldots$$

and it is certainly a model of **S**, for the ordering is transitive, connected and irreflexive, there is a 'least' member (viz. 2), and each member has a 'successor'. But furthermore each member is either the 'least' one or else the 'successor' of another: so it is a model of $\mathbf{S}^+$.

What *is* true, because of the completeness of $\mathbf{S}^+$, is that all its models, standard and non-standard alike, are 'elementarily equivalent': that is, they agree on all relevant sentence-forms—all assign $\mathbb{T}$ to any such form to which any does. So the non-standardness of *B* is not to be expressed in the way that of *A* was, by saying that it assigns $\mathbb{T}$ to a form that is not standardly assigned $\mathbb{T}$: for *B* assigns $\mathbb{T}$ to no such form. Rather, its non-standardness is to be expressed by saying that while it is true that

for any number *m*, there are only finitely many numbers *n* such that $\langle n, m \rangle$ is a member of what L is standardly assigned

it is false that

for any number *m*, there are only finitely many numbers *n* such that $\langle n, m \rangle$ is a member of what *B* assigns to L.

This entails that the English quantifier 'there are only finitely many' cannot be defined in the formal language in the way that the English quantifier 'there are only seven' can be (cf. *Beth*, pp. 334–5).

For an example of a model of $\mathbf{S}^+$ that, though non-standard, is as little so as mathematically possible, consider one with universe the set of finite ordinals that assigns to L the extension of

'*mn*.*m* is a member of (the finite ordinal) *n*'

(the *finite ordinals* are defined recursively as being the empty set, $\emptyset$, and, for each finite ordinal *m* the set $m \cup \{m\}$, so that they are

$$\emptyset \ , \ \{\emptyset\} \ , \ \{\emptyset, \{\emptyset\}\} \ , \ \{\emptyset, \{\emptyset\}, \{\emptyset, \{\emptyset\}\}\} \ , \ \ldots).$$

Such a model is not *mathematically* distinguishable from a standard model at all: the two are not merely elementarily equivalent, but even 'isomorphic'. To express the difference between them one has to say something like '17 is a natural number, not a finite ordinal', for the difference is one of the nature—the essence—of the members of the respective universes. Whether such a sentence really says anything, whether the difference between the two models is really expressible, whether indeed there really is a difference between them, are disputed problems—for discussion, see *Wittgenstein 1921*, 4.127–4.12721, *Ryle 1949* ch. 1 and *Benacerraf.*

II
Addition, Multiplication and Exponentiation

II.1 The fact that $\mathbf{S}^+$ is both sound and complete shows that the first-order truths involving only the concepts *natural number* and *less than* can be 'axiomatized': they can be shown all to follow logically from a small finite set of such truths—and indeed follow logically by means of inferences involving only the devices of first-order predicate logic.

But there are more arithmetical concepts than just these two—there are also, for example, the concepts *sum of*, *product of* and *power of*; so the question arises whether the first-order truths involving also these concepts can be axiomatized—not necessarily in exactly the same fashion, but at least in some similar fashion. One wild hope might be that they are already so axiomatized, but implicitly, as are the truths involving the concept *greater than* (which is definable in terms of *less than*). But it is not so, and the consequence is that we are forced to go beyond the concept *less than* to answer the question.

We have assumed (cf. A.5) that a, m, and e are the first, second and third binary descriptor-letters; for any expressions f, g we write

$$\ulcorner(f+g)\urcorner \qquad \ulcorner(f\times g)\urcorner \qquad \ulcorner(f^{g})\urcorner$$

in place of

$$\ulcorner \mathrm{a}fg \urcorner \qquad \ulcorner \mathrm{m}fg \urcorner \qquad \ulcorner \mathrm{e}fg \urcorner$$

Now we shall say that a predicate-form P *represents* an English predicate θ if, and only if, the only non-logical letters that occur in P are amongst $\mathrm{L}, \mathrm{a}, \mathrm{m}, \mathrm{e}$ and what P is standardly assigned is the extension of θ. Where the only non-logical letters that occur in P are members of a subset of $\{\mathrm{L}, \mathrm{a}, \mathrm{m}, \mathrm{e}\}$ we sometimes say, more precisely, that P *represents* θ *in terms of* the members of that subset.

Thus, for example,

— $xy.y<x$ represents '*mn.m* is greater than *n*' in terms of L;
— $xy.\exists z.(z \neq (z+z) \wedge x=(y+z))$ represents '*mn.m* is greater than *n*' in terms of a;
— $x.\exists y.x=(y+y)$ represents '*n.n* is an even number' in terms of a;
— $x.\exists y.x=(y \times \bar{2})$ represents '*n.n* is an even number' in terms of L, m;
— $x.\sim\exists y<x.\exists z<x.x=(y \times z)$ represents '*n.n* is a prime number' in terms of L, m;
— $xy.\exists z.y=(x^z)$ represents '*mn.m* is a root of *n*' in terms of e.

Note that representability is a wholly 'extensional' notion—any two co-extensive predicates are represented by the same predicate-forms; since to say that two predicates are co-extensive, have the same extension, is *not* to say that they have the same meaning, representability is only a distant cousin of definability, if a definition is taken to be a statement of meaning.

Now the predicate '*mnp.* the sum of *m* and *n* is *p*' is not representable in terms of L (though of course it is representable in terms of a—by $xyz.(x+y)=z$—and also in terms of L, m, e—by $xyz.((\bar{2}^x) \times (\bar{2}^y))=(\bar{2}^z)$): this is a corollary of Langford's result (cf. I.3 and *Enderton*, pp. 184–7), which entails that the only singulary predicates that are representable in terms of L alone are those that are either true only of finitely many numbers or false only of finitely many numbers. These predicates, for example,

'*m.* the sum of some number and 0 is *m*'
'*m.* the sum of some number and 1 is *m*'
'*m.* the sum of some number and 2 is *m*'
⋮

are all false only of finitely many numbers, and are obviously representable in terms of L, by

$$x.\exists y.y=x \qquad x.\exists y.y'=x \qquad x.\exists y.y''=x \qquad \ldots$$

But the predicate

'*m.* the sum of some number and itself is *m*'

is neither true only of finitely many numbers (for it is true of 0, 2, 4, 6, 8, ...) nor false only of finitely many numbers (for it is false of 1, 3, 5, 7, 9, ...), and is not representable in terms of L.

It has also been established that '*mnp.* the product of *m* and *n* is *p*' is not representable in terms of L and a. By contrast, it is an interesting result that '*mnp.* the nth power of *m* is *p*' *is* representable in terms of a and m: this is a special case of Theorem VII of *Gödel 1931*.

II.2 So what predicates are representable—in terms of L, a, m and e, that is? Those we have already seen to be representable were easily seen to be so; but not all are like this: certain predicates may turn out to be representable as it were by accident, for no logico-mathematical reason, such as

'*mn.m* is the number of women in America in the year *n* A.D.'

(if it turns out that from the year 3095 A.D. onward there are no women in America, the predicate will be represented by

$$\mathrm{xy}.((\mathrm{x}=\overline{0} \wedge \mathrm{y}=\overline{m_0}) \vee (\mathrm{x}=\overline{1} \wedge \mathrm{y}=\overline{m_1}) \vee \ldots \vee (\mathrm{x}=\overline{3094} \wedge \mathrm{y}=\overline{m_{3094}}))$$

where $m_0, m_1, \ldots, m_{3094}$ are respectively the numbers of women in America in the years $0, 1, \ldots, 3094$ A.D.); other predicates, which certainly look as if they ought to be representable, and not by accident, are not easily seen to be so, such as

'*mn.n* is $(m+1)!$'

(for any non-zero number m, $m!$ is the product of all the non-zero numbers less than $m+1$, each taken once only)—it is a useful exercise to see if one can find a representation of it.

Then again there are certain predicates that quite unexpectedly and for no easily understood reason, turn out not to be representable. One such might be called 'Cantor's diagonal predicate', in honour of his essentially similar use of such a predicate to demonstrate the uncountability of the continuum (*Hallett*, p. 77): we have assumed (cf. A.5) that the expressions, the finite sequences of letters of the formal language, can be enumerated as the first, the second, the third, etc.; now consider the singular predicate θ

'*n*. no singular predicate is both represented by the nth expression and true of *n*'.

This appears to be a perfectly ordinary predicate; thus, if the third, eighth and nineteenth expressions happen to be $\mathrm{x}.\exists\mathrm{y}.(\mathrm{y}+\mathrm{y})=\mathrm{x}$, $\mathrm{x}.\exists\mathrm{y}.\mathrm{x}=(\mathrm{y}^{\overline{3}})$ and $\mathrm{x}.\forall\mathrm{y}<\mathrm{x}.(\overline{2}\times\mathrm{y})<\mathrm{x}$, then θ is true of 3, false of 8 and true of 19—because 3 is not a member of $|\mathrm{x}.\exists\mathrm{y}.(\mathrm{y}+\mathrm{y})=\mathrm{x}|$, 8 is one of $|\mathrm{x}.\exists\mathrm{y}.\mathrm{x}=(\mathrm{y}^{\overline{3}})|$ and 19 is not one of $|\mathrm{x}.\forall\mathrm{y}<\mathrm{x}.(\overline{2}\times\mathrm{y})<\mathrm{x}|$. But θ is not representable—for, if it were, say by the kth expression, it would be the case that θ is true of k iff[1] no singular predicate is both represented by the kth expression and true of k, which is the case iff no singular predicate is both co-extensive with θ and true of k, which is the case iff θ is not true of k: that is, it would be the case that θ is true of k iff θ is not true of k, which is impossible.

[1] i.e. if, and only if,

These considerations make it clear that the problem posed at the beginning of the section is not easy: in IV.2 we shall see a *partial* answer proposed, one that is obtained by connecting the concept of representability with another, that of effectiveness.

II.3 It is convenient to introduce at this point a taxonomy of sentence-forms based upon the 'unifying notation' of Smullyan (see *Smullyan 1968*): the clarity and elegance of his technique lead to enormous simplification in the presentation of later results.

Thus let us say that i, U, V *are related in Smullyan's fashion* if, and only if, for some sentence-forms Y and Z, some singulary predicate-forms P and Q, some variable a such that a is the prefix of P and occurs freely in $Q[a]$, some subject-form s, some numbers m and n such that n is less than $m + 1$, and some numbers p and q; i, U, V are as in the following table—

i	U	V
0	$Q[(\bar{p}+\bar{q})]$	$Q[\overline{p+q}]$
0	$Q[(\bar{p}\times\bar{q})]$	$Q[\overline{p\times q}]$
0	$Q[(\bar{p}^{\bar{q}})]$	$Q[\overline{p^q}]$
0	$\exists a<\bar{0}.P[a]$	$\bar{0}\neq\bar{0}$
0	$\forall a<\bar{0}.P[a]$	$\bar{0}=\bar{0}$
0	$Q[\imath a<s.P[a]]$	$\left(\begin{array}{c}(\exists_1 a<s.P[a] \wedge \forall a<s.(P[a]\supset Q[a])) \\ \vee\,(\sim\exists_1 a<s.P[a] \wedge Q[\bar{0}])\end{array}\right)$
0	$\sim\sim Y$	Y
0	$\sim(Y\vee Z)$	$(\sim Y \wedge \sim Z)$
0	$\sim(Y\wedge Z)$	$(\sim Y \vee \sim Z)$
0	$\sim\exists a<\bar{m}.P[a]$	$\forall a<\bar{m}.\sim P[a]$
0	$\sim\forall a<\bar{m}.P[a]$	$\exists a<\bar{m}.\sim P[a]$
0	$\sim\exists a.P[a]$	$\forall a.\sim P[a]$
0	$\sim\forall a.P[a]$	$\exists a.\sim P[a]$
1	$(Y\vee Z)$	Y
1	$(Y\vee Z)$	Z
1	$\exists a<\overline{m+1}.P[a]$	$P[\bar{n}]$
2	$(Y\wedge Z)$	Y
2	$(Y\wedge Z)$	Z
2	$\forall a<\overline{m+1}.P[a]$	$P[\bar{n}]$
3	$\exists a.P[a]$	$P[\bar{n}]$
4	$\forall a.P[a]$	$P[\bar{n}]$

The *indices of* a sentence-form U are those numbers i such that i, U, V are related in Smullyan's fashion, for some V. If a sentence-form has no indices, it is *of type* **B** if, and only if, it is one of

$$\bar{m}=\bar{n} \qquad \bar{m}\neq\bar{n} \qquad \bar{m}<\bar{n} \qquad \sim\bar{m}<\bar{n}$$

for some numbers m and n; if it has indices, it is *of type* **R**, ∨, ∧, ∃, or ∀ according as its lowest index is 0, 1, 2, 3, or 4; the only *types* are **B**, **R**, ∨, ∧, ∃ and ∀ ('**B**' for 'basic'; '**R**' for 'reducible'). If a form U is of type **B**, it has no *immediate descendants*; if it is of type **R**, its only *immediate descendant* is the first sentence-form V such that $0, U, V$ are related in Smullyan's fashion; if it is type ∨, ∧, ∃ or ∀, its *immediate descendants* are those sentence-forms V such that i, U, V are related in Smullyan's fashion, i being its lowest index. Examples:

— $\bar{2}\neq\bar{3}$ and $\bar{3}<\bar{2}$ have no indices and are of type **B**;

— $(\bar{0}=\bar{3} \wedge \bar{2}=(\bar{1}+\bar{1}))$ has two indices, 0 and 2; so it's of type **R** and its immediate descendant is $(\bar{0}=\bar{3} \wedge \bar{2}=\bar{2})$;

— $\sim(\bar{0}=\bar{3} \wedge \bar{2}=(\bar{1}+\bar{1}))$ has only one index, 0; so it's of type **R** and its immediate descendant is the first of $(\bar{0}\neq\bar{3} \vee \bar{2}\neq(\bar{1}+\bar{1}))$ and $\sim(\bar{0}=\bar{3} \wedge \bar{2}=\bar{2})$;

— $\forall y.(y^{\bar{2}})<(y\times \imath x<\bar{3}.(x\times x)=x)$ has two indices, 0 and 4; so it's of type **R** and its immediate descendant is

$$\left(\begin{array}{c}(\exists_1 x<\bar{3}.(x\times x)=x \wedge \forall x<\bar{3}.((x\times x)=x \supset \forall y.(y^{\bar{2}})<(y\times x))) \\ \vee\, (\sim\exists_1 x<\bar{3}.(x\times x)=x \wedge \forall y.(y^{\bar{2}})<(y\times\bar{0}))\end{array}\right);$$

— $\exists y<\bar{3}.y=\bar{2}$ has two indices, 1 and 3 (because it is the same form as $\exists y.(y<\bar{3} \wedge y=\bar{2})$); so it's of type ∨ and its immediate descendants are $\bar{0}=\bar{2}$, $\bar{1}=\bar{2}$ and $\bar{2}=\bar{2}$;

— $(\bar{4}<\bar{0} \wedge \bar{0}<\bar{4})$ has only one index, 2; so it's of type ∧ and its immediate descendants are $\bar{4}<\bar{0}$ and $\bar{0}<\bar{4}$;

— $\forall y.\forall z.(y^z)<(y\times z)$ has only one index, 4; so it's of type ∀ and its immediate descendants are $\forall z.(\bar{0}^z)<(\bar{0}\times z)$, $\forall z.(\bar{1}^z)<(\bar{1}\times z)$, $\forall z.(\bar{2}^z)<(\bar{2}\times z)$, … ;

— $\bar{1}=\imath x.(x\times x)<(x+x)$ has no indices and is not of type **B**; so it's of no type and has no immediate descendants.

Notice that sentence-forms of type **R** have exactly one immediate descendant: those of type ∨ or ∧ have only finitely many; and those of type ∃ or ∀ have infinitely many. We have:

THEOREM II.3.1. *A form*

— *of type* **R** *is standardly assigned* $\mathbb{T}$ *iff its immediate descendant is;*

— *of type* ∨ *or* ∃ *is standardly assigned* $\mathbb{T}$ *iff at least one of its immediate descendants is;*

— *of type* ∧ *or* ∀ *is standardly assigned* $\mathbb{T}$ *iff every one of its immediate descendants is.*

A *descendance-chain for* a form is a sequence of forms each term of which, save the first, is an immediate descendant of its predecessor. Can such a chain be infinite—that is, can we go on indefinitely taking immediate descendants of immediate descendants of immediate ... descendants of a form? It is clear that we can't; we shall not prove this in detail, but merely state it officially as

THEOREM II.3.2. *All descendance-chains are finite; furthermore, there is a uniform effective procedure for associating with each sentence-form a number that is the maximum of the lengths of its descendance-chains.*

Thus consider the form $\forall x.(\forall y.y<(x^y) \supset \exists y.\forall z.(z\times x)=(y+x))$ —it is clear that each of its descendance-chains has to be, for some numbers m,n,p, an initial segment of one or the other of the two branches of this tree:

$$\forall x.(\forall y.y<(x^y) \supset \exists y.\forall z.(z\times x)=(y+x))$$

$$(\forall y.y<(\bar{m}^y) \supset \exists y.\forall z.(z\times \bar{m})=(y+\bar{m}))$$

$$\begin{array}{ll} \sim\forall y.y<(\bar{m}^y) & \exists y.\forall z.(z\times\bar{m})=(y+\bar{m}) \\ \exists y.\sim y<(\bar{m}^y) & \forall z.(z\times\bar{m})=(\bar{n}+\bar{m}) \\ \sim\bar{n}<(\bar{m}^{\bar{n}}) & \forall z.(z\times\bar{m})=\overline{n+m} \\ \sim\bar{n}<\overline{m^n} & (\bar{p}\times\bar{m})=\overline{n+m} \\ & \overline{p\times m}=\overline{n+m} \end{array}$$

Hence all its descendance-chains are finite, and their maximal length is 7.

The maximal length of the descendance-chains for a sentence-form is its *degree*; the terms of a descendance-chain for it are its *descendants* (so it is a descendant of itself); and a sentence-form is *grounded* if, and only if, each of its descendants is of some type (although $\forall y.(y=\bar{0} \supset y=\iota x.x=\bar{0})$ is of degree 3, it is not grounded because $\bar{0}=\iota x.x=\bar{0}$ is a descendant of it that is of no type).

THEOREM II.3.3. *A 'determinate' predicate that is true of all forms of type* B, *and true of any grounded form if it is true of all its immediate descendants, is true of every grounded form.*

PROOF. Suppose θ is such a predicate, and let η be
⌜$n.\theta$ is true of every grounded form of degree less than $n+2$⌝.
Then η is 'determinate', is true of 0, and is true of the successor of any number of which it is true. So η is true of every number, and thus θ is true of every grounded form.

Q.E.D.

It is worth observing that there is a uniform effective procedure for associating with each grounded form X another Υ such that (a) $\imath$ does not occur in Υ; (b) the same non-logical letters occur in both; and (c) $\mathbf{S} \vdash (X \equiv \Upsilon)$—for example,

$$\mathbf{S} \vdash (\exists x.(x^{\bar{2}}) = \bar{3} \equiv \forall y.(\exists_2 x.x < y \supset \forall z.(\exists_3 x.x < z \supset \exists x.(x^y) = z)));$$

—following Frege's suggestion (*1884*, §§55–6) one dispenses with the formal numerals using the numerical quantifiers defined in A.5: it is easy to see that, for each number n,

$$\mathbf{S} \vdash \forall y.(y = \bar{n} \equiv \exists_n x.x < y).$$

Finally, we have

THEOREM II.3.4. *A set of grounded forms is*

— *sound iff every relevant grounded form that is formally deducible from it is standardly assigned* $\mathbb{T}$*;*

— *complete iff every relevant grounded form that is standardly assigned* $\mathbb{T}$ *is formally deducible from it.*

PROOF. Let S be a set of grounded forms.

If every relevant grounded form that is formally deducible from S is standardly assigned $\mathbb{T}$, then every member of S is standardly assigned $\mathbb{T}$, and so, by theorem A.10.3, *every* form—relevant or not, grounded or not—that is formally deducible from S is standardly assigned $\mathbb{T}$, and thus S is sound.

If every relevant grounded form that is standardly assigned $\mathbb{T}$ is formally deducible from S, then every relevant form in which neither $\imath$ nor $*$ occurs that is standardly assigned $\mathbb{T}$ is formally deducible from S (for all such forms are grounded) and so, by the weakened form of the completeness condition mentioned at the end of A.10, S is complete.

Q.E.D.

II.4 The main question, raised in the second paragraph of II.1, can be put again in this way: is there a reasonable set of grounded forms that is sound and complete? (It can be put in this way provided one accepts that the devices of formal logic adequately codify the inferences of informal logic.) As usual, the concept of reasonableness had best remain unexplained, but one would hope such a set to be finite and small or, if either not finite or not small, then at least *simple* or 'surveyable' (cf. *Wittgenstein 1978*, III.§§1–39).

Three possible such sets play important roles in what follows—we shall refer to them as **R**, **Q** and **P**:

— **R** has as members the five forms in **S**, plus all those infinitely many forms X such that, for some numbers m,n, X is one of

$$(\bar{m}+\bar{n})=\overline{m+n} \qquad (\bar{m}\times\bar{n})=\overline{m\times n} \qquad (\bar{m}^{\bar{n}})=\overline{m^n}$$

Thus $(\bar{2}+\bar{3})=\bar{5}$, $(\bar{4}\times\bar{2})=\bar{8}$ and $(\bar{3}^{\bar{2}})=\bar{9}$ are amongst the members of **R**, but $(\bar{3}\times\bar{2})=\bar{9}$ and $(\bar{3}\times\bar{3})\neq\bar{9}$ are not. **R** is an amended version of the formal arithmetic given on pp. 52–3 of *Mostowski, Robinson & Tarski*; the amendment is described at the end of the next section.

— **Q** has as members the five forms in **S**, plus the following six:

$$\forall x.(x+\bar{0})=x \qquad \forall x.\forall y.(x+y')=(x+y)'$$
$$\forall x.(x\times\bar{0})=\bar{0} \qquad \forall x.\forall y.(x\times y')=((x\times y)+x)$$
$$\forall x.(x^{\bar{0}})=\bar{1} \qquad \forall x.\forall y.(x^{y'})=((x^{y})\times x)$$

It is an amended version of 'Robinson's Arithmetic', described on p. 51 of *Mostowski, Robinson & Tarski*: that it is an extension of **R** is tolerably obvious—to see that $\mathbf{Q}\vdash(\bar{2}+\bar{3})=\bar{5}$, observe that

$$\mathbf{Q}\vdash\left(\begin{array}{c}(\bar{2}+\bar{3})=(\bar{2}+\bar{2})'\wedge(\bar{2}+\bar{2})=(\bar{2}+\bar{1})'\\ \wedge(\bar{2}+\bar{1})=(\bar{2}+\bar{0})'\wedge(\bar{2}+\bar{0})=\bar{2}\end{array}\right)$$

—and is easily proved by mathematical induction.

— **P** has as members the eleven forms in **Q**, plus all those infinitely many grounded forms X such that, for some singulary predicate-form P, X is

$$(P[\bar{0}]\supset\forall x.(P[x]\supset P[x'])\supset\forall P)$$

It is a version of 'Peano's Arithmetic', traditionally so-called despite the facts first that the axioms Peano gave in *1889* were not his but Dedekind's (as he later acknowledged) and second that **P** is only a poor formalization of them (for a better one, see IX.2 *inf.*, note (3)). The restriction to singulary predicate-forms is not significant—suppose, for example, P is a ternary predicate-form, and let Q be

$$x.\forall y.\forall z.(P[\bar{0},y,z]\supset\forall x.(P[x,y,z]\supset P[x',y,z])\supset P[x,y,z]);$$

then

$$\mathbf{P}\vdash(Q[\bar{0}]\supset\forall x.(Q[x]\supset Q[x'])\supset\forall Q)$$

and it is obvious that

$$\vdash Q[\bar{0}] \qquad \text{and} \qquad \vdash\forall x.(Q[x]\supset Q[x'])$$

so that

$$\mathbf{P}\vdash\forall Q$$

and therefore

$$\mathbf{P}\vdash\forall y.\forall z.(P[\bar{0},y,z]\supset\forall x.(P[x,y,z]\supset P[x',y,z])\supset\forall x.P[x,y,z]).$$

The merit of Smullyan's taxonomy is clearly displayed in the simplicity of the statement of the next theorem:

THEOREM II.4.1. *Suppose S is an extension of* **R**; *then a form*

— *of type* R *is formally deducible from S if, and only if, its immediate descendant is;*

— *of type* $\vee$ *is formally deducible from S if at least one of its immediate descendants is;*

— *of type* $\wedge$ *is formally deducible from S if, and only if, every one of its immediate descendants is;*

— *of type* $\exists$ *is formally deducible from S if at least one of its immediate descendants is;*

— *of type* $\forall$ *is formally deducible from S only if every one of its immediate descendants is.*

PROOF. We examine some of the twenty-one separate cases in the table at the beginning of II.3.

Suppose given sentence-forms Y and Z, singulary predicate-forms P and Q, a variable α that is the prefix of P and occurs freely in $Q[\alpha]$, a subject-form s, numbers m and n such that n is less than $m+1$, and numbers p and q; then

— $S \vdash Q[(\bar{p}+\bar{q})]$ if, and only if, $S \vdash Q[\overline{p+q}]$
: since $\mathbf{R} \vdash (\bar{p}+\bar{q})=\overline{p+q}$ and so $S \vdash (Q[(\bar{p}+\bar{q})] \equiv Q[\overline{p+q}])$;

— $S \vdash \exists\alpha<\bar{0}.P[\alpha]$ if, and only if, $S \vdash \bar{0}\neq\bar{0}$
: since $\vdash (\exists\alpha<\bar{0}.P[\alpha] \equiv \exists\alpha.(\alpha<\bar{0} \wedge P[\alpha]))$ and $\mathbf{S} \vdash \sim\exists\alpha.\alpha<\bar{0}$, so that $S \vdash (\exists\alpha<\bar{0}.P[\alpha] \equiv \bar{0}\neq\bar{0})$;

— $S \vdash Q[\iota\alpha<s.P[\alpha]]$ if, and only if, $S \vdash ((\exists_1\alpha<s.P[\alpha] \wedge \forall\alpha<s.(P[\alpha] \supset Q[\alpha])) \vee (\sim\exists_1\alpha<s.P[\alpha] \wedge Q[\bar{0}]))$
: since $\exists_1\alpha<s.P[\alpha] \vdash (Q[\iota\alpha<s.P[\alpha]] \equiv \forall\alpha<s.(P[\alpha] \supset Q[\alpha]))$ and $\sim\exists_1\alpha<s.P[\alpha] \vdash (Q[\iota\alpha<s.P[\alpha]] \equiv Q[\bar{0}])$, because (by Theorem I.1.1) $\exists_1\alpha<s.P[\alpha] \vdash \iota\alpha<s.P[\alpha]=\iota\alpha.(\alpha<s \wedge P[\alpha])$ and $\sim\exists_1\alpha<s.P[\alpha] \vdash \iota\alpha<s.P[\alpha]=\bar{0}$;

— $S \vdash \sim(Y \vee Z)$ if, and only if, $S \vdash (\sim Y \wedge \sim Z)$
: since $\vdash (\sim(Y \vee Z) \equiv (\sim Y \wedge \sim Z))$;

— $S \vdash \sim\forall\alpha<\bar{m}.P[\alpha]$ if, and only if, $S \vdash \exists\alpha<\bar{m}.\sim P[\alpha]$
: since $\vdash (\sim\forall\alpha<\bar{m}.P[\alpha] \equiv \sim\forall\alpha.(\alpha<\bar{m} \supset P[\alpha]))$ and also $\vdash (\exists\alpha.(\alpha<\bar{m} \wedge \sim P[\alpha]) \equiv \exists\alpha<\bar{m}.\sim P[\alpha])$;

— $S \vdash (Y \vee Z)$ if either $S \vdash Y$ or $S \vdash Z$

— $S \vdash \exists\alpha<\overline{m+1}.P[\alpha]$ if, for some number n less than $m+1$, $S \vdash P[\bar{n}]$
: in view of Theorem I.2.1;

— $S \vdash \forall\alpha < \overline{m+1}.P[\alpha]$ if, and only if, for every number n less than $m+1$, $S \vdash P[\bar{n}]$

: in view first of Theorem I.2.1 and second of the fact that, for every number n less than $m+1$, $\mathbf{S} \vdash \bar{n} < \overline{m+1}$ and therefore $\mathbf{S}, \forall\alpha < \overline{m+1}.P[\alpha] \vdash P[\bar{n}]$;

— $S \vdash \exists\alpha.P[\alpha]$ if, for some number n, $S \vdash P[\bar{n}]$

— $S \vdash \forall\alpha.P[\alpha]$ only if, for every number n, $S \vdash P[\bar{n}]$.

The conclusion follows easily.

Q.E.D.

Theorem II.4.1 leaves some obvious questions; to examine them, let us say that a set of grounded forms S *has the* $\vee$*-property* just in case any relevant grounded form of type $\vee$ is formally deducible from S only if at least one of its immediate descendants is; *has the* $\exists$*-property* just in case any relevant grounded form of type $\exists$ is formally deducible from S only if at least one of its immediate descendants is; and *has the* $\forall$*-property* just in case any relevant grounded form of type $\forall$ is formally deducible from S if every one of its immediate descendants is (this last is conventionally called the property of ω*-completeness*).

Before examining the residual questions alluded to, let us note some connexions between these three properties.

THEOREM II.4.2. *A set of grounded forms that is an extension of* **S** *has the* $\vee$*-property if it has the* $\exists$*-property.*

PROOF. Suppose S is a set of grounded forms that is an extension of **S** and has the $\exists$-property, and let X be a relevant grounded form of type $\vee$ that is formally deducible from S: then either

(a) there are forms Y and Z such that X is $(Y \vee Z)$, in which case $\exists x.((x = \bar{0} \wedge Y) \vee (x \neq \bar{0} \wedge Z))$ is formally deducible from S and thus, for some number n, $((\bar{n} = \bar{0} \wedge Y) \vee (\bar{n} \neq \bar{0} \wedge Z))$ is formally deducible from S; but if n is 0, then $S \vdash {\sim}\bar{n} \neq \bar{0}$, and so Y is an immediate descendant of X that is formally deducible from S, whereas if n is not 0, then $S \vdash {\sim}\bar{n} = \bar{0}$, and so Z is an immediate descendant of X that is formally deducible from S; or

(b) there is a variable α, a predicate-form P and a number m such that X is $\exists\alpha < \overline{m+1}.P[\alpha]$, so that $\exists\alpha.(\alpha < \overline{m+1} \wedge P[\alpha])$ is formally deducible from S and thus, for some number n, $(\bar{n} < \overline{m+1} \wedge P[\bar{n}])$ is formally deducible from S; now if n is less than $m+1$, then $P[\bar{n}]$ is an immediate descendant of X that is formally deducible from S; on the other hand if n is not less than $m+1$, then $S \vdash \sim \bar{n} < \overline{m+1}$ and so (since also $S \vdash \bar{n} < \overline{m+1}$) $S \vdash P[\bar{0}]$ and thus $P[\bar{0}]$ is an immediate descendant of X that is formally deducible from S.

Q.E.D.

It was Tarski who first drew attention to the ∀-property, in his famous paper 'The concept of truth in formalized languages' (*1933*, p. 259 f.) and he pointed out the second of the following facts:

THEOREM II.4.3. *A set of grounded forms that is an extension of* **R** *is*
— *sound if it has the ∃-property and every form of type* B *that is formally deducible from it is standardly assigned* $\mathbb{T}$*;*
— *complete if it has the ∀-property.*

PROOF. 1. Suppose S is a set of grounded forms, is an extension of **R**, has the ∃-property, and is such that every form of type B that is formally deducible from it is standardly assigned $\mathbb{T}$.

Let θ be the predicate

⌜$X.X$ is standardly assigned $\mathbb{T}$ if it is formally deducible from S⌝

Clearly, θ is 'determinate' and is true of every form of type B.

Now θ is true of a form X of type R, ∨, ∧, ∃ or ∀ if it is true of every immediate descendant of X; for, if X is formally deducible from S, then either

(a) X is of type ∨ or ∃, in which case (as S has the ∃-property and thus also the ∨-property) at least one of X's immediate descendants is formally deducible from S, so that (as θ is true of it) that immediate descendant is standardly assigned $\mathbb{T}$, and therefore X is standardly assigned $\mathbb{T}$; or

(b) X is of type ∧ or ∀, in which case every one of X's immediate descendants is formally deducible from S, so that (as θ is true of them all) they are all standardly assigned $\mathbb{T}$, and therefore X is standardly assigned $\mathbb{T}$; or else

(c) X is of type R, in which case too X is standardly assigned $\mathbb{T}$.

Therefore, by Theorem II.3.3, θ is true of every grounded form and so, by Theorem II.3.4, S is sound.

2. Similarly; but observe that every form of type B that is standardly assigned $\mathbb{T}$ is formally deducible from S, by Theorem I.2.1. (By contrast, not every form of type B that is formally deducible from S need be standardly assigned $\mathbb{T}$—for example, if S has as members those of **R** plus $\bar{3} < \bar{2}$.)

Q.E.D.

THEOREM II.4.4. *Consider a set of grounded forms that is an extension of* **R** *and is sound; the following conditions are equivalent:*

— *it has the* ∨*-property;* — *it has the* ∀*-property;*

— *it has the* ∃*-property;* — *it is complete.*

PROOF. If it has the ∀-property, it is complete (by Theorem II.4.3).

If it is complete, it has the ∃-property: because if *X* is a grounded form of type ∃ that is formally deducible from it, then (as it is sound) *X* is standardly assigned 𝕋, whence at least one of *X*'s descendants is standardly assigned 𝕋, and so (as it is complete) that immediate descendant is formally deducible from it.

If it has the ∃-property, it has the ∨-property (by Theorem II.4.2).

If it has the ∨-property, it has the ∀-property: because if *X* is a grounded form of type ∀ all of whose immediate descendants are formally deducible from it, then (as it is sound) all the immediate descendants of *X* are standardly assigned 𝕋, whence *X* is standardly assigned 𝕋, and so ∼*X* is not, and thus (as it is sound) ∼*X* is not formally deducible from it, so that (as it has the ∨-property and (*X* ∨ ∼*X*) is formally deducible from it) *X* is formally deducible from it.

Q.E.D.

Returning now to our main project, the quest for a reasonable set of forms that is both sound and complete, let us note that **Q** at least is not complete because the 'rogue' form $\sim\exists x.(x \neq \bar{0} \wedge \forall y < x.y' < x)$ is not formally deducible from it—see II.5. That form is, however, deducible from **P**, and so are the vast numbers of others that one would hope to be—as, for example, these:

$$\forall x.(x \neq \bar{0} \supset \forall w.\exists_1 y.\exists_1 z < x.w = ((x \times y) + z))$$
$$\forall v.\exists w.(v < w \wedge \mathrm{Pr}[w])$$
$$\forall x.(x < \bar{2} \vee \mathrm{Pr}[x] \vee \exists y.(\mathrm{Pr}[y] \wedge \mathrm{Div}[x, y]))$$
$$\forall x.(\mathrm{Pr}[x] \supset \forall y.\mathrm{Div}[\imath z.(z + y) = (y^x), x])$$
$$\forall v.\exists w.\exists x.\exists y.\exists z.v = ((((w^{\bar{2}}) + (x^{\bar{2}})) + (y^{\bar{2}})) + (z^{\bar{2}}))$$

(Pr, Div being $x.(\bar{1} < x \wedge \sim\exists y < x.\mathrm{Div}[x, y])$, $xy.\exists z < x.x = (y \times z)$ respectively)—consult, for instance, *Kleene 1952* §§38–40. As one works with **P** one becomes increasingly convinced of its completeness, even though the known proofs that given grounded forms are standardly assigned 𝕋 may resist immediate recasting as formal deductions from **P**—for example, what standardly fits

$$\forall y.\forall z.(\sim\exists x.(\mathrm{Div}[y, x] \wedge \mathrm{Div}[z, x]) \supset \forall v.\exists x.(v < x \wedge \mathrm{Pr}[((x \times y) + z)]))$$

expresses something proved by Dirichlet in 1837 using techniques from analysis, and it was not until 1948 that it became possible to *exhibit* a formal deduction of the form from **P** (cf. *LeVeque*, chs. 6–7). Nevertheless, provided one believed that Dirichlet's Theorem and other analogous ones could be proved using techniques of elementary number-theory, one could be in no serious doubt about **P**'s completeness—before 1931: but in that year Gödel published his extraordinary findings, which do indeed entail that **P** is not complete (unless unsound).

II.5 To see that **Q** is not complete, that in particular $\sim\exists x.(x \neq \bar{0} \wedge \forall y < x.y' < x)$ is not formally deducible from it, one can simply adapt the technique of section I.3 and show that there is a model of **Q** in which the form is not assigned $\mathbb{T}$. It is more interesting, however, to use a constructive method that is closer in form to the precursors of metalogical independence proofs, those obtained by Klein and Poincaré in their studies of non-Euclidean geometry.

Poincaré, for instance, gives a "kind of dictionary" by means of which he "translates" Lobatschewsky's theorems: "*We shall then obtain the theorems of ordinary geometry* ... Thus, however far the consequences of Lobatschewsky's hypotheses are carried, they will never lead to contradiction; in fact, if two of Lobatschewsky's theorems were contradictory, the translations of these two theorems made by the aid of our dictionary would be contradictory also. But these translations are theorems of ordinary geometry, and no one doubts that ordinary geometry is exempt from contradiction." (*Poincaré 1902*, pp. 42–3.) It is precisely a formalization of this method that we use to prove

Theorem II.5.1. $\sim\exists x.(x \neq \bar{0} \wedge \forall y < x.y' < x)$ *is not formally deducible from* **Q**.

Proof. Define predicate- and descriptor-forms as follows:

O	$x.\exists y.x = (y + y)'$
h	$x.\imath y.(x = (y + y)' \vee x = (y + y))$
$\underline{L}$	$xy.((O[x] \equiv O[y]) \wedge x < y) \vee (O[x] \wedge \sim O[y]))$
$\underline{a}$	$xy.\imath z.(h[z] = (h[x] + h[y]) \wedge (O[z] \equiv O[x]))$
$\underline{m}$	$xy.\imath z.(h[z] = (h[x] \times h[y]) \wedge (O[z] \equiv O[y]))$
$\underline{e}$	$xy.\imath z.(h[z] = (h[x]^{h[y]}) \wedge (O[z] \equiv (O[x] \vee y = \bar{1})))$

Now it is an easy exercise to show that each of the following twelve forms is formally deducible from **P** (for help with details, consult *Mendelson*, ch. 3, §1):

$$\forall x.\forall y.\forall z.(\underline{L}[x,y] \supset \underline{L}[y,z] \supset \underline{L}[x,z])$$

$$\forall x.\forall y.(\underline{L}[x,y] \vee x = y \vee \underline{L}[y,x])$$

$$\sim \exists x.\underline{L}[x,x]$$

$$\sim \exists y.\underline{L}[y,\bar{1}]$$

$$\forall x.(\underline{L}[x,x''] \wedge \sim \exists z.(\underline{L}[x,z] \wedge \underline{L}[z,x'']))$$

$$\forall x.\underline{a}[x,\bar{1}] = x$$

$$\forall x.\forall y.\underline{a}[x,y''] = \underline{a}[x,y]''$$

$$\forall x.\underline{m}[x,\bar{1}] = \bar{1}$$

$$\forall x.\forall y.\underline{m}[x,y''] = \underline{a}[\underline{m}[x,y],x]$$

$$\forall x.\underline{e}[x,\bar{1}] = \bar{3}$$

$$\forall x.\forall y.\underline{e}[x,y''] = \underline{m}[\underline{e}[x,y],x]$$

$$\forall y.(\underline{L}[y,\bar{0}] \supset \underline{L}[y'',\bar{0}])$$

Consider a formal translation that provides $x.x = x$ as universal-form and associates $\underline{L}, \underline{a}, \underline{m}, \underline{e}$ with L, a, m, e respectively: suppose it translates a sentence-form X into another $\underline{X}$, and let $\underline{\mathbf{Q}}$ be the set of forms into which it translates the eleven members of **Q**. Then, by what's just been said, each of the eleven forms in $\underline{\mathbf{Q}}$, and $\underline{\exists x.(x \neq \bar{0} \wedge \forall y < x.y' < x)}$, is formally deducible from **P**. It follows that $\underline{\sim \exists x.(x \neq \bar{0} \wedge \forall y < x.y' < x)}$ is not formally deducible from **P**, and hence not from $\underline{\mathbf{Q}}$. Thus $\sim \exists x.(x \neq \bar{0} \wedge \forall y < x.y' < x)$ is not formally deducible from **Q**, by Theorem A.9.1.

Q.E.D.

So if one lets $\mathbf{Q}^+$ be the set whose members are the forms in **Q** plus the rogue form, and **Q**! be that whose members are the forms in **Q** plus its negation, we see that $\mathbf{Q}^+$ and **Q**! stand to one another as do Euclid's and Lobatschewsky's geometries[1]: neither is inconsistent, yet they are formally incompatible. A corollary is that there are models of **Q** in which the rogue form is not assigned $\mathbb{T}$: viz. those that assign $|\underline{L}|, |\underline{a}|, |\underline{m}|, |\underline{e}|$ to L, a, m, e (and have the

[1] The analogy is only exact if the geometries are formal systems—mere sets of sentence-forms, such as those of Tarski (cf. *Schwabhäuser et al.*). It has frequently been argued that there is a genuine question which geometry is true, Euclid's or Lobatschewsky's—a question *not* to be settled by empirical investigation: no such question arises regarding formal systems—as Frege says, no one will imagine that he understands sentence-*forms*, or finds thoughts expressed in them (*1906*, p. 389).

usual universe). There are also of course models of **Q** in which the rogue form *is* assigned $\mathbb{T}$: the standard models.

A second corollary is that **Q** doesn't have the ∨-, ∃- or ∀-properties: in fact, letting P be $x.\sim(x \neq \bar{0} \wedge \forall y<x.y'<x)$, we see that

— $(\forall P \vee \sim\forall P)$ is formally deducible from **Q** although neither of its immediate descendants is;

— $\exists x.(\forall P \vee \sim P[x])$ is formally deducible from **Q** although none of its immediate descendants is;

— $\forall P$ is not formally deducible from **Q** although every one of its immediate descendants is;

— $(P[\bar{0}] \supset \forall x.(P[x] \supset P[x']) \supset \forall P)$ is not formally deducible from **Q** (because $P[\bar{0}]$ and $\forall x.(P[x] \supset P[x'])$ are formally deducible from it).

Note that the role of **P** in the proof can be played by that one of its finite subsystems that has as members the forms in **Q** plus $\forall x.(O[x'] \equiv \sim O[x])$—$\mathbf{Q}^{O}$, say: what the proof then shows is how the rogue form's being formally deducible from **Q** (or even $\mathbf{Q}^{O}$) would entail the inconsistency of $\mathbf{Q}^{O}$; or again, how the inconsistency of **Q**! (or even $\mathbf{Q}^{O}$!) would entail that of $\mathbf{Q}^{O}$. Of course, $\mathbf{Q}^{O}$ is not inconsistent since it is sound.

Finally, it is worth qualifying the description of **Q** as an 'amended version' of Robinson's Arithmetic—call it **Q**′—because the latter has received exhaustive examination and it has even been said of it that "this beautiful and much studied theory is in a sense a minimal axiomatization of arithmetic" (*Nelson*, p. 9, cf. p. 80; *Jones & Shepherdson*). **Q** is stronger than **Q**′ in that $\forall x.(x^{\bar{0}})=\bar{1}$ and $\forall x.\forall y.(x^{y'})=((x^{y})\times x)$ are formally deducible from **Q** but not from **Q**′, but weaker than it in that the rogue form is formally deducible from **Q**′ but not from **Q**. The justification of the description is that, for the purposes of the present work, all that is required of **Q** is that it be finite and yield Theorem III.1.2 (and hence Theorem IX.3.6), and all that Mostowski, Robinson and Tarski needed to require of **Q**′ was that it be finite and yield the corresponding Theorem 6 of their paper. Similar remarks apply to **R**, of which all we require is that it yield Theorem III.1.2.

III
The Theory of Σ-Forms

III.1 The Δ-*sentence-forms* are those grounded forms none of whose descendants is of type ∀ or ∃. The Δ-*predicate-forms* are those predicate-forms the results of applying which to formal numerals are Δ-sentence-forms. The Δ-*subject-forms* are those subject-forms s such that $\alpha.s=\alpha$ is a Δ-predicate-form (α being the first variable). The Δ-*descriptor-forms* are those descriptor-forms d such that, for some positive number n, $\alpha_1 \ldots \alpha_n\alpha_{n+1}.d[\alpha_1,\ldots,\alpha_n]=\alpha_{n+1}$ is a Δ-predicate-form ($\alpha_1,\ldots,\alpha_{n+1}$ being the first $n+1$ variables).

The Σ-*sentence-forms* are those grounded forms none of whose descendants is of type ∀. The Σ-*predicate-*, *subject-* and *descriptor-forms* are defined as above (though we have no use for the latter two notions, there being no Σ-subject-forms that are not Δ-subject-forms).

For example, $\forall x<(\bar{2}+\bar{3}).\exists y<(x^x).(x\times y)<x$ is a Δ-sentence-form and $\forall x<(\bar{2}+\bar{3}).\exists y.(x\times y)<x$ is a Σ-sentence-form, although $\forall x.\exists y<(x^x).(x\times y)<x$ is neither. Clearly, all sentence- or predicate-forms that are Δ-forms are Σ-forms, and we shall frequently use the following result implicitly:

Theorem III.1.1. *Suppose α is a variable, X a sentence-form, P a singulary predicate form, Q an n-ary one ($n>0$), and $s,s_1,\ldots,s_n$ are Δ-subject-forms: then*
—if Q is a Δ-form, so is $Q[s_1,\ldots,s_n]$;
—if Q is a Σ-form, so is $Q[s_1,\ldots,s_n]$;
—if P is a Δ-form, so are $\exists\alpha<s.P[\alpha]$, $\forall\alpha<s.P[\alpha]$ and $\iota\alpha<s.P[\alpha]$;
—if P is a Σ-form, so are $\exists\alpha<s.P[\alpha]$, $\forall\alpha<s.P[\alpha]$ and $\exists\alpha.P[\alpha]$;
—if X is a Δ-form, so is $\sim X$.

We know that **R** is sound, but doesn't have the ∀-property, and so isn't complete: however, no descendant of a Σ-form is of type ∀, and so we have:

Theorem III.1.2. *The Σ-forms that are formally deducible from* **R** *are those that are standardly assigned* $\mathbb{T}$.

Proof. By Theorem A.10.3, every form, and hence *a fortiori* every Σ-form, that is formally deducible from **R** is standardly assigned $\mathbb{T}$.

On the other hand, let θ be the 'determinate' predicate

'*X*.*X* is formally deducible from **R** if it is a Σ-form that is standardly assigned $\mathbb{T}$';

clearly, θ is true of every form of type B, and it is true of any grounded form all of whose immediate descendants it is true of: for, if *X* is a Σ-form that is standardly assigned $\mathbb{T}$, then either

— *X* is of type ∨ or ∃, in which case at least one of its immediate descendants is standardly assigned $\mathbb{T}$, so that (as θ is true of it) that immediate descendant is formally deducible from **R**, and therefore so is *X*; or

— *X* is of type ∧, in which case every one of its immediate descendants is standardly assigned $\mathbb{T}$, so that (as θ is true of them all) they are all formally deducible from **R**, and therefore so is *X*; or

— *X* is of type R, in which case similarly *X* is formally deducible from **R**.

Thus, by Theorem II.3.3, θ is true of every grounded form, and so every Σ-form that is standardly assigned $\mathbb{T}$ is formally deducible from **R**.

Q.E.D.

Theorem III.1.2 should be credited to Gödel: it is the essence obtained by refining Theorem V of *Gödel 1931*.

III.2 For reasons that will not become entirely clear until later in the book, we now introduce a second kind of tableau, the Σ-*tableaux*. Like the other kind, the regular tableaux defined in A.7, they are given in terms of extension rules and a conception of branch closure: thus a Σ-tableau is a tableau that is obtained from a one-point tableau for a Σ-form by successively applying the following *Rules for* Σ-*tableaux*; a branch of a Σ-tableau is *closed* just in case there is a form of type B on it that is standardly assigned $\mathbb{T}$; a Σ-tableau is *closed* just in case all its branches are closed (an example is given in Fig. 1 opposite); and a form is Σ-*provable* just in case there is a closed Σ-tableau for it.

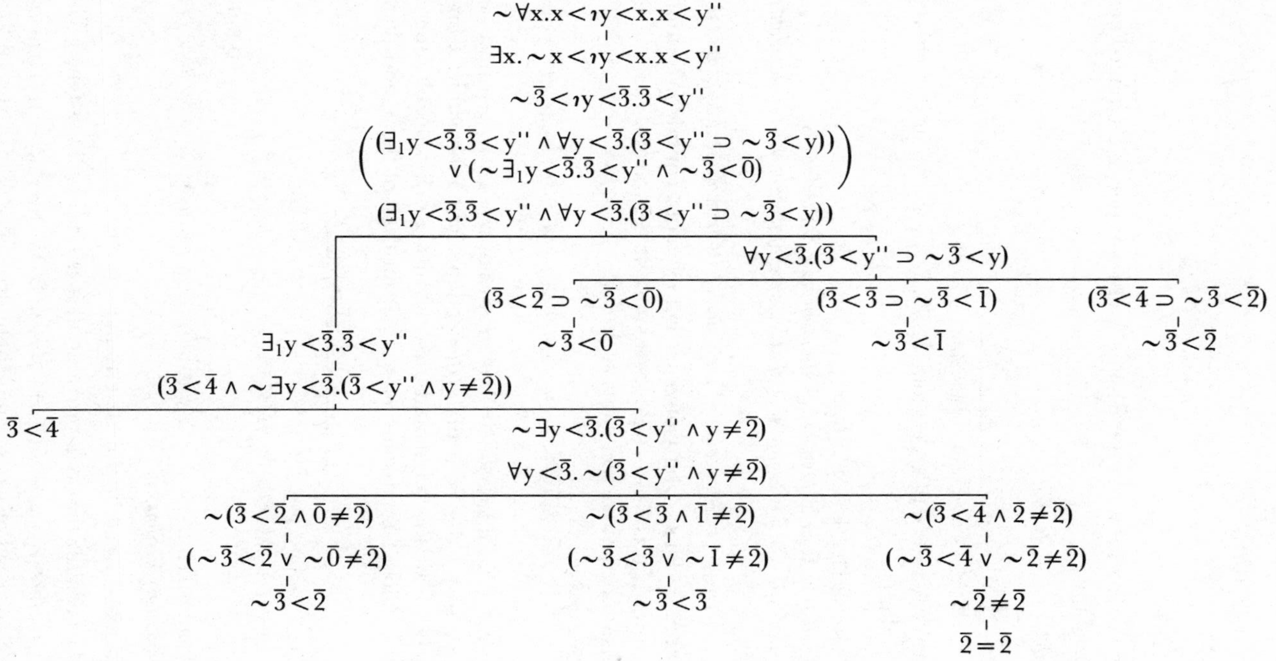
$\sim \forall x. x < \imath y < x. x < y''$
$\exists x. \sim x < \imath y < x. x < y''$
$\sim \bar{3} < \imath y < \bar{3}. \bar{3} < y''$
$\left(\begin{array}{c} (\exists_1 y < \bar{3}. \bar{3} < y'' \wedge \forall y < \bar{3}. (\bar{3} < y'' \supset \sim \bar{3} < y)) \\ \vee (\sim \exists_1 y < \bar{3}. \bar{3} < y'' \wedge \sim \bar{3} < \bar{0}) \end{array} \right)$
$(\exists_1 y < \bar{3}. \bar{3} < y'' \wedge \forall y < \bar{3}. (\bar{3} < y'' \supset \sim \bar{3} < y))$
$\forall y < \bar{3}. (\bar{3} < y'' \supset \sim \bar{3} < y)$
$(\bar{3} < \bar{2} \supset \sim \bar{3} < \bar{0})$
$(\bar{3} < \bar{3} \supset \sim \bar{3} < \bar{1})$
$(\bar{3} < \bar{4} \supset \sim \bar{3} < \bar{2})$
$\sim \bar{3} < \bar{0}$
$\sim \bar{3} < \bar{1}$
$\sim \bar{3} < \bar{2}$
$\exists_1 y < \bar{3}. \bar{3} < y''$
$(\bar{3} < \bar{4} \wedge \sim \exists y < \bar{3}. (\bar{3} < y'' \wedge y \neq \bar{2}))$
$\bar{3} < \bar{4}$
$\sim \exists y < \bar{3}. (\bar{3} < y'' \wedge y \neq \bar{2})$
$\forall y < \bar{3}. \sim (\bar{3} < y'' \wedge y \neq \bar{2})$
$\sim (\bar{3} < \bar{2} \wedge \bar{0} \neq \bar{2})$
$\sim (\bar{3} < \bar{3} \wedge \bar{1} \neq \bar{2})$
$\sim (\bar{3} < \bar{4} \wedge \bar{2} \neq \bar{2})$
$(\sim \bar{3} < \bar{2} \vee \sim \bar{0} \neq \bar{2})$
$(\sim \bar{3} < \bar{3} \vee \sim \bar{1} \neq \bar{2})$
$(\sim \bar{3} < \bar{4} \vee \sim \bar{2} \neq \bar{2})$
$\sim \bar{3} < \bar{2}$
$\sim \bar{3} < \bar{3}$
$\sim \bar{2} \neq \bar{2}$
$\bar{2} = \bar{2}$

Fig. 1: a closed Σ-tableau

The rules are:

R-, ∨- *and* ∃-*Rule*

$$\begin{array}{c} X \\ | \\ Y \end{array}$$

where X is a form of type R, ∨ or ∃ and Y is one of its immediate descendants;

∧-*Rule*

$$\begin{array}{cccc} & & X & \\ \hline Y_1 & Y_2 & \dots & Y_k \end{array}$$

where X is a form of type ∧ and $Y_1, Y_2, \ldots, Y_k$ are all its immediate descendants.

THEOREM III.2.1. *A Σ-form*

— *of type* R *is Σ-provable iff its immediate descendant is;*

— *of type* ∨ *or* ∃ *is Σ-provable iff at least one of its immediate descendants is;*

— *of type* ∧ *is Σ-provable iff every one of its immediate descendants is.*

PROOF. This is pretty obvious. For example, consider a form X of type ∧. If it is Σ-provable there must be Σ-tableaux $\tau_1, \tau_2, \ldots, \tau_k$ for its immediate descendants such that

$$\begin{array}{cccc} & & X & \\ \hline \tau_1 & \tau_2 & \dots & \tau_k \end{array}$$

is a closed Σ-tableau for it; but then each of $\tau_1, \tau_2, \ldots, \tau_k$ must be closed; so all the immediate descendants are Σ-provable. Conversely, if all the immediate descendants are Σ-provable, there must be closed Σ-tableaux $\tau_1, \tau_2, \ldots, \tau_k$ for each of them, and then

$$\begin{array}{cccc} & & X & \\ \hline \tau_1 & \tau_2 & \dots & \tau_k \end{array}$$

is a closed Σ-tableau for X.

Q.E.D.

THEOREM III.2.2. *The Σ-provable-forms are those Σ-forms that are standardly assigned* $\mathbb{T}$.

PROOF. Let θ be the 'determinate' predicate

'X.X is a form that is Σ-provable iff it is standardly assigned $\mathbb{T}$'.

Clearly, θ is true of every form of type B. Furthermore, it is true of any Σ-form all of whose immediate descendants it is true of: for, given such a form, either

— it is of type ∨ or ∃, in which case it is Σ-provable iff at least one of its immediate descendants is; that is (as θ is true of all of them) iff at least one of them is standardly assigned 𝕋; that is, iff it is standardly assigned 𝕋; or
— it is of type ∧, in which case it is Σ-provable iff every one of its immediate descendants is; that is (as θ is true of all of them) iff every one of them is standardly assigned 𝕋; or else
— it is of type **R**, in which case similarly it is Σ-provable iff it is standardly assigned 𝕋.
Thus, by Theorem II.3.3, θ is true of every Σ-form.

Q.E.D.

III.3 The last theorem assures us that, for every Σ-form that is standardly assigned 𝕋, there is a closed Σ-tableau. But we can be a good deal more definite: we can show that there is a closed Σ-tableau of a specific kind, a *systematically generated* Σ-tableau. To explain this, we need some new concepts.

First, a sentence-form is *fulfilled in* a set of sentence-forms if, and only if, either
— it is of type **B**; or
— it is of type **R**, and its immediate descendant is a member of the set; or
— it is of type ∨ or ∃, and every one of its immediate descendants is a member of the set; or
— it is of type ∧ or ∀, and at least one of its immediate descendants is a member of the set.
Then, a set is *replete* if, and only if, its members are all grounded forms that are fulfilled in it.

Some examples of replete sets are:
— the set of all grounded forms that are not standardly assigned 𝕋 (see Theorem II.3.1);
— the set of all Σ-forms that are not formally deducible from *S*, *S* being an extension of **R** (see Theorem II.4.1);
— the set of all Σ-forms that are not Σ-provable (see Theorem III.2.2);
— the set whose members are the eight forms
$\forall x.(x=\bar{0} \vee \exists y<x.\sim y'<x)$, $(\bar{4}=\bar{0} \vee \exists y<\bar{4}.\sim y'<\bar{4})$, $\exists y<\bar{4}.\sim y'<\bar{4}$, $\sim\bar{1}<\bar{4}$, $\sim\bar{2}<\bar{4}$, $\sim\bar{3}<\bar{4}$, $\sim\bar{4}<\bar{4}$, $\bar{4}=\bar{0}$.

THEOREM III.3.1. *None of the members of a replete set are standardly assigned 𝕋 if none of its members of type* **B** *are standardly assigned 𝕋.*

PROOF. Let S be a replete set, and θ the 'determinate' predicate

$\ulcorner X.X$ is not standardly assigned $\mathbb{T}$ if it is a member of $S\urcorner$.

Then by hypothesis θ is true of every form of type B. Furthermore, it is true of every grounded form all of whose immediate descendants it is true of—for, if X is a member of S, then either

— X is of type $\vee$ or $\exists$, in which case (as X is fulfilled in S) every one of its immediate descendants is a member of S and so (as θ is true of them all) none of them are standardly assigned $\mathbb{T}$, whence X isn't either; or

— X is of type $\wedge$ or $\forall$, in which case (as X is fulfilled in S) at least one of its immediate descendants is a member of S and so (as θ is true of it) that one is not standardly assigned $\mathbb{T}$, whence X isn't either; or else

— X is of type R, in which case similarly X isn't standardly assigned $\mathbb{T}$.

Q.E.D.

Now, speaking roughly, we can say that *a systematically generated Σ-tableau is one constructed in stages, at each stage using the rules to fulfil all the fulfillable points and increase the degree of fulfilment of the unfulfillable points;* but this is vague and potentially misleading, and we need to be more precise.

(1) Suppose given a Σ-tableau τ, a branch β of τ, and a point π on τ: let X be the form at π. Then the *systematic extensions of τ relative to π and β* are those Σ-tableaux σ such that either

(i) β is closed; or π is not on β; or π is on β and is fulfilled on it (i.e. the form at π is fulfilled in the set of forms at points on β): and σ is τ itself; or else

(ii) β is not closed; and π is on β; and π is not fulfilled on β; and either

— X is of type R or $\vee$: and σ is just like τ except for having the branch

$$\begin{array}{c}\beta\\ |\\ Y_1\\ |\\ Y_2\\ |\\ \vdots\\ |\\ Y_k\end{array}$$

where τ has β, $Y_1, Y_2, \ldots, Y_k$ being those immediate descendants of X that are not at points on β; or

— X is of type $\exists$: and σ is just like τ except for having the branch

$$\begin{array}{c} \beta \\ | \\ \Upsilon_1 \\ | \\ \Upsilon_2 \\ | \\ \vdots \\ | \\ \Upsilon_k \end{array}$$

where τ has β, $\Upsilon_1, \Upsilon_2, \ldots, \Upsilon_k$ being those immediate descendants of X amongst $P[\bar{0}], P[\bar{1}], \ldots, P[\bar{m}]$ that are not at points on β, P being the singulary predicate-form such that X is $\exists P$, and m being the least number greater than all those numbers n such that $P[\bar{n}]$ is at a point on β; or

— X is of type $\wedge$: and σ is just like τ except for having the branches

$$\begin{array}{cccc} & \beta & & \\ \hline \Upsilon_1 & \Upsilon_2 & \ldots & \Upsilon_k \end{array}$$

where τ has β, $\Upsilon_1, \Upsilon_2, \ldots, \Upsilon_k$ being the immediate descendants of X.

(2) Suppose given a Σ-tableau τ and a point π on τ. Then the *systematic extensions of* τ *relative to* π are those Σ-tableaux σ such that σ is the last term of a finite sequence $\langle \sigma_0, \sigma_1, \ldots, \sigma_n \rangle$, where σ_0 is τ and, for each number j less than n, σ_{j+1} is a systematic extension of σ_j relative to π and β_{j+1}, $\beta_1, \beta_2, \ldots, \beta_n$ being the branches of τ.

(3) Suppose given a Σ-tableau τ. Then the *systematic extensions of* τ are those Σ-tableaux σ such that σ is the last term of a finite sequence $\langle \sigma_0, \sigma_1, \ldots, \sigma_m \rangle$, where σ_0 is τ and, for each number i less than m, σ_{i+1} is a systematic extension of σ_i relative to π_{i+1}, $\pi_1, \pi_2, \ldots, \pi_m$ being the points on τ.

To illustrate, consider the following sequence of seventeen Σ-tableaux $\langle \tau_1, \tau_2, \ldots, \tau_{17} \rangle$. In it, τ_5 is an extension of τ_4 relative to the $\exists x.(x \neq \bar{0} \wedge \forall y < x.(y^{\bar{2}}) < x)$-point and the left branch, whereas τ_6 is an extension of τ_5 relative to the same point and the right branch; thus τ_6 is an extension of τ_4 relative to that point—similarly, τ_8 is an extension of τ_6 relative to the $(\bar{1} \neq \bar{0} \wedge \forall y < \bar{1}.(y^{\bar{2}}) < \bar{1})$-point. Also, τ_9 is a systematic extension *simpliciter* of τ_4, as is τ_{12} of τ_9: in fact, in the sequence

$$\langle \tau_1, \tau_2, \tau_4, \tau_9, \tau_{12}, \tau_{17} \rangle$$

each non-initial term is a systematic extension of its predecessor and is different from that predecessor.

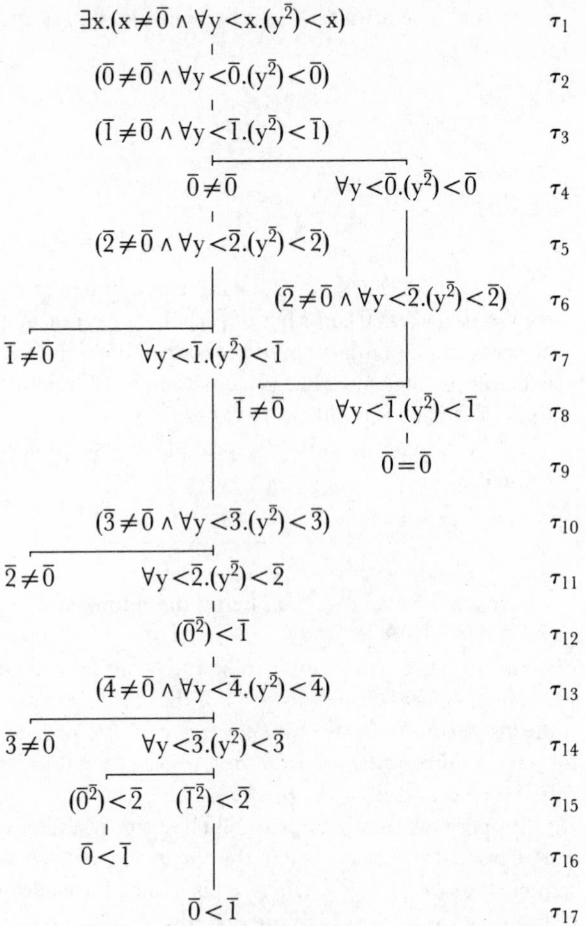
∃x.(x≠0̄ ∧ ∀y<x.(y²̄)<x)   τ1
(0̄≠0̄ ∧ ∀y<0̄.(y²̄)<0̄)   τ2
(1̄≠0̄ ∧ ∀y<1̄.(y²̄)<1̄)   τ3
0̄≠0̄   ∀y<0̄.(y²̄)<0̄   τ4
(2̄≠0̄ ∧ ∀y<2̄.(y²̄)<2̄)   τ5
(2̄≠0̄ ∧ ∀y<2̄.(y²̄)<2̄)   τ6
1̄≠0̄   ∀y<1̄.(y²̄)<1̄   τ7
1̄≠0̄   ∀y<1̄.(y²̄)<1̄   τ8
0̄=0̄   τ9
(3̄≠0̄ ∧ ∀y<3̄.(y²̄)<3̄)   τ10
2̄≠0̄   ∀y<2̄.(y²̄)<2̄   τ11
(0̄²̄)<1̄   τ12
(4̄≠0̄ ∧ ∀y<4̄.(y²̄)<4̄)   τ13
3̄≠0̄   ∀y<3̄.(y²̄)<3̄   τ14
(0̄²̄)<2̄   (1̄²̄)<2̄   τ15
0̄<1̄   τ16
0̄<1̄   τ17

Since all the branches of τ_{17} are closed, it is itself its only systematic extension. Thus, in this case, the process of taking systematic extensions of systematic extensions of systematic ... extensions of τ_1 grinds to a halt at the sixth stage. But that is not true in every case; for a counterexample, consider the following *infinite* sequence of Σ-tableaux $\langle \sigma_1, \sigma_2, \sigma_3, \ldots \rangle$, which is such that, for each number *n*, σ_{3n+12} is a systematic extension of σ_{3n+9} and is different from it: in fact, in the sequence

$$\langle \sigma_1, \sigma_2, \sigma_4, \sigma_9, \sigma_{12}, \ldots, \sigma_{3n+9}, \sigma_{3n+12}, \ldots \rangle$$

each non-initial term is a systematic extension of its predecessor and is different from that predecessor.

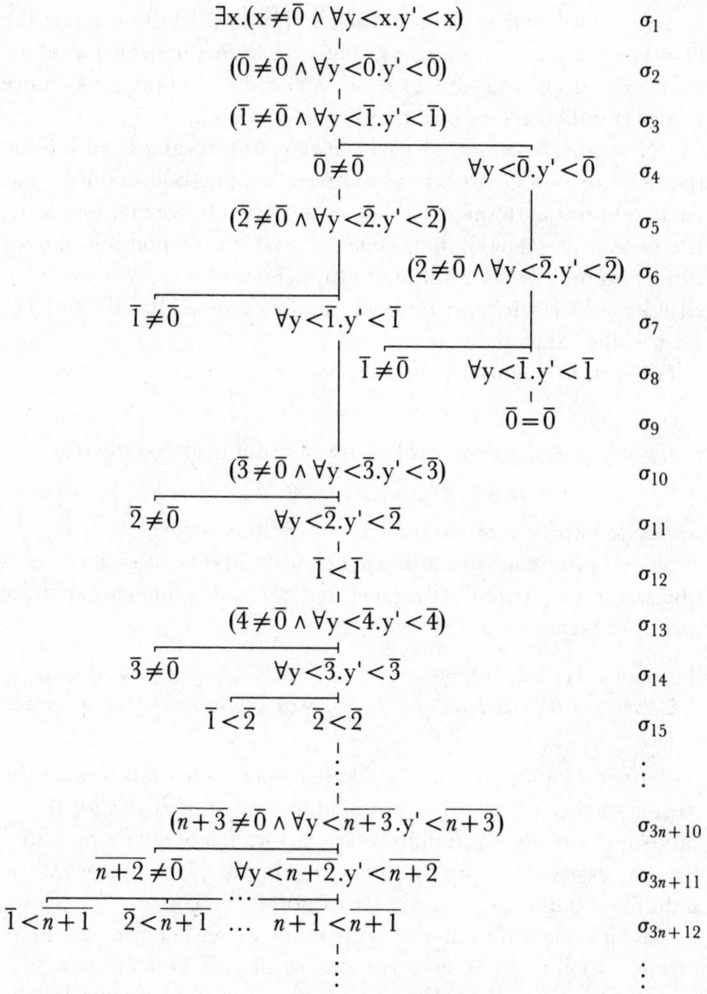
∃x.(x≠0̄ ∧ ∀y<x.y'<x) σ1
(0̄≠0̄ ∧ ∀y<0̄.y'<0̄) σ2
(1̄≠0̄ ∧ ∀y<1̄.y'<1̄) σ3
0̄≠0̄ ∀y<0̄.y'<0̄ σ4
(2̄≠0̄ ∧ ∀y<2̄.y'<2̄) σ5
(2̄≠0̄ ∧ ∀y<2̄.y'<2̄) σ6
1̄≠0̄ ∀y<1̄.y'<1̄ σ7
1̄≠0̄ ∀y<1̄.y'<1̄ σ8
0̄=0̄ σ9
(3̄≠0̄ ∧ ∀y<3̄.y'<3̄) σ10
2̄≠0̄ ∀y<2̄.y'<2̄ σ11
1̄<1̄ σ12
(4̄≠0̄ ∧ ∀y<4̄.y'<4̄) σ13
3̄≠0̄ ∀y<3̄.y'<3̄ σ14
1̄<2̄ 2̄<2̄ σ15
(n+3≠0̄ ∧ ∀y<n+3.y'<n+3) σ3n+10
n+2≠0̄ ∀y<n+2.y'<n+2 σ3n+11
1̄<n+1 2̄<n+1 … n+1<n+1 σ3n+12

Before proceeding, we should encapsulate the point of the introduction of the concept of systematic extensions in the following result, which is either obvious or at least very easy to prove:

THEOREM III.3.2. *Suppose π is a point on an open branch β of a Σ-tableau τ, and σ is a systematic extension of τ:*
— if π is not of type $\exists$, then it is fulfilled on those branches of σ that extend β;
— if π is of type $\exists$, then it is 'more nearly' fulfilled on each of those branches than it was on β.

Thus consider the 'main' branch β of σ_9 in the last example: the $(\bar{2} \neq \bar{0} \wedge \forall y < \bar{2}.y' < \bar{2})$-point is fulfilled on both the branches of σ_{12} that extend β; and the $\exists x.(x \neq \bar{0} \wedge \forall y < x.y' < x)$-point is 'more nearly' fulfilled on each of them than it is on β.

(4) Now a *systematically generated chain of* Σ-tableaux is an infinite sequence of Σ-tableaux whose first term is a one-point tableau and each non-initial term of which is a systematic extension of its predecessor. Such a chain is *of infinite order* if each non-initial term differs from its predecessor; and otherwise is *of finite order*, in which case its *order* is the least positive number n such that the $(n+1)^{\text{th}}$ term is the same as the nth.

For instance, considering the above examples, we see that

$$\langle \tau_1, \tau_2, \tau_4, \tau_9, \tau_{12}, \tau_{17}, \tau_{17}, \ldots \rangle$$

is a systematically generated chain of finite order 6, whereas

$$\langle \sigma_1, \sigma_2, \sigma_4, \sigma_9, \sigma_{12}, \ldots, \sigma_{3n+9}, \sigma_{3n+12}, \ldots \rangle$$

is a systematically generated chain of infinite order.

Since Δ-sentence-forms have no descendants of type $\exists$, it is obvious that systematically generated chains for them are of finite order; in fact, we have

THEOREM III.3.3. *Suppose given a systematically generated chain of Σ-tableaux for a Δ-form of degree n; then it is of finite order no greater than n.*

PROOF. Let us say that the *degree of* a point on a Σ-tableau is the degree of the form at that point; that the point is *fulfilled on* the tableau iff the point is fulfilled on every branch of the tableau; and that the *degree of* the tableau is the maximum of the degrees of the unfulfilled points on it, if any (1, if none).

Now it is clear that, if σ is a systematic extension of τ, and there are no $\exists$-points on τ, then the degree of τ, if greater than 1, is greater than that of σ: this is a consequence of Theorem III.3.2.

So suppose $\langle \tau_1, \tau_2, \tau_3, \ldots \rangle$ is a systematically generated chain for a Δ-form of degree n. The degree of τ_1 is obviously either 1 or n, and hence is no greater than n. Thus at least one of $\tau_1, \tau_2, \ldots, \tau_n$ must be of degree 1—for, if none were, there would be $n+1$ numbers between 1 and n, which is absurd. Hence τ_n must be of degree 1, so that there are no unfulfilled points on it. And then τ_{n+1} must be the same as τ_n, so that the order of the chain is no greater than n.

Q.E.D.

(5) Now suppose given a systematically generated chain of Σ-tableaux; then a *chain of branches through* it is an infinite sequence

such that, for each positive number n, the nth term of the sequence is a branch of the nth tableau in the chain; such a chain of branches is *monotonic* iff each of its non-initial terms extends its predecessor (for one finite sequence to *extend* another is for the former to be the concatenation of one whose first term is the latter: so any finite sequence extends itself and thus it is not necessary that an extension of a branch of a tableau have more points on it than does the branch).

THEOREM III.3.4. *Suppose given a systematically generated chain of Σ-tableaux, and a monotonic chain of branches through it. Then the set of forms at points on those branches is either closed or replete.*

PROOF. Let $\langle\tau_1,\tau_2,\tau_3,\ldots\rangle$ be the chain of tableaux, $\langle\beta_1,\beta_2,\beta_3,\ldots\rangle$ the chain of branches, and S the set of forms at points on those branches.

Suppose S is not closed, and consider one of its members, X, say. — Suppose that X is not of type $\exists$. Then there is a number k such that X is at a point on β_k; since S is not closed, nor is β_k; hence, by Theorem III.3.2, the X-point is fulfilled on all those branches of τ_{k+1} that extend β_k, and so fulfilled on β_{k+1}. Thus X is fulfilled in S. — Suppose that X is of type $\exists$—let P be the singular predicate-form such that X is $\exists P$. We observe that, for any number m, $P[\overline{m+1}]$ is a member of S if all of $P[\bar{0}],\ldots,P[\bar{m}]$ are (for then there is a number k such that all of $\exists P, P[\bar{0}],\ldots,P[\bar{m}]$ are at points on β_k and so, reasoning as above, $P[\overline{m+1}]$ is at a point on β_{k+1}); thus by mathematical induction we conclude that every immediate descendant of X is a member of S. Thus X is fulfilled in S.

Q.E.D.

Thus consider the systematically generated chain

$$\langle\sigma_1,\sigma_2,\sigma_4,\sigma_9,\sigma_{12},\ldots,\sigma_{3n+9},\sigma_{3n+12},\ldots\rangle$$

of Σ-tableaux for $\exists x.(x\neq\bar{0} \wedge \forall y<x.y'<x)$, the second of our two examples: there are infinitely many monotonic chains of branches through it, but they are all closed with the exception of the 'main' one, which is replete.

THEOREM III.3.5. **THE BROUWER-KÖNIG INFINITY LEMMA.** *Suppose given a systematically generated chain of Σ-tableaux, no one of which is closed; then there is a monotonic chain of open branches through it.*

PROOF. Let $\langle\tau_1,\tau_2,\tau_3,\ldots\rangle$ be the chain of tableaux, and let us say that a branch of one of the tableaux is *infinitely extensible* if each tableau later in the chain has open branches that extend the given branch.

Clearly, the only branch of τ_1 is infinitely extensible, because every tableau in the chain has open branches, and they all extend the branch of τ_1.

Secondly, for every positive number k and every infinitely extensible branch β of τ_k, there is an infinitely extensible branch of τ_{k+1} that extends β. Because, since β is infinitely extensible, τ_{k+1} has open branches that extend β—let $\gamma_1, \gamma_2, \ldots, \gamma_l$ be a complete list of them: now at least one of $\gamma_1, \gamma_2, \ldots, \gamma_l$ is infinitely extensible—for, if none were, there would be numbers $n_1, n_2, \ldots, n_l$, all greater than $k+1$, such that

$$\begin{aligned} &\tau_{n_1} \text{ has no open branches that extend } \gamma_1 \\ \text{and } &\tau_{n_2} \text{ has no open branches that extend } \gamma_2 \\ &\vdots \\ \text{and } &\tau_{n_l} \text{ has no open branches that extend } \gamma_l; \end{aligned}$$

but then, letting m be the largest of $n_1, n_2, \ldots, n_l$, it would be the case that

$$\begin{aligned} &\tau_m \text{ has no open branches that extend } \gamma_1 \\ \text{and } &\tau_m \text{ has no open branches that extend } \gamma_2 \\ &\vdots \\ \text{and } &\tau_m \text{ has no open branches that extend } \gamma_l: \end{aligned}$$

and then, as $\gamma_1, \gamma_2, \ldots, \gamma_l$ are *all* the open branches of τ_{k+1} that extend β, it would follow that τ_m has no open branches that extend β—which is impossible, as β is infinitely extensible and τ_m is later in the chain than τ_k.

Finally, let β_1 be the only branch of τ_1 and, for each positive number k, β_{k+1} be the left-most infinitely extensible branch of τ_{k+1} that extends β_k. Then, by mathematical induction, $\langle \beta_1, \beta_2, \beta_3, \ldots \rangle$ is a monotonic chain of open branches through $\langle \tau_1, \tau_2, \tau_3, \ldots \rangle$.

The result is now established, but it is illuminating to put the matter in a different way: let θ be the 'determinate' predicate

'$k\beta.k$ is a positive number and β an infinitely extensible branch of τ_k'.

The second and third paragraphs establish, respectively, that θ is true of $\langle 1, \beta_1 \rangle$ and that, for every k and β, if θ is true of $\langle k, \beta \rangle$ then, for some γ that extends β, θ is true of $\langle k+1, \gamma \rangle$. So, for every positive number k, let β_{k+1} be the left-most branch γ that extends β_k and is such that θ is true of $\langle k+1, \gamma \rangle$; then θ, if true of $\langle k, \beta_k \rangle$, is true of $\langle k+1, \beta_{k+1} \rangle$. Thus, for every positive number k, θ is true of $\langle k, \beta_k \rangle$.

Q.E.D.

The above theorem is due independently to Brouwer and König, but the relationship between their proofs is complicated, and the epistemological status of the proofs is different—indeed, Brouwer would not have acknowledged this theorem as a proper statement of what he had proved. (For discussion of the two proofs, see *Parsons* and *Dummett 1977*, pp. 66–78.) Brouwer's doubts about this theorem would be due to the fact that it is not constructively true: rather than explain this concept, consider a Σ-form that is known not to be Σ-provable; one can of course begin to construct a systematically generated chain $\langle \tau_1, \tau_2, \tau_3, \ldots \rangle$ for it; now suppose one pauses after constructing, say, the first thirteen terms, so that one has laid out before one the whole of τ_{13}.

At this stage, one already knows that τ_{13} has open branches; and that τ_{14}, when constructed, will have open branches; and that τ_{15} will have open branches; and indeed that all the remaining yet-to-be-constructed terms will have open branches (for, if any of them didn't, the top-form would be Σ-provable, which it is *ex hypothesi* known not to be). Thus according to the Infinity Lemma it is already known that at least one of these branches—i.e. those of τ_{13}—is infinitely extensible; it does not, however, follow that at least one of these branches is already known to be infinitely extensible (compare: it is already known that someone has killed Cock Robin, but it doesn't follow that anyone is already known to have killed Cock Robin). Nor does the proof of the Infinity Lemma supply any effective procedure for deciding which of these branches is infinitely extensible: and that is because there may be no such effective procedure (whether there is or not depends upon the choice of top-form).

In these particular circumstances, where the top-form is *known* not to be Σ-provable, reflection on the nature of this knowledge assures one that at least one of these branches is *going to be* known to be infinitely extensible. However, were it the case that the top-form is neither known to be Σ-provable nor known not to be—had the top-form been, for example, 'Fermat's Form'

$$\exists w.\exists x.\exists y.\exists z.(\overline{2} < w \wedge \overline{0} < x \wedge \overline{0} < y \wedge ((x^w) + (y^w)) = (z^w))$$

(for which see *Edwards 1977*)—one would not have even this assurance: as it is only a pious hope or a philosophical dogma that Fermat's Last Theorem is either going to be known to be true or going to be known to be false, so it is only a pious hope or a philosophical dogma that either at least one of these branches is going to be known to be infinitely extensible or else at least one of the yet-to-be-constructed tableaux is going to be known to be closed.

We can now draw together the results of this section to attain our objective:

THEOREM III.3.6. *Suppose given a systematically generated chain of Σ-tableaux for a form that is standardly assigned* $\mathbb{T}$*; then at least one of the tableaux is closed.*

PROOF. If none of the tableaux were closed then, by the Infinity Lemma, there would be a monotonic chain of open branches through the chain of tableaux; then, by Theorem III.3.4, the set of forms at points on those branches would be either closed or else replete; yet it couldn't be closed, else some of the branches would be; so it would be replete; furthermore, none of its members of type B would be standardly assigned $\mathbb{T}$; hence, by Theorem III.3.1, none of its members would be standardly assigned $\mathbb{T}$; so in particular the top-form wouldn't be assigned $\mathbb{T}$: which contradicts the hypothesis.

Q.E.D.

Since it is clear that we can always construct, for a given Σ-form, as much as we wish of a systematically generated chain for it, it follows that, if it is standardly assigned $\mathbb{T}$, we can construct a closed systematically generated tableau for it. Following Smullyan again—for these are essentially his methods (cf. *Smullyan 1968*, ch. V)—we shall speak of this technique of construction as the 'Systematic Procedure'; it enables us to search systematically for a closed Σ-tableau for a Σ-form in the assurance that, if there is one, we shall find it (given world enough and time).

IV
Effectiveness

IV.1 Let us recapitulate. We introduced, in section II.1, the notion of representability, in order to be able to deal formally with those arithmetical concepts, such as that of oddness, that cannot be dealt with explicitly in the formal language. In the following section, we wondered what predicates were representable, seeking a satisfactory understanding of the class of representable predicates; and the considerations raised there, especially Cantor's argument, forced us to recognize that there are difficulties in the way of this understanding. In the succeeding sections we travelled down what may have seemed a side-track by considering the theory of Σ-forms; it is now time to see that this was no side-track.

What then was the point of the introduction of the notion of a Σ-form? It was to enable us to construct a mathematical model of a somewhat more imprecise notion, that of effectiveness, which has only recently entered mathematics. In this chapter we shall draw together the three concepts, of representability, of being a Σ-form, and of effectiveness, to see how they illuminate one another.

The Systematic Procedure described in the last section is an example of an *effective procedure*: the central characteristics of an effective procedure are that it is a procedure designed for a certain project of an agent of finite intellectual and physical prowess; it is given as a finite set of instructions such that the agent can recognize each instruction and obey it within a finite amount of time, and can recognize whether or not there remain instructions whose application will advance the project; the agent applies the instruction in a discrete, step-wise, fashion—the procedure is of the 'digital' type rather than the 'analogue' type (cf. *D. Lewis* and *Haugeland*); the order of application of the instructions is logically determinate (or, at least, any scope left in the instructions for choice is not logically of the essence); and the application of an instruction requires no intelligence beyond that required to grasp what it is an instruction to do, and certainly no insight, intuition or niceness of judgement, nor any recourse to random procedures (such as the tossing of coins), nor any appeals to higher authorities (such as oracles or gods).

This determination of what it is to be an effective procedure is couched entirely in terms of extra-mathematical concepts, but it is not for that reason that the concept of effectiveness is imprecise, if it is; it is rather because the concepts in terms of which it is couched are imprecise, although it is by no means necessary that a concept is imprecise if extra-mathematical (nor conversely). This imprecision does not, however, mean that we are incapable of recognizing procedures to be effective when they are: on the contrary there are numerous examples in all branches of mathematics of procedures that are obviously effective in this sense, most notably the procedures taught to us in the earliest years of our education for adding, subtracting, multiplying and dividing numbers.

An effective procedure is necessarily general: the agent's project is necessarily one of a type, and it is for that type of project that the procedure is designed. The Systematic Procedure is designed to result in a closed Σ-tableau for *any* Σ-form that is standardly assigned $\mathbb{T}$; the 'addition procedure' is designed to result in the sum of *any* pair of numbers. Now let us say that a procedure, as applied to a given object, *halts* if, and only if, a stage in the project is reached in which there remains no procedural instruction whose application would advance the project. The Systematic Procedure, for example, as applied to a particular Σ-form, halts when a tableau all of whose branches are either closed or replete is reached—as applied to $\exists x.(x \neq \bar{0} \wedge \forall y < x.(y^{\bar{2}}) < x)$ it halts at the sixth stage, whereas as applied to $\exists x.(x \neq \bar{0} \wedge \forall y < x.y' < x)$ it never halts. Similarly, the 'divisibility procedure' (simple-minded version: 'Given a pair $\langle m, n \rangle$ of numbers, work through the numbers r one by one asking each time whether $m \times r = n$; if so, halt; if not, go on.') as applied to $\langle 24, 312 \rangle$ halts at the thirteenth stage, whereas as applied to $\langle 23, 312 \rangle$ it never halts.

The Systematic Procedure has the following property: there is a logical guarantee—Theorem III.3.6—that, as applied to a Σ-form that is standardly assigned $\mathbb{T}$, it will sooner or later halt; furthermore, when it halts, it halts with a closed tableau—that is, in a state that enables us to recognize that the top-form is standardly assigned $\mathbb{T}$. Thus it is a *confirmation procedure* for the predicate

'$X.X$ is a Σ-form that is standardly assigned $\mathbb{T}$' .

because application of the procedure to a Σ-form enables the agent to *confirm* that the form is standardly assigned $\mathbb{T}$, if it is.

In similar fashion, for the simple-minded 'divisibility procedure' mentioned above there is a logical guarantee that, as applied to a pair $\langle m,n \rangle$ for which m divides n, it must sooner or later halt; furthermore, when it halts, it does so in a state that enables us to recognize that m divides n. Thus it is a confirmation procedure for the predicate

'$mn.m$ divides n'.

In general then an effective procedure is a *confirmation procedure for* a predicate θ if, and only if, there is a logical guarantee that θ is true of a given object just in case the procedure, as applied to that object, will sooner or later halt in a state enabling the agent to recognize that θ is true of the object—by doing so he *confirms* that θ is true of the object.

A confirmation procedure is by definition an effective procedure, but it is not required that applying the procedure be always a practical ('effective') way of confirming a fact; what is required is only that applying the procedure be always a theoretical ('in principle') way of confirming a fact—given world enough and time. It would be entirely impractical—indeed, quite absurd—to apply the 'divisibility procedure' in order to confirm that $10^{10^{10}}$ divides $10 \times 10^{10^{10}}$, if that is taken to entail writing out the numbers in Arabic notation and then performing various multiplications. Similarly, it would be entirely impractical to apply the Systematic Procedure in order to confirm that $\forall x < (\overline{10}^{(\overline{10}^{\overline{10}})}).(x+x) \neq \overline{5}$ is standardly assigned $\mathbb{T}$, if that is taken to entail writing out all the branches of the appropriate Σ-tableaux. The distinction between a confirmation procedure's being effective in a theoretical sense and in a practical one, only superficially adverted to here, is essential to drawing the boundaries between various philosophies of mathematics such as finitism, intuitionism and Platonism; for discussion of these issues, see *Wright 1982*, esp. sect. II. The various degrees of practicality are discussed non-technically from a mathematical point of view in *Lewis & Papadimitriou* and *Stockmeyer & Chandra*.

Related to this point about practicality is the following one: if C is a confirmation procedure for a predicate that is true of an object, then there is a logical guarantee only that C, as applied to that object, will *sooner or later* halt; there is not necessarily any logical guarantee that it will have halted by any particular stage. Consider the Systematic Procedure: Theorem III.3.3 is a logical guarantee that, as applied to a Δ-form of degree *n*, it will have halted by the nth stage; but there is no logical guarantee that, as applied to an arbitrary Σ-form, it will have halted by any particular stage—more precisely put, the following is not true:

> There is an effective procedure that, as applied to an arbitrary Σ-form *X*, results in a number *n* such that the Systematic Procedure, as applied to *X*, will have halted by the nth stage.

(This follows from Theorem IX.3.1.)

IV.2 The concept of effectiveness is, no doubt, relatively imprecise and hence so is the concept of a *confirmable* predicate, that is, of a predicate for which there is a confirmation procedure: some such predicates are clearly confirmable, some clearly not so, but an uncomfortably large number are neither clearly confirmable nor clearly not so. To eliminate—or at least reduce—the discomfort we turn our attention instead to the relatively precise concept of a Σ-*representable* predicate, that is, of a predicate of natural numbers for which there is a Σ-representation (as $\text{xy}.\exists\text{z}.\text{x}=(\text{y}^{\text{z}})$ is a Σ-representation of '*mn.m* is a power of *n*').

The proposal that *the confirmable predicates (of natural numbers) are the* Σ-*representable ones* is *Church's Thesis*—that is to say, we shall call that proposal by that name: the situation is that three men, Post, Church and Turing, working quite independently, reached equivalent conclusions, Post in the '20s, Church and Turing more or less simultaneously in the '30s; Church, however, was the first to publish. (The relevant papers are all reprinted in *Davis*.)

The word 'thesis', due to Kleene (*op. cit.* p. 274) but now traditional, is mildly misleading as it does rather suggest that there is some question of *verification* or *proof* of the proposal: Church was fairly clear that there was not ("This definition is thought to be justified by the considerations which follow, so far as positive justification can ever be obtained for the selection of a formal definition to correspond to an intuitive notion", p. 100), Turing rather less so ("All arguments which can be given are bound to be, fundamentally, appeals to intuition, and for this reason rather unsatisfactory mathematically", p. 135), and Post least of all ("But for full generality a complete analysis would have to be made of all the possible ways in which the human mind could set up finite processes for generating sequences ... In the meantime, however, assuming the correctness of our characterization ...", p. 408; "Establishing this ... is not a matter for mathematical proof, but of psychological analysis of the mental processes involved in combinatory mathematical processes", p. 418; cf. also pp. 291, 344).

The proper analogues to Church's Thesis are such things as 'limitations by statute' and 'standardizations': as for example that mentioned by the *Oxford English Dictionary* under 'Acre'—"A definite measure of land, originally as much as a yoke of oxen could plough in a day; afterwards limited by statutes ... to a piece 40 poles long by 4 broad ..., or its equivalent of any shape"—or that hypothesized by Wittgenstein—"Let us imagine samples of colour being preserved in Paris like the standard metre. We define: "sepia" means the colour of the standard sepia which is there kept hermetically sealed" (*Wittgenstein 1953* §50). A concept—measuring an acre, being coloured sepia—already exists but in an uncomfortably large number of normally occurring cases what falls under it is not entirely and indisputably obvious; to decrease this number to a bearable minimum the concept is then 'limited by statute'. As a result, it is right to say that the concept was vague and is precise: such precision may or may not be an advantage and whether it is or not will normally be shown by whether or not we decide to carry out the limitation (for *acre* we have, for *sepia* we haven't). "And if you want to say "But still, before that it wasn't an exact measure", then I reply: very well, it was an inexact one.—Though you still owe me a definition of exactness" (ib., §69).

Since the concept that is a candidate for limitation already exists, there is no question that the limitation can be *arbitrary*: it would have been absurd to fix the acre as a piece 100 poles long by 100 broad, or to keep as the standard sepia some pieces of ultramarine cloth. (The metre is an entirely different case, as it was never *limited* by statute: it was *introduced* by statute—as one forty-millionth part of the Paris meridian—and then *re-introduced* by statute—as the length of a certain bar. But the yard is like the acre.) So there is a genuine question whether the statutory limitation is right or not, but its being right is not a matter of its being true or fitting the facts: for it makes no claim about the facts. Rather, a fact underlies, and is presupposed by, the limitation, which, if it were not a fact, would render the limitation idle and useless: the fact that a piece 40 poles long by 4 broad, or its equivalent of any shape, is as much as a yoke of oxen could plough in a day, or again the fact that the colour of the samples kept in Paris is sepia.

Kleene, in his classic *Introduction to Metamathematics*, while unguardedly saying that Church's Thesis "has seemed ... to be true" (p. 300), and incorrectly saying that "Since our original notion of [confirmability] is a somewhat vague intuitive one, the thesis cannot be proved" (p. 317), nevertheless accurately depicts the situation: "While we cannot prove Church's Thesis, since its role is to delimit precisely an hitherto vaguely conceived totality, we require evidence that it cannot conflict with the intuitive notion which it is supposed to complete" (p. 318). What we require is evidence that the confirmable predicates are the Σ-representable ones: and that, if obtained, will be evidence of the *rightness* of the statutory limitation which is Church's Thesis (evidence that the colour of the samples is sepia is evidence that 'sepia' is *rightly* defined as meaning the colour of the samples!).

That what is Σ-representable is confirmable has seemed obvious, on the basis of the following argument: given a Σ-representable predicate *a confirmation procedure for it is supplied by the Systematic Procedure*—for (supposing it is singulary) to confirm that it is true of a number n one need only confirm that $P[\bar{n}]$ is standardly assigned $\mathbb{T}$, which we can do by applying the Systematic Procedure to the sentence-form (P being a Σ-representation of the predicate). Certainly it is true that if we have a Σ-representation of a predicate then we have a confirmation procedure for it: and we see that the Systematic Procedure is *universal*, in the sense of Turing's 'universal computing machine' (*Turing*, p. 127).

The converse, that what is confirmable is Σ-representable, is more difficult to argue. The necessary but brutal labour of showing that particular confirmable predicates (of natural numbers) are Σ-representable, and that particular confirmability-preserving modes of transformation are also Σ-representability-preserving, has been carried out over half a century without a single counter-example emerging. Furthermore, the conditions of confirmability have been examined by a number of thinkers—amongst them Post, Church and Turing, but also Gödel, Kleene and Markov—in an effort to account 'transcendentally' for this lack of emergence, and each such examination has resulted in the definition of a mathematical predicate that has turned out to be co-extensive with '$\theta.\theta$ is Σ-representable'. This work, summarized in §62 of Kleene's book, enables us to claim that we are in the presence of a fact.

Thus, to the question asked in section II.2—what predicates are representable?—, we have a partial answer: confirmable predicates are representable, in fact Σ-representable. But that is only a *partial* answer because, as will become clear, there are representable predicates that are not Σ-representable and so, by Church's Thesis, not confirmable.

IV.3 Since confirmability is a concept of predicates, and—at least on most views of mathematical knowledge—it is possible for two predicates to be co-extensive without our knowing that they are, it is *a fortiori* possible that we should know that one predicate is confirmable but not know that another, co-extensive, one is. For example, if Fermat's Last Theorem were, unknown to us, true, then it would be the case that the two predicates

'*n.n* is less than 1 or greater than 2'

'*n.* there are no positive integers p, q, r such that $p^n + q^n = r^n$'

were, unknown to us, co-extensive; and then it would be the case that we would know the former to be confirmable but not know the latter to be so. Just as we needn't know who killed Cock Robin even if we know someone did, so we needn't know what is a confirmation procedure for a predicate even if we know something is; just as there can be a man for the job without our having one, so there can be a confirmation procedure for a predicate without our having one; etc. (The imagery is that of the mathematical realist and is to be found in most expositions of the topic—for example, in *Rogers*, §1.3.)

But there are no serious problems here: as Church pointed out, it all depends upon how one takes the existential quantifier used in defining 'confirm*able*' (and 'Σ-represent*able*'), whether in a constructive sense or not; and, as he judiciously adds, "What the criterion of constructiveness shall be is left to the reader" (*1936*, p. 95). Some superficially serious problems turn out to be no more than mildly diverting paralogisms generated by shuffling back and forth between constructive and non-constructive senses of the quantifier. One such is this: it is easy to see that

'*n.* either Fermat was right and *n* is even, or he wasn't and *n* is odd'

is decidable, so it follows that we have a way of deciding whether Fermat was right or not!

In any case it is clear that there is no harm in affirming that *a predicate is confirmable if it is co-extensive with a confirmable predicate*: for each person will regard the two assertions, that the first predicate is co-extensive with the second, and that the second is confirmable, with the same scepticism or lack of it.

IV.4 A *decision procedure* for a predicate θ is an effective procedure that is both a confirmation and a disconfirmation procedure for it (i.e. one such that there is a logical guarantee that θ is not true of a given object just in case the procedure, as applied to that object, will sooner or later halt in a state enabling the agent to recognize that θ is not true of the object). Such a decision procedure, as applied to an object, will sooner or later halt: and when it does it will halt in a state enabling the agent to recognize either that θ is true of the object or that θ is not true of it—thus the procedure enables the agent to *decide* whether θ is true of it.

By way of example, notice that the Systematic Procedure is a decision procedure *as far as Δ-forms are concerned*: that is, it is a disconfirmation procedure, as well as a confirmation procedure, for the predicate

'$X.X$ is a Δ-form that is standardly assigned $\mathbb{T}$';

by Theorem III.3.3, the Procedure, as applied to a Δ-form, eventually halts; and when it does so it will halt either with all branches closed or with at least one open and replete.

It is perhaps not quite obvious that *a predicate that is both confirmable and disconfirmable is decidable*—but suppose given a confirmation procedure for it and a disconfirmation procedure for it; then we can get a decision procedure for it simply by 'interlacing' the two (say by transferring attention from one to the other after each discrete step has been performed).

Since the negations of Δ-sentence-forms are themselves Δ-forms, it follows that Δ-representable predicates are—given Church's thesis—both confirmable and disconfirmable, and hence decidable: but the converse is not true, as we shall see (cf. X.2).

IV.5 Effectiveness is not usually discussed in terms of predicates, but in terms of relations and functions over, and operations on, the set of natural numbers—these are defined in A.3: we say that such a relation is *effectively enumerable* just in case it is the extension of a confirmable predicate; and *effective* just in case both it and its complement are effectively enumerable. We note immediately

THEOREM IV.5.1. *The effective relations are those that are the extensions of decidable predicates.*

PROOF. An effective relation is one such that both it and its complement are the extensions of confirmable predicates: hence one that is both the extension of a confirmable predicate and that of a disconfirmable one: hence (as in IV.3) one that is the extension of a predicate both confirmable and disconfirmable: hence finally (as in IV.4) one that is the extension of a decidable predicate.

Q.E.D.

Since, according to Church (*1936*, p. 100), his 'effectively calculable functions' are those for which there exist algorithms for the calculation of the values, it is clear that they are our effective operations.

We shall shortly need the following result, which is independently interesting:

THEOREM IV.5.2. *A relation is effectively enumerable if it is the domain of another effectively enumerable relation, but only if it is the domain of an effective function.*

PROOF. Let our relation, R say, be binary.

As to the first claim, suppose R is the domain of an effectively enumerable relation S; then there is a confirmation procedure C for the ternary predicate

$$\ulcorner mnp.\ \langle m,n,p\rangle \text{ is a member of } S\urcorner.$$

Now define an effective procedure D so that, as applied to $\langle m,n\rangle$, its $q+1^{\text{th}}$ step is

> Perform the 1st C-step towards confirming whether
> $\langle m,n,q-0\rangle$ is a member of S; and then
> perform the 2nd C-step towards confirming whether
> $\langle m,n,q-1\rangle$ is a member of S; and then
> ⋮
> perform the $q+1^{\text{th}}$ C-step towards confirming whether
> $\langle m,n,q-q\rangle$ is a member of S.

It is clear that D is a confirmation procedure for

$$\ulcorner mn.\ \text{for some } p,\ \langle m,n,p\rangle \text{ is a member of } S\urcorner$$

and so R, which is the domain of S and hence the extension of this predicate, is effectively enumerable.

As to the second claim, suppose R is effectively enumerable, so that there is a confirmation procedure E for

$$\theta : \ulcorner mn.\ \langle m,n\rangle \text{ is a member of } R\urcorner;$$

but now it is part of the definition of an effective procedure that

$$\eta : \ulcorner mnp.\ E, \text{ as applied to } \langle m,n\rangle, \text{ halts at the } p+1^{\text{th}} \text{ step and no sooner}\urcorner$$

should be decidable; hence its extension—which is a function—is effective. But it is clear that θ is co-extensive with

$$\ulcorner mn. \text{ for some } p,\ \eta \text{ is true of } \langle m,n,p\rangle\urcorner$$

and so R is the domain of an effective function.

Q.E.D.

So the domain of an effectively enumerable function must be effectively enumerable, but it need not be effective (indeed, even the domain of an *effective* function need not be effective—consider the predicate '$X\tau$. X is Σ-provable and τ is the closed Σ-tableau for it with smallest Gödel number' and see IX.4, penultimate paragraph); however, if it is effective, then the function is effective: so all effectively enumerable *operations* are effective.

IV.6 Turning now to the concept of recursiveness, we say that a relation is *recursively enumerable* just in case it is the extension of a Σ-representable predicate, and *recursive* just in case both it and its complement are recursively enumerable.

The possibility of such a definition appears to have been first noted, simultaneously but independently, by Feferman and Smullyan (*Feferman 1960*, pt. 3; *Smullyan 1961*, ch. IV, §11). It should be observed that our recursively enumerable functions are what are usually called 'partial recursive functions', and our recursive operations are what are usually called 'recursive functions'; what *we* would call 'recursive functions' occupy an intermediate position and have no usual name. We shall need

THEOREM IV.6.1. *A relation is recursively enumerable if it is the domain of another recursively enumerable relation, but only if it is the domain of a recursive function.*

PROOF. Let our relation, R say, be binary.

As to the first claim, suppose R is the domain of a recursively enumerable relation S; then there is a Σ-representation P of the ternary predicate

$$\ulcorner mnp.\ \langle m,n,p\rangle \text{ is a member of } S\urcorner;$$

but then xy.∃z.P[x, y, z] is a Σ-representation of

$$\ulcorner mn. \text{ for some } p, \langle m,n,p\rangle \text{ is a member of } S\urcorner$$

and so R, which is the domain of S and hence the extension of this predicate, is recursively enumerable.

As to the second claim, suppose R is recursively enumerable, so that there is a Σ-representation P of

$$\theta : \ulcorner mn.\ \langle m,n\rangle \text{ is a member of } R\urcorner;$$

but now consider the predicate

$$\eta : \ulcorner mnp. \text{ the Systematic Procedure, as applied to } P[\bar{m},\bar{n}], \text{ halts at the } p+1^{\text{th}} \text{ step and no sooner}\urcorner$$

—it will become clear later (cf. VI.6) that both

$$\ulcorner mnp.\ \eta \text{ is true of } \langle m,n,p\rangle\urcorner \text{ and } \ulcorner mnp.\ \eta \text{ is not true of } \langle m,n,p\rangle\urcorner$$

are Σ-representable; hence the extension of η—which is a function—is recursive. And it is obvious that θ is co-extensive with

$$\ulcorner mn. \text{ for some } p,\ \eta \text{ is true of } \langle m,n,p\rangle\urcorner$$

and so R is the domain of a recursive function.

Q.E.D.

The only reason for giving Theorems IV.5.2 and IV.6.1 was to be able to give a simple proof of the following, which is included in deference to the tradition:

Theorem IV.6.2. *Church's Thesis is equivalent to each of the following:*
— *the effectively enumerable relations are the recursively enumerable ones;*
— *the effective relations are the recursive ones;*
— *the effective functions are the recursive ones;*
— *the effective operations are the recursive ones.*

Proof. That Church's Thesis is equivalent to the first, and that the first entails the second, are obvious. That the second, third and fourth are equivalent follows from the facts
— that operations are functions;
— that functions are relations;
— that a relation is effective if, and only if, its characteristic function is; and
— that a relation is recursive if, and only if, its characteristic function is.
(The *characteristic function of* a relation is that operation whose value is 1 for members of the relation as arguments, and 0 for other arguments).

So we need only show that the second entails the first. But

suppose the effective relations are the recursive ones: then, if R is an effectively enumerable relation, it is (by Theorem IV.5.2) the domain of an effective function, which function is then (*ex hypothesi*) recursive, so that R is the domain of a recursive function, and thus (by Theorem IV.6.1) recursively enumerable; and conversely.

Q.E.D.

Since the effective operations are Church's effectively calculable functions, and the recursive operations his recursive functions, this theorem justifies the hijacking of the title 'Church's Thesis'—unless, indeed, there was any significance in Church's defining the *notion* of the one by identifying it with the *notion* of the other (*1936*, p. 100): but I do not think there was.

V
Recursively Defined Predicates

V.1 Church's Thesis is a most remarkable proposal. Why on earth should one suggest that, for *any* confirmable predicate of natural numbers, there is a Σ-representation? Why should one even suggest that it is representable—that is, in terms of L, a, m, e? Or in any terms at all?

Consider, for example, the predicate

'*n.n* is $(m+1)!$, for some number *m*',

which is true of $1, 2, 6, 24, 120, 720, 5040, \ldots$. It is clear that it is confirmable (just keep calculating $1, 2 \times 1, 3 \times 2 \times 1, 4 \times 3 \times 2 \times 1, \ldots$) but it is certainly not *clear* that it is Σ-representable. Or consider

'*mn.m* is the nth digit in the decimal expansion of π',

which is true of $\langle 3,1\rangle, \langle 1,2\rangle, \langle 4,3\rangle, \langle 1,4\rangle, \langle 5,5\rangle, \ldots$: the decimal expansion of π is settled by an effective procedure and, for any number *n*, it is simple to compute the nth digit; but—is the predicate Σ-representable?

These are characteristic specimens of a broad class of predicates that, on the face of it, poses grave problems to representability—the class of predicates that are introduced by 'recursive definition'. It is not, for our purposes, necessary to give a general account of recursive definition: a few examples, and an historical excursus, will suffice to make it clear that such predicates are usually easily shown to be representable. The work will at the same time introduce some necessary concepts and provide a firmer grasp of the concept of representability.

Begin with the concept of even-ness: a number-theorist *might* introduce the predicate '*n.n* is an even number' by the following recursive definition:

'0 is even, and whenever m is even, so is $(2+m)$'.

And the question is, whether there is a suitable representation of it. In this case of course there is no problem, because our understanding of recursive definition enables us to see that the predicate, so introduced, is co-extensive with

'$n.n$ is $(m+m)$, for some number m'

and so we know that $x.\exists y.x=(y+y)$ represents it.

But now consider a more tricky case: a number-theorist might introduce the predicate '$n.n$ is a beth-number' by the following recursive definition:

'0 is a beth-number, and whenever m is, so is (2^m)',

so that it is true just of $0, 1, 2, 4, 16, 65536, \ldots$.

In §80 of *Foundations of Arithmetic*, Frege says: "Only by means of the definition of following in a series is it possible to reduce the argument from n to $(n+1)$, which on the face of it is peculiar to mathematics, to the general laws of logic." The definition he refers to was such that the predicate

'$n.n$ falls under every concept such that
— 0 falls under it; and
— 2^m falls under it whenever m does'

would have given the sense of the predicate '$n.n$ is a beth-number'—or at least an acceptable paraphrase thereof. In terms we understand better, his predicate would be

'n.every singular predicate that is
— true of 0; and
— true of 2^m whenever it's true of m;
is true of n'.

It is clear that this predicate is true of all and only the beth-numbers, so that a representation of it would solve our problem: however, the quantification involved is not over numbers but over singulary predicates, and we have no way of handling such quantification.

Dedekind, working quite independently, arrived at a very similar thesis: he cited as one of "the essential fundamental ideas" of his *The Nature and Meaning of Numbers* "the proof that the form of argument known as complete induction (or the inference from n to $n+1$) is really conclusive, and that therefore definition by induction (or recursion) is determinate and consistent" (pp. 32–3). For him, an acceptable paraphrase of the sense of '$n.n$ is a beth-number' is given by

'*n*.*n* is a member of every set of which
— 0 is a member; and
— 2^m is a member whenever *m* is';

here the quantification involved is over sets, and so we're apparently no further forward.

Indeed, the quantification involved is essentially over *infinite* sets (because a set of which 0 is a member, and of which 2^m is a member whenever *m* is, clearly has all the infinitely many beth-numbers as members): so in §241 of *The Principles of Mathematics*, Russell complains against Dedekind "that theorems concerning the finite class of numbers not greater than *n* as a rule have to be deduced from corresponding theorems concerning the infinite class of numbers greater than *n*"—which complaint, if I understand it correctly, is the same as that on pp. 75–6 of Quine's *Set Theory and its Logic*. Yet Dedekind could easily have avoided the criticism by considering instead the predicate

'*n*.*n* is a term of a finite sequence of which
— the first term is 0; and
— any other term is $2^{\text{its predecessor}}$'

—for here the quantification, though admittedly over sequences, is at least over *finite* sequences. (For other possible side-steps open to Dedekind, consult Quine's footnote, loc. cit.)

Yet still our formal language seems inadequate, for it permits only quantification over numbers.

V.2 Even apart from issues specifically associated with recursive definition, it is apparent that the number-theorist often wishes to talk about, and quantify over, finite sequences of numbers. For example, a well-known truth is that

a number is divisible by 3 iff the sum of its digits is

—which could be put thus:

a number is divisible by 3 iff the sum of the terms of the sequence of its digits is.

Again, a famous (and, as far as I know, unsolved) problem of number-theory is whether

some odd number is perfect

—i.e. whether

some odd number is such that the sum of the terms
of the sequence of its divisors is double itself.

It also soon becomes obvious that the number-theorist wishes to talk, not only of finite sequences whose terms are numbers, but of those whose terms are themselves finite sequences of numbers. For example, of a matrix, such as

9	14	7	2	31
41	22	0	7	3
3	7	14	15	5
6	9	3	0	100,

the number-theorist might want to say that the sum of the sums of the individual rows is the same as the sum of the sums of the individual columns: if he identifies the matrix with (say) the sequence of length 5 whose i^{th} term is the ith column of the matrix, he can say what he wants to say while talking of finite sequences of finite sequences of numbers.

In general, we can say that the number-theorist wishes to talk about (*finite*) *numerical sequents*, where we introduce that predicate recursively:

— each number is a *numerical sequent*;

— whenever $\sigma_1, \ldots, \sigma_n$ are *numerical sequents*, so is the finite sequence $\langle \sigma_1, \ldots, \sigma_n \rangle$.

(Of course, there is much else he also wishes to talk about—finite sets of numbers, for example, and even arbitrary infinite sets and sequences of numbers; though here his interest overlaps that of the analyst.) Here are some numerical sequents:

0	3	110
$\langle 0,0 \rangle$	$\langle 0,3,0 \rangle$	$\langle 1,1,0 \rangle$
$\langle \langle 0,0 \rangle, 3 \rangle$	$\langle \langle 0,0 \rangle, \langle 0,3,0 \rangle \rangle$	$\langle 1, \langle 1,1 \rangle, \langle \langle 1,1 \rangle, 0 \rangle \rangle$

An important corollary of the explanation of numerical sequents is that each can be fully and uniquely described by an expression of mathematical English that involves just signs from among the following thirteen:

‘0’ ‘1’ ‘2’ ‘3’ ‘4’ ‘5’ ‘6’ ‘7’ ‘8’ ‘9’ ‘$\langle$’ ‘$\rangle$’ ‘,’ .

This thought is the key to what follows: for whatever can be fully and uniquely described using only signs from a finite list can be given a code-number in such a way that each such thing has one and only one code-number, and the ‘encoding’ is decidable. There are infinitely many possible ‘encodings’ of numerical sequents as numbers and, although we settle on a particular one, nothing special hangs upon the choice.

The encoding we use is introduced recursively:

— for any number n, the *code-number of n* is that number whose numeral is $\ulcorner 1\underbrace{0\ldots0}_{n}\urcorner$ in the conventional Hindu-Arabic denary notation;

— for any numerical sequents $\sigma_1, \sigma_2, \ldots, \sigma_n$, with respective *code-numbers* $c_1, c_2, \ldots, c_n$, the *code-number of* the sequent $\langle\sigma_1, \sigma_2, \ldots, \sigma_n\rangle$ is that number whose numeral is $\ulcorner 2a_1 3a_2 3\ldots 3a_n 4\urcorner$, $a_1, a_2, \ldots, a_n$ being the numerals for $c_1, c_2, \ldots, c_n$.

And we say that a number *encodes* a sequent iff it is its code-number. Some examples:

sequent	code-number
0	1
12	1000000000000
$((3+1)\times 4)$	10000000000000000
$\langle 2,1,2\rangle$	210031031004
$\langle 3,3,3,3\rangle$	21000310003100031 0004
$\langle 2,\langle 2\rangle,\langle\langle 2\rangle\rangle\rangle$	2100321004322100444
$\langle 2,\langle\langle 2\rangle\rangle,\langle 2\rangle\rangle$	2100322100443210044
$\langle 2,\langle 2,\langle 2\rangle\rangle\rangle$	21003210032100444

THEOREM V.2.1. *The binary predicate 'nσ.n encodes σ' is decidable; each number encodes at most one numerical sequent; and each numerical sequent is encoded by exactly one number.*

PROOF. Merely reflect that to convert a full and unique description of a sequent in terms of the thirteen signs mentioned into a conventional Hindu-Arabic denary numeral, one simply has to replace numerals $\ulcorner n\urcorner$ by numerals $\ulcorner 1\underbrace{0\ldots0}_{n}\urcorner$, and the signs '⟨', '⟩' and ',' by '2', '4' and '3'.

Q.E.D.

Finally, the *size of* the code-number of a finite sequence is the length of the sequence, and the *parts—first, second, third, fourth …—of* the code-number are the code-numbers of the terms—first, second, third, fourth …—of the sequence. Thus the number 2100321004322100444 encodes $\langle 2,\langle 2\rangle,\langle\langle 2\rangle\rangle\rangle$, so its size is 3, and its first, second and third parts are 100, 21004 and 2210044.

V.3 We left the problem of representing '*n.n* is a beth-number' when we had reduced it to that of representing

'*n.n* is a term of a sequent of which
— the first term is 0; and
— any other term is $2^{\text{its predecessor}}$'

and we can now further reduce it, in virtue of the encoding just described, to that of representing

'*n.n* is encoded by a part of a code-number of which
— the first part encodes 0; and
— any other part encodes $2^{\text{what its predecessor encodes}}$'.

So we are now a considerable way towards solving our problem, since the quantification here is over numbers—with which we can cope.

To crack the problem finally, we need to know that *a ternary* Δ*-predicate-form* Pt *has been found that represents*

'lmn.l is positive, m is a code-number with at least l parts, and n is the lth part of m'.

We are indebted for this fact essentially to Gödel—see the eighth entry in the catalogue in Section 2 of *1931*. A proof is fairly demanding, but purely an exercise in number-theory: to construct one appropriate to this particular encoding of sequents—which is quite unlike Gödel's (but very like Turing's: cf. *Turing* pp. 126–7)—consult *Smullyan 1961*, ch. IV #B. We don't use Pt itself, but rather a couple of Δ-descriptor-forms derived from it: we write

'sz' for '$\mathrm{y}.\iota\mathrm{x}<\mathrm{y}.(\exists\mathrm{z}<\mathrm{y}.\mathrm{Pt}[\mathrm{x},\mathrm{y},\mathrm{z}] \wedge \sim\exists\mathrm{z}<\mathrm{y}.\mathrm{Pt}[\mathrm{x}',\mathrm{y},\mathrm{z}])$'

and 'pt' for '$\mathrm{xy}.\iota\mathrm{z}<\mathrm{y}.\mathrm{Pt}[\mathrm{x},\mathrm{y},\mathrm{z}]$'

so that the following are Δ-forms that are standardly assigned 𝕋—

$$\mathrm{sz}[\overline{210032103104321313144}]=\overline{3}$$
$$\mathrm{pt}[\overline{2},\overline{210032103104321313144}]=\overline{2103104}$$
$$\mathrm{pt}[\overline{3},\overline{210032103104321313144}]=\overline{2131314}$$
$$\mathrm{sz}[\overline{2103104}]=\overline{2}$$
$$\mathrm{pt}[\overline{2},\overline{2103104}]=\overline{10}.$$

Also, we write

'enc' for '$\mathrm{y}.\iota\mathrm{x}<\mathrm{y}.\mathrm{y}=(\overline{10}^{\mathrm{x}})$'.

Now we can solve our problem by considering the form

$$\mathrm{w}.\exists\mathrm{y}.(\exists\mathrm{x}.\mathrm{w}=\mathrm{enc}[\mathrm{pt}[\mathrm{x},\mathrm{y}]] \wedge$$
$$\mathrm{enc}[\mathrm{pt}[\overline{1},\mathrm{y}]]=\overline{0} \wedge$$
$$\forall\mathrm{x}<\mathrm{sz}[\mathrm{y}].(\overline{0}<\mathrm{x} \supset \mathrm{enc}[\mathrm{pt}[\mathrm{x}',\mathrm{y}]]=(\overline{2}^{\mathrm{enc}[\mathrm{pt}[\mathrm{x},\mathrm{y}]]}))).$$

It is clear that it represents the predicate mentioned at the beginning of this section, and so represents the co-extensive predicate '*n.n* is a beth-number'.

V.4 Although we have shown that '*n.n* is a beth-number' is representable, indeed Σ-representable, we ought to be able to do better—for it is clearly decidable: so we ought also to be able to show that '*n.n* is not a beth-number' is Σ-representable. In fact, we can show something stronger still, viz. that '*n.n* is a beth-number' is Δ-representable. To do so, we avail ourselves of a simple result:

THEOREM V.4.1. *The size, and each of the parts, of a code-number is less than it; furthermore, if its size is less than a number m, and each of its parts less than* 10^m*, then it is less than* 10^{m^2}.

PROOF. The first part is obvious. As to the second, consider an example:

$$2\ 10\ 3\ 100\ 3\ 21004\ 3\ 214\ 4$$
$$< 1\ 0\ \underbrace{00}_{2}\ 0\ \underbrace{000}_{3}\ 0\ \underbrace{00000}_{5}\ 0\ \underbrace{000}_{3}\ 0$$
$$= 10^{1+(2+1)+(3+1)+(5+1)+(3+1)}$$
$$\leqslant 10^{1+(5+1)+(5+1)+(5+1)+(5+1)}$$
$$= 10^{5^2}$$

Q.E.D.

So let us write

'bd' for 'w.($\overline{10}^{(w^2)}$)'

as we shall be needing this descriptor-form often.

Now a moment's reflexion reveals that the first predicate mentioned at the beginning of the last section is co-extensive with

'*n.n* is a term of a sequent of which
— the length and each of the terms is less than $n+2$;
— the first term is 0; and
— any other term is $2^{\text{its predecessor}}$'

so that it is represented by

$$\begin{aligned}&\text{w}.\exists\text{y} < \text{bd}[(\text{w}+\bar{2})].(\exists\text{x} < \text{sz}[\text{y}].\text{w} = \text{enc}[\text{pt}[\text{x},\text{y}]] \wedge \\ &\quad \text{enc}[\text{pt}[\bar{1},\text{y}]] = \bar{0} \wedge \\ &\quad \forall\text{x} < \text{sz}[\text{y}].(\bar{0} < \text{x} \supset \text{enc}[\text{pt}[\text{x}',\text{y}]] = (\bar{2}^{\text{enc}[\text{pt}[\text{x},\text{y}]]}))).\end{aligned}$$

And this is a Δ-form, because all of pt, sz, enc and bd are.

V.5 It would not, I think, occur to a working mathematician to introduce '*n.n* is a beth-number' by the recursive definition we have been considering. It is much more likely that such a person would have said

'The first beth-number is 0, and the $m+2^{\text{th}}$ is $2^{\text{the } m+1^{\text{th}}}$'

to introduce the singulary *descriptor* '*m.* the $m+1^{\text{th}}$ beth-number'. This way of proceeding would have posed no problems for the technique of finding a Δ-representation: we should merely have noted that, where *B* is the binary predicate-form

$$\text{vw}.\exists \text{y} < \text{bd}[(\text{w}+\bar{2})].(\text{sz}[\text{y}]=\text{v}' \wedge \text{w}=\text{enc}[\text{pt}[\text{v}',\text{y}]] \wedge \text{enc}[\text{pt}[\bar{1},\text{y}]]=\bar{0} \wedge \forall \text{x} < \text{sz}[\text{y}].(\bar{0}<\text{x} \supset \text{enc}[\text{pt}[\text{x}',\text{y}]]=(\bar{2}^{\text{enc}[\text{pt}[\text{x},\text{y}]]}))),$$

'*mn.* the $m+1^{\text{th}}$ beth-number is *n*' is represented by *B*, so that '*n.n* is a beth-number' is represented by w.∃v<w'.*B*[v, w]. However, it would have brought sharply into focus a further question, viz.: Is there a singulary Δ-*descriptor*-form *b* such that vw.*b*[v]=w represents '*mn.* the $m+1^{\text{th}}$ beth-number is *n*'? This is equivalent to the question whether there is a singulary Δ-descriptor-form *c* such that

$$\forall \text{v}.\forall \text{w}.(B[\text{v},\text{w}] \supset \text{w} < c[\text{v}])$$

is standardly assigned 𝕋—for if there is, v.ɿw<*c*[v].*B*[v, w] will do for *b*.

I suspect, without being sure, that the answer is negative—there is no such form *b* (cf. *Ritchie*): the point of posing the question is simply to give an example of a type that continually arises.

For another example, one sees easily enough that, where *F* is the binary predicate-form

$$\text{vw}.\exists \text{y} < \text{bd}[\text{w}'].(\text{sz}[\text{y}]=\text{v}' \wedge \text{w}=\text{enc}[\text{pt}[\text{v}',\text{y}]] \wedge \text{enc}[\text{pt}[\bar{1},\text{y}]]=\bar{1} \wedge \forall \text{x} < \text{sz}[\text{y}].(\bar{0}<\text{x} \supset \text{enc}[\text{pt}[\text{x}',\text{y}]]=(\text{x}' \times \text{enc}[\text{pt}[\text{x},\text{y}]]))),$$

F represents '*mn.n* is $(m+1)!$' and so, since

$$\forall \text{v}.\forall \text{w}.(F[\text{v},\text{w}] \supset \text{w} < (\text{v}^{\text{v}})''')$$

is standardly assigned 𝕋, one sees that the predicate is also represented by

$$\text{vw}.\text{ɿw} < (\text{v}^{\text{v}})'''.F[\text{v},\text{w}]=\text{w}.$$

Parenthetically, we note that it is clear from some work of Grzegorczyk (*1953*, esp. Theorem 4.10) that

— a relation is elementary in Kalmár's relational sense just in case it is standardly assigned to a Δ-predicate-form; and

— a relation is elementary in Kalmár's operational sense just in case it is standardly assigned to a Δ-descriptor-form:
so, to put matters in these terms, we have seen that the extension of '*mn.n* is $(m+1)!$' is elementary in Kalmár's operational sense, and have doubted that the same is true of '*mn*. the $m+1^{\text{th}}$ beth-number is *n*', although its extension is certainly an operation and, as we have observed, elementary in the relational sense. We shall later come across an operation that is undoubtedly elementary in the weaker sense but not in the stronger (cf. X.2).

V.6 It should now be clear that we have here a technique of wide application for associating with a recursively-defined predicate, a co-extensive one that is representable: speaking roughly, *any predicates introduced by recursive definition in terms of Σ-representable predicates are themselves Σ-representable.* This fact is evidence for the claim underlying and presupposed by Church's Thesis, the claim that the confirmable predicates are Σ-representable: and it justifies the use of the word 'recursive' in the context 'recursive relation'.

It might be supposed that it has been shown that talk about sequents is dispensable and need not occur in mathematics, because reducible to talk about code-numbers. However, the very definitions of 'sequent' and 'code-number' show this idea to be false; and the reason given is inadequate. The reduction proceeds by replacing predicates by co-extensive predicates: but they're *only* co-extensive (though indeed necessarily so) and the replacements do not generally preserve sense—to admit that '*n.n* is twice some number' and '*n.n* is the sum of some number and itself' are co-extensive does not commit one to saying that either is dispensable (if either were, what would become of the theorem that a number is twice some number just in case it is the sum of some number and itself?).

Nor, *a fortiori*, ought one to draw from this chapter, in particular from the opening paragraphs of V.2, the conclusion that number-theorists are somehow unable to talk about sequents except by talking about code-numbers: the point is simply that they can say something like some of what they want to say about sequents by saying something instead about code-numbers—some of the facts about code-numbers mirror some of the facts about sequents, and they can exploit that mirroring (but the fact *of* the mirroring is also a number-theoretical fact).

V.7 By way of appendix to the chapter, it is convenient to introduce at this point a binary Δ-descriptor-form *d* that plays a minor role in what follows:

$$\text{xy.}\iota\text{z} < \text{bd}[(\text{x}+\text{y})].\exists\text{u}<\text{z}.\exists\text{v}<\text{z}.((\text{u}+\text{v})=\text{sz}[\text{z}] \wedge \bar{0}<\text{u} \wedge \text{u}=\text{sz}[\text{x}] \wedge \forall\text{w}<\text{u}.\text{pt}[\text{w}',\text{x}]=\text{pt}[\text{w}',\text{z}] \wedge \bar{0}<\text{v} \wedge \text{v}=\text{sz}[\text{y}] \wedge \forall\text{w}<\text{v}.\text{pt}[\text{w}',\text{y}]=\text{pt}[(\text{u}+\text{w}'),\text{z}]);$$

if $e_1, e_2, \ldots, e_n$ are expressions of the formal language, we write

$$\ulcorner(e_1{}^\frown e_2{}^\frown\ldots{}^\frown e_n)\urcorner \text{ for } \ulcorner d[e_1, d[e_2, d[\ldots, e_n]\ldots]]\urcorner.$$

Despite its curious mode of introduction, $|\text{xy.}(\text{x}^\frown\text{y})|$ is as ordinary a binary recursive operation as $|\text{xy.}(\text{x}\times\text{y})|$: note, for example, that each of these pairs of analogous forms is standardly assigned 𝕋—

$$(\overline{2104}{}^\frown\overline{22144})=\overline{21032144}$$
$$(\overline{2104}\times\overline{22144})=\overline{46590976}$$

$$\forall\text{x}.\forall\text{y}.((\text{sz}[\text{x}]=\bar{0} \vee \text{sz}[\text{y}]=\bar{0}) \supset (\text{x}^\frown\text{y})=\bar{0})$$
$$\forall\text{x}.\forall\text{y}.((\text{x}=\bar{0} \vee \text{y}=\bar{0}) \supset (\text{x}\times\text{y})=\bar{0})$$

$$\forall\text{x}.\forall\text{y}.\forall\text{z}.(\text{x}^\frown(\text{y}^\frown\text{z}))=((\text{x}^\frown\text{y})^\frown\text{z})$$
$$\forall\text{x}.\forall\text{y}.\forall\text{z}.(\text{x}\times(\text{y}\times\text{z}))=((\text{x}\times\text{y})\times\text{z})$$

In general, if $c_1, c_2, \ldots, c_n$ are the code-numbers of finite sequences $\sigma_1, \sigma_2, \ldots, \sigma_n$, then $|(\bar{c}_1{}^\frown\bar{c}_2{}^\frown\ldots{}^\frown\bar{c}_n)|$ is the code-number of the concatenation of $\langle\sigma_1, \sigma_2, \ldots, \sigma_n\rangle$.

VI
The 'Arithmetization of Syntax'

VI.1 The formal objects under discussion in mathematical logic include such things as letters, forms and various kinds of tableaux. Forms are expressions, i.e. finite sequences of letters (A.5); and tableaux are finite sequences of finite sequences of forms (A.7). For instance, if p and q are sentence-letters, the sentence-form $((p \vee q) \vee \sim(q \vee p))$ is the finite sequence

$$\langle (, (, p, \vee, q,), \vee, \sim, (, q, \vee, p,),) \rangle$$

of length 14, each of whose terms is a letter. (A form that consists of a letter alone is the finite sequence of length 1 whose only term is that letter.) Again, the tableau

$$((p \vee q) \vee \sim(q \vee p))$$
$$\sim(q \vee p)$$
$$(\sim q \wedge \sim p)$$
$$\sim q \qquad\qquad\qquad\qquad \sim p$$
$$(p \vee q)$$
$$q$$

is the finite sequence of length 2 whose first term

$$\langle ((p \vee q) \vee \sim(q \vee p)), \sim(q \vee p), (\sim q \wedge \sim p), \sim q, (p \vee q), q \rangle$$

is the left-hand branch, and whose second term

$$\langle ((p \vee q) \vee \sim(q \vee p)), \sim(q \vee p), (\sim q \wedge \sim p), \sim p \rangle$$

is the right-hand branch; each branch being itself a finite sequence of sentence-forms.

To generalize, we can say that the formal objects under discussion in mathematical logic include all the *(finite) syntactical sequents*, where we introduce that predicate recursively:

— each letter is a *syntactical sequent*;
— whenever $\sigma_1, \ldots, \sigma_n$ are *syntactical sequents*, so is the finite sequence $\langle \sigma_1, \ldots, \sigma_n \rangle$.

It is obvious that the syntactical sequents and the numerical sequents are in one-to-one correspondence in such a way that the $m+1^{\text{th}}$ letter corresponds to the $m+1^{\text{th}}$ number (i.e. m), and, if $\sigma_1, \ldots, \sigma_n$ respectively correspond to $\rho_1, \ldots, \rho_n$, then $\langle \sigma_1, \ldots, \sigma_n \rangle$ corresponds to $\langle \rho_1, \ldots, \rho_n \rangle$: the *Gödel number of* a syntactical sequent is the code-number of the numerical sequent to which it corresponds.[1]

Examples: suppose $p, q, \wedge, (,)$ are the first five letters, in that order; then

—cor-$(p \wedge q)$ is : cor-$\langle (, p, \wedge, q,) \rangle$
i.e. : $\langle$cor-(, cor-p, cor-$\wedge$, cor-q, cor-)$\rangle$
i.e. : $\langle 3, 0, 2, 1, 4 \rangle$

—Gn-$(p \wedge q)$ is : cn-cor-$(p \wedge q)$
i.e. : cn-$\langle 3, 0, 2, 1, 4 \rangle$
i.e. : 210003131003103100004

—cor-$\begin{array}{c}(p \wedge q)\\ \overline{p \quad q}\end{array}$ is : cor-$\langle \langle (p \wedge q), p \rangle, \langle (p \wedge q), q \rangle \rangle$
i.e. : $\langle$cor-$\langle (p \wedge q), p \rangle$, cor-$\langle (p \wedge q), q \rangle \rangle$
i.e. : $\langle \langle$cor-$(p \wedge q)$, cor-$p \rangle$, $\langle$cor-$(p \wedge q)$, cor-$q \rangle \rangle$
i.e. : $\langle \langle \langle 3, 0, 2, 1, 4 \rangle, \langle 0 \rangle \rangle, \langle \langle 3, 0, 2, 1, 4 \rangle, \langle 1 \rangle \rangle \rangle$

—Gn-$\begin{array}{c}(p \wedge q)\\ \overline{p \quad q}\end{array}$ is : cn-cor-$\begin{array}{c}(p \wedge q)\\ \overline{p \quad q}\end{array}$
i.e. : cn-$\langle \langle \langle 3, 0, 2, 1, 4 \rangle, \langle 0 \rangle \rangle, \langle \langle 3, 0, 2, 1, 4 \rangle, \langle 1 \rangle \rangle \rangle$
i.e. : 2221000313100310310000432144322100031 31-
003103100004321 0444.

[1] For the history of the idea of Gödel numbering, see *Tarski 1933*, pp. 184–5 and 249–50, *Church 1936*, p. 94 n. and *Tarski 1956*, p. 12 fn. Kreisel's characteristically *de haut en bas* remark that "contrary to a widespread misunderstanding, there was nothing particularly novel in Gödel's numbering of formulae or derivations, that is, finite sequences of formulae: this was implicit in Cantor's well-known enumeration of finite sequences of elements taken from an enumerated set" (*1980*, p. 170) is misleading—no-one since Cantor has thought that the numbering of finite sequences of mathematical objects, as in V.2, was novel: what *was* novel was the thought that "proofs, from a formal point of view, are nothing but finite sequences of formulas" (*Gödel 1931*, p. 147)—the thought that *language can be seen as part of reality*. It is true that Hilbert had had the same idea a quarter of a century earlier and made it the foundation of his philosophy (we need to "consider the proof itself to be a mathematical object": *1904*, p. 137) but—as with the closely related thought that actions, *from a certain point of view*, are nothing but movements of the body—the praise is due not so much for having the idea as for demonstrating the fecundity of looking at the phenomena from that point of view.

Now, for any syntactical sequent σ, in place of

$\ulcorner$the formal numeral for the Gödel number of $\sigma\urcorner$

we write

$$\ulcorner *\sigma* \urcorner$$

—so that, while σ is a syntactical sequent, $*\sigma*$ is a formal numeral—that is, one of $\overline{0}, \overline{1}, \overline{2}, \overline{3}, \ldots$: in the above example, $*(p \wedge q)*$ would be the formal numeral $\overline{21000313100310310004}$. We have

Theorem VI.1.1. *For any syntactical sequent σ, $|*\sigma*|$ is the Gödel number of σ; and, if σ is not a letter, $|\mathrm{sz}[*\sigma*]|$ is its length and $|\mathrm{pt}[\bar{n}, *\sigma*]|$ the Gödel number of its nth term if it has one.*

Also, for any syntactical sequents $\sigma_1, \sigma_2, \ldots, \sigma_n$ that are not letters, $|(*\sigma_1*{}^\frown*\sigma_2*{}^\frown\ldots{}^\frown*\sigma_n*)|$ is the Gödel number of the concatenation of $\langle\sigma_1, \sigma_2, \ldots, \sigma_n\rangle$.

Proof. To consider one claim only, let σ be a syntactical sequent that is not a letter and has an nth term: then

$|\mathrm{pt}[\bar{n}, *\sigma*]|$ is: the $|\bar{n}|^{\mathrm{th}}$ part of $|*\sigma*|$
i.e. : the nth part of Gn-σ
i.e. : the nth part of cn-cor-σ
i.e. : cn-the nth term of cor-σ
i.e. : cn-cor-the nth term of σ
i.e. : Gn-the nth term of σ.

Q.E.D.

Hence, by the theorem, these are standardly assigned $\mathbb{T}$:

$$\mathrm{sz}[*(p \wedge q)*] = \overline{5} \qquad \mathrm{pt}[\overline{3}, *(p \wedge q)*] = *\wedge*$$

$$(*(*{}^\frown*(p \wedge q)*{}^\frown*\wedge\sim*{}^\frown*(q \wedge p)*{}^\frown*)*) = *((p \wedge q) \wedge \sim(q \wedge p))*$$

VI.2 As an example of what becomes possible by means of the results of VI.1 we shall now give a detailed derivation of a singulary Δ-descriptor-form **fn** such that the form xy.**fn**[x] = y represents the predicate

'*mn*. the Gödel number of the formal numeral for *m* is *n*'.

We recall, first of all, that the formal numerals are recursively defined: the formal numeral for 0 is $\overline{0}$; the formal numeral for $n+1$ is the result of 'dashing' the formal numeral for *n*—the *result of dashing* an expression *e* being *e*', that is, the result of applying to *e* the singulary descriptor-form σ of I.1.

Now the form σ is

$$\mathrm{x.\iota y.(Lxy \wedge \sim\exists z.(Lxz \wedge Lzy))}$$

and so, for an expression *e* to which it is applicable, the result of dashing *e* is the expression

$$\mathrm{\iota y.(L}e\mathrm{y \wedge \sim\exists z.(L}e\mathrm{z \wedge Lzy)),}$$

which is the concatenation of the five-termed syntactical sequent

$$\langle\ \mathrm{\iota y.(L}\ ,\ e\ ,\ \mathrm{y \wedge \sim\exists z.(L}\ ,\ e\ ,\ \mathrm{z \wedge Lzy))}\ \rangle;$$

hence, if we let **dash** be the singulary descriptor-form

$$\mathrm{x.(*\iota y.(L*{}^\frown x^\frown{}*y \wedge \sim\exists z.(L*{}^\frown x^\frown{}*z \wedge Lzy))*)}$$

we see that, for such an expression *e*, the sentence-form

$$\mathbf{dash}[*e*] = *e'*$$

is standardly assigned $\mathbb{T}$. As a consequence, if *n* is the Gödel number of such an expression, the value of the operation |**dash**| for *n* as argument is the Gödel number of the result of dashing that of which *n* is the Gödel number.

Now let **Fnsq** be the form

$$\begin{aligned}&\mathrm{yv.(sz[y]=(v+\bar{1})} \wedge \\ &\quad \mathrm{pt[\bar{1},y]=*\bar{0}*} \wedge \\ &\quad \mathrm{\forall x<sz[y].(\bar{0}<x \supset pt[x',y]=}\mathbf{dash}\mathrm{[pt[x,y]]));}\end{aligned}$$

then, for any pair of numbers *g* and *m*, $\mathbf{Fnsq}[\bar{g},\bar{m}]$ is standardly assigned $\mathbb{T}$

iff— the size of *g* is $m+1$; and

— the first part of *g* is the Gödel number of $\bar{0}$; and

— any other part of *g* is the value of |**dash**| for the preceding part as argument : i.e.

iff *g* is a code-number of which

— the size is $m+1$; and

— the first part is the Gödel number of $\bar{0}$; and

— any other part is the Gödel number of the result of dashing that of which the preceding part is the Gödel number : i.e.

iff *g* is the code-number of the numerical sequent of which

— the length is $m+1$; and

— the first term is the correspondent of $\bar{0}$; and

— any other term is the correspondent of the result of dashing that of which the preceding term is the correspondent : i.e.

iff *g* is the Gödel number of the syntactical sequent of which

— the length is $m+1$; and

— the first term is $\bar{0}$; and

— any other term is the result of dashing the preceding

term : i.e.
iff g is the Gödel number of $\langle\bar{0},\bar{1},\bar{2},\ldots,\bar{m}\rangle$.

Thus at this point we already know that

$$\mathrm{vw}.\exists\mathrm{y}.(\mathrm{w}=\mathrm{pt}[\mathrm{v}',\mathrm{y}]\wedge\mathbf{Fnsq}[\mathrm{y},\mathrm{v}])$$

represents

'*mn.* the Gödel number of the formal numeral for m is n'.

But to deliver the goods promised, we need to enter into further detail. What we shall now show is that

$$\forall\mathrm{y}.\forall\mathrm{v}.(\mathbf{Fnsq}[\mathrm{y},\mathrm{v}]\supset\mathrm{y}<\mathrm{bd}[(((\bar{2}^{\mathrm{v}})\times\overline{30})+\bar{k})])$$

is standardly assigned $\mathbb{T}$, where k is the least number such that all the letters that occur in either $\bar{0}$ or σ are among the first k letters.

To see this, observe that the length of the formal numeral for a number m is $(2^m\times30)-20$, and each letter that occurs in it is among the first k (this follows by mathematical induction from the facts

— that the length of $\bar{0}$, which is ${\imath}\mathrm{x}.\sim\exists\mathrm{y}.\mathrm{Lyx}$, is 10, and each letter that occurs in $\bar{0}$ is among the first k;

— that, for an expression e to which σ is applicable, the length of e' is twice that of e, plus 20 (because e' is ${\imath}\mathrm{y}.(\mathrm{L}e\mathrm{y}\wedge\sim\exists\mathrm{z}.(\mathrm{L}e\mathrm{z}\wedge\mathrm{Lzy})))$, and each letter that occurs in e' occurs in either e or σ); thus the Gödel number of the formal numeral for a number m is of size less than $(2^m\times30)+k$ and each of its parts—being the Gödel number of one of the first k letters—is less than $10^{(2^m\times30)+k}$: so the result follows by Theorem V.4.1.

Now we write

'**fn**' for '$\mathrm{v}.\mathrm{pt}[\mathrm{v}',{\imath}\mathrm{y}<\mathrm{bd}[(((\bar{2}^{\mathrm{v}})\times\overline{30})+\bar{k})].\mathbf{Fnsq}[\mathrm{y},\mathrm{v}]]$'

and so see that $\mathrm{vw}.\mathbf{fn}[\mathrm{v}]=\mathrm{w}$ is a Δ-representation of the predicate. Hence, for any formal numeral ν,

$$\mathbf{fn}[\nu]=*\nu*$$

is a Δ-form that is standardly assigned $\mathbb{T}$: by way of example, both $\mathbf{fn}[\bar{2}]=*\bar{2}*$ and $\mathbf{fn}[\overline{22}]=*\overline{22}*$ are standardly assigned $\mathbb{T}$; and so are both $\mathbf{fn}[*\wedge*]=**\wedge**$ and $\mathbf{fn}[*(p\wedge q)*]=**(p\wedge q)**$. Observe, incidentally, that

$$\forall\mathrm{x}.\mathrm{x}<\mathbf{fn}[\mathrm{x}]$$

is standardly assigned $\mathbb{T}$.

Next, an example of a Δ-representation of

'*n.n* is the Gödel number of a form of type B
that is standardly assigned $\mathbb{T}$'.

Remember that a form of type B is one that is $\bar{m}=\bar{n}$, $\bar{m}\neq\bar{n}$, $\bar{m}<\bar{n}$ or $\sim\bar{m}<\bar{n}$, for some numbers m and n. So X is a form of type B that is standardly assigned 𝕋 just in case there are numbers m and n such that either m is the same as n and X is $\bar{m}=\bar{n}$ or m is not the same as n and X is $\bar{m}\neq\bar{n}$ or m is less than n and X is $\bar{m}<\bar{n}$ or m is not less than n and X is $\sim\bar{m}<\bar{n}$; and both m and n are less than the Gödel number of X (each is less than the Gödel number of its own formal numeral, which is actually part of, and so less than, the Gödel number of X). Thus the form

$$\begin{aligned}\mathrm{x}.\exists\mathrm{y}<\mathrm{x}.\exists\mathrm{z}<\mathrm{x}.((&\mathrm{y}=\mathrm{z}\wedge\mathrm{x}=(\mathbf{fn}[\mathrm{y}]^\frown{*}=*^\frown\mathbf{fn}[\mathrm{z}]))\vee\\ (&\mathrm{y}\neq\mathrm{z}\wedge\mathrm{x}=(*\sim*^\frown\mathbf{fn}[\mathrm{y}]^\frown{*}=*^\frown\mathbf{fn}[\mathrm{z}]))\vee\\ (&\mathrm{y}<\mathrm{z}\wedge\mathrm{x}=(*\mathrm{L}*^\frown\mathbf{fn}[\mathrm{y}]^\frown\mathbf{fn}[\mathrm{z}]))\vee\\ (&\sim\mathrm{y}<\mathrm{z}\wedge\mathrm{x}=(*\sim*^\frown*\mathrm{L}*^\frown\mathbf{fn}[\mathrm{y}]^\frown\mathbf{fn}[\mathrm{z}])))\end{aligned}$$

—for which we write '$\mathbf{Tr}_{\mathsf{B}}$'—does the trick.

As a final example we shall see how, given a Δ-representation of

'*n*.*n* is the Gödel number of a sentence letter'

to construct a Δ-representation of

'*n*.*n* is the Gödel number of a simple form'

—the simple forms being those sentence-forms in which occur no letter other than (,), $\sim$, $\wedge$, $\vee$ and sentence letters $p, q, r, s, \ldots$.

One sees easily enough that a simple form is a term of a sequent each of whose terms is either an atomic simple form (i.e. a one-termed sequent whose only term is a sentence letter) or else the negation of an earlier term or else the conjunction of earlier terms or else the disjunction of earlier terms; and whose length is no greater than that of the form itself; and each of whose terms occurs in the last term—an example of such a sequent is

$$\langle q, \sim q, p, (p\vee q), r, s, (r\wedge s), (\sim q\vee(r\wedge s)),\\ \sim(\sim q\vee(r\wedge s)), ((p\vee q)\wedge\sim(\sim q\vee(r\wedge s)))\rangle.$$

The last two conditions ensure that, where g is the Gödel number of the sequent and n that of the form, the size of g is no greater than n and each of its parts is no greater than n, so that g is less than $10^{(n+1)^2}$.

We write

'**ngn**' for '$\mathrm{x}.(*\sim*^\frown\mathrm{x})$'
'**dsjn**' for '$\mathrm{xy}.(*(*^\frown\mathrm{x}^\frown*\vee*^\frown\mathrm{y}^\frown*)*)$'
'**cnjn**' for '$\mathrm{xy}.(*(*^\frown\mathrm{x}^\frown*\wedge*^\frown\mathrm{y}^\frown*)*)$'
and '**hk**' for '$\mathrm{xy}.\mathbf{dsjn}[\mathbf{ngn}[\mathrm{x}],\mathrm{y}]$'

so that, e.g., these are Δ-forms that are standardly assigned 𝕋:

$$\mathbf{ngn}[*(p \wedge q)*] = * \sim (p \wedge q)*$$
$$\mathbf{dsjn}[* \sim p*, *(p \wedge q)*] = *(\sim p \vee (p \wedge q))*.$$

Now suppose P is a Δ-representation of

'*n.n* is the Gödel number of a sentence letter'

and let Q be

$$\text{w.}(\text{sz}[\text{w}] = \bar{1} \wedge P[\text{pt}[\bar{1}, \text{w}]]);$$

then

$$\begin{aligned} &\text{w.}\exists \text{y} < \text{bd}[\text{w}'].(\exists \text{x} < \text{sz}[\text{y}].\text{w} = \text{pt}[\text{x}', \text{y}] \wedge \\ &\quad \forall \text{x} < \text{sz}[\text{y}].(Q[\text{pt}[\text{x}', \text{y}]] \vee \\ &\qquad \exists \text{w} < \text{x}.\text{pt}[\text{x}', \text{y}] = \mathbf{ngn}[\text{pt}[\text{w}', \text{y}]] \vee \\ &\qquad \exists \text{u} < \text{x}.\exists \text{v} < \text{x}.\text{pt}[\text{x}', \text{y}] = \mathbf{cnjn}[\text{pt}[\text{u}', \text{y}], \text{pt}[\text{v}', \text{y}]] \vee \\ &\qquad \exists \text{u} < \text{x}.\exists \text{v} < \text{x}.\text{pt}[\text{x}', \text{y}] = \mathbf{dsjn}[\text{pt}[\text{u}', \text{y}], \text{pt}[\text{v}', \text{y}]])) \end{aligned}$$

is a Δ-representation of

'*n.n* is the Gödel number of a simple form'.

So what is generally involved in the 'arithmetization of syntax' is this: one moves from a syntactical predicate, such as

'*X.X* is a simple form',

to the associated predicate of numerical sequents, in this case

'$\sigma.\sigma$ is the numerical sequent that corresponds to a simple form',

from there to the appropriate predicate of numbers,

'*n.n* is the Gödel number of a simple form',

and thence finally to a form that represents the last predicate, which may be called an 'arithmetization' of the first one.

What, though, is a 'syntactical' predicate? The obvious answer—a predicate of syntactical sequents—is not at all what Carnap, who is responsible for the phrase 'arithmetization of syntax',[1] would have said: what he meant by 'syntax' is "the systematic statement of the formal rules which govern [the language] together with the development of the consequences which follow from these rules. / A theory, a rule, a definition, or the like is to be called *formal* when no reference is made in it either to the meaning of the symbols ... or to the sense of the expressions ..., but simply and solely to the kinds and order of the symbols from which the expressions are constructed"; furthermore, "*truth and*

[1] Though the idea of arithmetization goes further back: fifty years earlier, the ur-intuitionist Kronecker claimed that "someday people will succeed in 'arithmetizing' all of mathematics, that is, founding it on the single foundation of the number-concept in its narrowest sense" (*Edwards 1988*, p. 141).

falsehood are not proper syntactical properties; whether a sentence is true or false cannot generally be seen by its design, that is to say, by the kinds and serial order of its symbols" (*1937*, pp. 1, 216; Tarski's independent, slightly earlier, but much more condensed, meditation on the theme is in *1933*, p. 237, fn. 2). Yet it is unclear whether or not the predicate

'*X*.*X* is a form of type **B** that is standardly assigned 𝕋'

is syntactical by Carnap's lights: on the first criterion it is not, for "reference is made in it" to the notions involved in understanding what it is to be standardly assigned 𝕋; on the second criterion it is, for whether or not it is true of a form *can* "be seen by [the form's] design" (as is incidentally demonstrated in the construction of $\mathbf{Tr}_{\mathsf{B}}$). This unclarity makes it best not to use the word 'syntax' except in heavily guarded situations.

VI.3 We stipulate, in A.5, that the letters are given according to some fixed and standard well-ordering. We here make a further stipulation, that Δ-representations are to hand of each of

'*mn*. the Gödel number of the mth variable is *n*'
'*mn*. the Gödel number of the mth subject-letter is *n*'
'*mn*. the Gödel number of the mth sentence-letter is *n*'
'*lmn*. the Gödel number of the mth *l*-ary descriptor-letter is *n*'
'*lmn*. the Gödel number of the mth *l*-ary predicate-letter is *n*'.

Is justification of this either necessary or desirable? Church tells us, of a slightly weaker stipulation, that it is necessary if "the system is to serve at all the purposes for which a system of symbolic logic is usually intended" (*1936*, p. 101) but does not say what he takes these purposes to be: later, he imposes further "requirements of effectiveness" and remarks that "a structure which is analogous to a logistic system except that it fails to satisfy these requirements ... is unsuitable for use or interpretation as a language. For, however indefinite or imprecisely fixed the common idea of a language may be, it is at least fundamental to it that a language shall serve the purpose of communication. And to the extent that requirements of effectiveness fail, the purpose of communication is defeated. Consider, in particular, the situation which arises if the definition of well-formedness is non-effective. There is then no certain means by which when an alleged expression of the language is uttered (spoken or written), say as an asserted sentence, the auditor (reader or hearer) may determine whether it is well-formed, and thus whether any actual assertion has been made" (*1956*, pp. 52–3).

It is pretty clear that Church has at the back of his mind a picture of language, based perhaps on some remarks of Frege (cf. *1918–19*, pp. 65–6, 77), according to which each speaker has his own language, but one that can be at least partially understood by others in virtue of rough coincidences in the senses of words, coincidences that can be observed or detected to hold or fail to hold. This picture seems to be without merit but, even if it were correct, it would by no means follow that an auditor must have effective procedures, or even '*certain* means', for determining the meaningfulness and the meaning of a speaker's utterances. Nor is there independent reason for any such consequence, *pace* Davidson (*1965*, p. 8; *1980*, p. 5) and Chomsky (*passim*). The Effective Decidability of Meaning is indeed a requirement, as Church says—and not, as he suggests, a *result of investigation* (cf. *Wittgenstein 1953*, §107).

And even had the Effective Decidability of Meaning been a result of investigation, its application to 'logistic systems' would still depend upon the idea that such a system must be "suitable for use or interpretation as a language", in Church's words. But must it? Church tells us: "There is no reason in principle why a first language ... should not be one of the formalized languages of this book, instead of one of the natural languages" (ib., p. 47), again following Frege, who certainly thought of his *Begriffsschrift* as a possible natural language: but, as van Heijenoort has often pointed out (*1967a*, *1987*), this way of thinking about a logistic system is actually *incompatible* with the way of thinking about it that enquires into its completeness and decidability.

So it seems to me, though I am aware that detailed arguments need to be advanced, that the stipulation is unjustifiable and that no justification is required—except perhaps the observation that the Gödelian results depend upon the formal language's being as stipulated!

VI.4 Following the definition of the predicates, and using the techniques illustrated in VI.2, it is easy—though laborious—to write down, in terms of the stipulated Δ-representations of VI.3, further Δ-representations as follows:

—**Sbjfm**, of '*n.n* is the Gödel number of a subject-form';

—**Dscfm**, of '*ln.n* is the Gödel number of an *l*-ary descriptor-form';

—**Sntfm**, of '*n.n* is the Gödel number of a sentence-form';
—**Prdfm**, of '*ln.n* is the Gödel number of an *l*-ary predicate-form';
—**Δfm**, of '*n.n* is the Gödel number of a Δ-form';
—**Σfm**, of '*n.n* is the Gödel number of a Σ-form';
—**Rgtb**, of '*n.n* is the Gödel number of a regular tableau';
—**Σtb**, of '*n.n* is the Gödel number of a Σ-tableau';
and also a singulary Δ-descriptor-form **ap** with the property that, for any number $l>0$, any l-ary predicate- or descriptor-form f, and any expressions $e_1,\ldots,e_l$, $|\mathbf{ap}[*\langle f,e_1,\ldots,e_l\rangle*]|$ is the Gödel number of $f[e_1,\ldots,e_l]$—that is, of the result of applying f to $e_1,\ldots,e_l$.

Thus, by way of illustration, the following are Δ-forms that are standardly assigned 𝕋:

$$\mathbf{\Sigma fm}[*\exists x.\forall y<x.y=(x^{\bar{2}})*]$$
$$\sim\mathbf{\Sigma fm}[*\forall x.\exists y<x.y=(x^{\bar{2}})*]$$
$$\mathbf{ap}[*\langle x.\imath y.y<(x^{\bar{2}}),((z\times\bar{3})+x)\rangle*]=*\imath y.y<(((z\times\bar{3})+x)^{\bar{2}})*.$$

It is convenient to write

$$\text{'}\mathbf{ap}_1\text{' for 'wx.}\mathbf{ap}[(\iota[w]^\frown\iota[x])]\text{'}$$
$$\text{'}\mathbf{ap}_2\text{' for 'wxy.}\mathbf{ap}[(\iota[w]^\frown\iota[x]^\frown\iota[y])]\text{'}$$
$$\text{'}\mathbf{ap}_3\text{' for 'wxyz.}\mathbf{ap}[(\iota[w]^\frown\iota[x]^\frown\iota[y]^\frown\iota[z])]\text{'}$$

and so forth, where ι is $v.\imath w<\mathrm{bd}[v].(\mathrm{sz}[w]=\bar{1}\wedge\mathrm{pt}[\bar{1},w]=v)$, so that, if f, $e_1,\ldots,e_l$ are as before, then

$$(\iota[*f*]^\frown\iota[*e_1*]^\frown\ldots{}^\frown\iota[*e_l*])=*\langle f,e_1,\ldots,e_l\rangle*,$$

and hence

$$\mathbf{ap}_l[*f*,*e_1*,\ldots,*e_l*]=*f[e_1,\ldots,e_l]*,$$

is standardly assigned 𝕋—for instance, this is:

$$\mathbf{ap}_2[*xy.\imath u.\exists v.(u^x)<(v+y)*,*x'*,*x*]=*\imath u.\exists v.(u^{x'})<(v+x)*.$$

Notice that the first example in VI.2 could have been simplified by using $x.\mathbf{ap}_1[*\sigma*,x]$ in place of **dash**; and the second could have been put more illuminatingly as

$$\begin{aligned}x.\exists y<x.\exists z<x.((y=z\wedge x=\mathbf{ap}_2[*yz.y=z*,\mathbf{fn}[y],\mathbf{fn}[z]])\vee\\(y\neq z\wedge x=\mathbf{ap}_2[*yz.y\neq z*,\mathbf{fn}[y],\mathbf{fn}[z]])\vee\\(y<z\wedge x=\mathbf{ap}_2[*yz.y<z*,\mathbf{fn}[y],\mathbf{fn}[z]])\vee\\(\sim y<z\wedge x=\mathbf{ap}_2[*yz.\sim y<z*,\mathbf{fn}[y],\mathbf{fn}[z]]))\end{aligned}$$

or even as

$$\begin{aligned}x.\exists y<x.\exists z<x.((P[y,z]\wedge x=\mathbf{ap}_2[*P*,\mathbf{fn}[y],\mathbf{fn}[z]])\vee\\(Q[y,z]\wedge x=\mathbf{ap}_2[*Q*,\mathbf{fn}[y],\mathbf{fn}[z]])\vee\\(R[y,z]\wedge x=\mathbf{ap}_2[*R*,\mathbf{fn}[y],\mathbf{fn}[z]])\vee\\(S[y,z]\wedge x=\mathbf{ap}_2[*S*,\mathbf{fn}[y],\mathbf{fn}[z]]))\end{aligned}$$

where P is $yz.y=z$, Q is $yz.y\neq z$, and so on.

VI.5 The singulary predicate-form from VI.2 just alluded to is $\mathbf{Tr}_{\mathrm{B}}$; using it, let us write

'$\mathbf{\Sigma cl}$' for '$\mathrm{x}.\exists \mathrm{y} < \mathrm{sz}[\mathrm{x}].\mathbf{Tr}_{\mathrm{B}}[\mathrm{pt}[\mathrm{y}',\mathrm{x}]]$'
'$\mathbf{Cl\Sigma tb}$' for '$\mathrm{y}.(\mathbf{\Sigma tb}[\mathrm{y}] \wedge \forall \mathrm{x} < \mathrm{sz}[\mathrm{y}].\mathbf{\Sigma cl}[\mathrm{pt}[\mathrm{x}',\mathrm{y}]])$'
'$\mathbf{tpfm}$' for '$\mathrm{y}.\mathrm{pt}[\bar{1},\mathrm{pt}[\bar{1},\mathrm{y}]]$'
and '$\mathbf{\Sigma pr}$' for '$\mathrm{x}.\exists \mathrm{y}.(\mathbf{Cl\Sigma tb}[\mathrm{y}] \wedge \mathrm{x} = \mathbf{tpfm}[\mathrm{y}])$'

so that we have

THEOREM VI.5.1. $\mathbf{\Sigma pr}$ *is a* Σ*-representation of*

'n.n is the Gödel number of a Σ*-provable form'.*

and thus

COROLLARY VI.5.2. *'X.X is* Σ*-provable' is effectively confirmable.*

—although we knew this already, since the Systematic Procedure is a confirmation procedure for '*X.X* is Σ-provable'.

Of more interest is the implication of the theorem that, for any Σ-sentence-form X, $\mathbf{\Sigma pr}[*X*]$ is standardly assigned $\mathbb{T}$ just in case X is Σ-provable—which, by Theorem III.2.2, is so just in case X is standardly assigned $\mathbb{T}$. Hence:

COROLLARY VI.5.3. *For any* Σ*-sentence-form* X,

$$(\mathbf{\Sigma pr}[*X*] \equiv X)$$

is standardly assigned $\mathbb{T}$.

Next, consider a Σ-predicate-form P that is, say, ternary: for any formal numerals κ, λ, μ we have that

$$\mathbf{fn}[\kappa] = *\kappa* \qquad \mathbf{fn}[\lambda] = *\lambda* \qquad \mathbf{fn}[\mu] = *\mu*$$

and $$\mathbf{ap}_3[*P*, *\kappa*, *\lambda*, *\mu*] = *P[\kappa, \lambda, \mu]*$$

are standardly assigned $\mathbb{T}$, and therefore, by Corollary VI.5.3,

$$(\mathbf{\Sigma pr}[\mathbf{ap}_3[*P*, \mathbf{fn}[\kappa], \mathbf{fn}[\lambda], \mathbf{fn}[\mu]]] \equiv P[\kappa, \lambda, \mu])$$

is also standardly assigned $\mathbb{T}$; consequently, so is

$$\forall \mathrm{x}.\forall \mathrm{y}.\forall \mathrm{z}.(\mathbf{\Sigma pr}[\mathbf{ap}_3[*P*, \mathbf{fn}[\mathrm{x}], \mathbf{fn}[\mathrm{y}], \mathbf{fn}[\mathrm{z}]]] \equiv P[\mathrm{x}, \mathrm{y}, \mathrm{z}]).$$

More generally, we have

COROLLARY VI.5.4. *For any n-ary* Σ*-predicate-form* P $(n>0)$ *and variables* $\alpha_1, \ldots, \alpha_n$,

$$\forall \alpha_1.\ldots.\forall \alpha_n.(\mathbf{\Sigma pr}[\mathbf{ap}_n[*P*, \mathbf{fn}[\alpha_1], \ldots, \mathbf{fn}[\alpha_n]]] \equiv P[\alpha_1, \ldots, \alpha_n])$$

is standardly assigned $\mathbb{T}$.

—which is, in essence, Kleene's 'enumeration theorem' (*1952*, p. 281): the function whose value for a number m as argument is $|\mathrm{x}.\mathbf{\Sigma pr}[\mathbf{ap}_1[\bar{m}, \mathbf{fn}[\mathrm{x}]]]|$ is an enumeration, with repetitions, of the recursively enumerable sets. In the abstract theory of computing machines one very soon comes across the existence of a *universal* machine, which mimics the action of any given machine if primed with an acceptable description of it: in just the same way, the predicate-form

$$\text{zx}.\mathbf{\Sigma pr}[\mathbf{ap}_1[\text{z}, \mathbf{fn}[\text{x}]]]$$

'mimics the action of' any given singulary Σ-predicate-form *P* if 'primed with' **P**, which is an 'acceptable description of' it. (This is why the Systematic Procedure was said in IV.2 to be 'universal'.) It is perhaps worth mentioning here that the results Kleene derives using his famous elementary relation T_1 can just as easily be derived using, instead of S_1 (which it replaces),

$$|\text{zxy}.(\mathbf{Cl\Sigma tb}[\text{y}] \wedge \mathbf{ap}_1[\text{z}, \mathbf{fn}[\text{x}]] = \mathbf{tpfm}[\text{y}])|,$$

which is also elementary.

VI.6 In the course of the proof of Theorem IV.6.1, certain claims were made that can now be justified. Let *P* be a binary predicate-form: we shall see that there is a Δ-representation of

$$\ulcorner mnp. \text{ the Systematic Procedure, as applied to } P[\bar{m}, \bar{n}], \text{ halts at the } p+1^{\text{th}} \text{ step and no sooner}\urcorner.$$

It isn't difficult to find a Δ-representation **Systext** of

'*mn.n* is the Gödel number of a systematic extension of a Σ-tableau with Gödel number *m*'

and we let **Systchn** be

$$\text{x}.(\exists \text{w} < \text{x}.(\mathbf{\Sigma fm}[\text{w}] \wedge \text{pt}[\bar{1}, \text{x}] = \iota[\iota[\text{w}]]) \wedge \forall \text{z} < \text{sz}[\text{x}].(\bar{0} < \text{z} \supset \mathbf{Systext}[\text{pt}[\text{z}, \text{x}], \text{pt}[\text{z}', \text{x}]]))$$

which therefore represents

'*m.m* is the Gödel number of a systematic chain of Σ-tableaux of finite order'.

Also, we can find a binary Δ-descriptor-form *c* such that

$$\forall \text{x}.(\mathbf{Systchn}[\text{x}] \supset \text{x} < c[\text{pt}[\bar{1}, \text{x}], \text{sz}[\text{x}]])$$

is standardly assigned $\mathbb{T}$.

Hence **SystProc**, or

$$\text{wy}.\exists \text{x} < c[\iota[\iota[\text{w}]], \text{y}].(\mathbf{Systchn}[\text{x}] \wedge \text{pt}[\bar{1}, \text{x}] = \iota[\iota[\text{w}]] \wedge \text{sz}[\text{x}] = \text{y} \wedge \mathbf{Cl\Sigma tb}[\text{pt}[\text{y}, \text{x}]])$$

represents

'*mn.m* is the Gödel number of a form applied to which the Systematic Procedure halts no later than the nth step'.

So the following does the trick:

uvy.(**SystProc**[**ap**$_2$[**P**,**fn**[u],**fn**[v]],y'] ∧
~∃z<y.**SystProc**[**ap**$_2$[**P**,**fn**[u],**fn**[v]],z']).

VI.7 Let us write '**Rgcl**' for

'x.(∃y<sz[x].∃u<x.(**Sbjfm**[u] ∧ pt[y',x]=(u⌒*=*⌒u))
∨ ∃y<sz[x].∃z<sz[x].pt[y',x]=**ngn**[pt[z',x]])'

and '**Clrgtb**' for

'y.(**Rgtb**[y] ∧ ∀x<sz[y].**Rgcl**[pt[x',y]])'.

THEOREM VI.7.1. **Clrgtb** *is a Δ-representation of*

'm.m is the Gödel number of a closed regular tableau'.

Recall that a formal deduction of a sentence-form *X* from a set of sentence-forms is a closed regular tableau for the hook-up of a finite sequence whose last term is *X* and whose other terms (if any) are all members of the set. Clearly, we can find a singulary Δ-descriptor-form **hkup** such that, for any finite sequence σ of sentence-forms, |**hkup**[*σ*]| is the Gödel number of the hook-up of σ.

For any singulary predicate-form *P*, we write ⌜**Fmddn**$_P$⌝ for

⌜yx.(**Clrgtb**[y] ∧
∃z<bd[y].(**hkup**[z]=**tpfm**[y] ∧
pt[sz[z],z]=x ∧
∀w<sz[z].($\bar{0}$<w ⊃ *P*[pt[w,z]])))⌝.

THEOREM VI.7.2. **Fmddn**$_P$ *is a Δ-form if P is, and a Σ-form if P is. Also, if P represents ⌜n.n is the Gödel number of a member of S⌝, then* **Fmddn**$_P$ *represents ⌜mn.m is the Gödel number of a formal deduction from S of a form with Gödel number n⌝.*

PROOF. All is obvious except the bound: but suppose δ is a tableau for the hook-up of σ: then the length of σ is less than that of the top-form of δ, so less than the Gödel number of the top-form of δ, so less than the Gödel number of δ; furthermore, each term of σ occurs in the top-form of δ and so its Gödel number is less than that of the top-form of δ and so less than that of δ. Hence the Gödel number of σ is less than |bd[*δ*]|.

Q.E.D.

Next, for any singular predicate-form P, we write

$$\ulcorner \mathbf{Fmdbl}_P \urcorner \quad \text{for} \quad \ulcorner \text{x}.\exists \text{y}.\mathbf{Fmddn}_P[\text{y},\text{x}] \urcorner \,;$$

so we have

THEOREM VI.7.3. $\mathbf{Fmdbl}_P$ *is a Σ-form if P is. Also, if P represents* $\ulcorner$*n.n is the Gödel number of a member of S*$\urcorner$*, then* $\mathbf{Fmdbl}_P$ *represents* $\ulcorner$*n.n is the Gödel number of a form that is formally deducible from S*$\urcorner$.

and hence, using Church's Thesis,

COROLLARY VI.7.4. *If* $\ulcorner$*X.X is a member of S*$\urcorner$ *is effectively confirmable, then so is* $\ulcorner$*X.X is formally deducible from S*$\urcorner$.

As with the analogous VI.5.2, the proof of VI.7.4 is a bit roundabout. A more direct way to see that it is true would be to construct a confirmation procedure *C* for the predicate '*X*. there is a closed regular tableau for *X*' by making minor modifications to the Systematic Procedure (for help with the details, consult *Smullyan 1968*, ch. V); then if one has *ex hypothesi* a confirmation procedure *D* for $\ulcorner$*X.X* is a member of *S*$\urcorner$, one can easily construct from *C* and *D* a confirmation procedure for $\ulcorner$*X.X* is formally deducible from *S*$\urcorner$—for to confirm that *X* is formally deducible from *S* one need only confirm that there are members $Y_1, \ldots, Y_n$ of *S* such that there is a closed regular tableau for $(Y_1 \supset \ldots \supset Y_n \supset X)$.

Finally, it is pretty obvious that, if *S* is one of **P**, **Q**, **R**, **S**, then $\ulcorner$*X.X* is a member of *S*$\urcorner$ is not merely confirmable, but decidable: in fact by following I.1 and II.4 we can construct Δ-representations of the appropriate predicates—write

'**S**' for 'w.(w = *∀x.∀y.∀z.(x < y ⊃ y < z ⊃ x < z)* ∨ …
… ∨ w = *∀x.∃y.(x < y ∧ ~∃z.(x < z ∧ z < y))*)'

'**R**' for 'w.(**S**[w] ∨ ∃x < w.∃y < w.
(w = $\mathbf{ap}_3$[*xyz.(x + y) = z*, **fn**[x], **fn**[y], **fn**[(x + y)]] ∨
w = $\mathbf{ap}_3$[*xyz.(x × y) = z*, **fn**[x], **fn**[y], **fn**[(x × y)]] ∨
w = $\mathbf{ap}_3$[*xyz.(x^y) = z*, **fn**[x], **fn**[y], **fn**[(x^y)]]))'

'**Q**' for 'w.(**S**[w] ∨ w = *∀x.(x + $\bar{0}$) = x* ∨ …
… ∨ w = *∀x.∀y.($\text{x}^{\text{y}'}$) = ((x^y) × x)*)'

'**P**' for 'w.(**Q**[w] ∨ ∃p < w.∃t < w.∃u < w.∃v < w.(**Prdfm**[$\bar{1}$, p] ∧
t = $\mathbf{ap}_1$[p, *$\bar{0}$*] ∧
u = (*∀x.*⌒**hk**[$\mathbf{ap}_1$[p, *x*], $\mathbf{ap}_1$[p, *x'*]]) ∧
v = (*∀*⌒p) ∧
w = **hk**[t, **hk**[u, v]]))'.

Thus, by Corollary VI.7.4, the predicate $\ulcorner$*X.X* is formally deducible from *S*$\urcorner$ is effectively confirmable.

VII
Diagonalization

VII.1 The abrupt ending to the last chapter was deliberate: we can go no further along the road until we have a firm grasp of the concept of diagonalization and its uses in constructing paradoxical sentences—those involved in the so-called 'semantical paradoxes' studied by philosophers since antiquity.

Let us begin by recalling the relationships between subjects, singulary predicates,[1] sentences and application—the application, that is, of predicates *of English* to subjects *of English* to obtain sentences *of English*. Some of the facts are displayed in Fig. 2, in which the sentence (right) is the result of applying the predicate (left) to the subject (centre); using the concept of quotation, the same facts—though not the first—are displayed in Fig. 3, in which the sentence is the result of applying the same predicate to *the quotation of* a different subject. ('Though not the first' because there is no such thing as the quotation of Jones—for our purposes only expressions of mathematical English can have quotations.)

In the light of these facts, we see that the sentence

''$\eta.\eta$ contains an archaism' contains an archaism'

is the result of applying the predicate

'$\eta.\eta$ contains an archaism'

to its own quotation. Such a sentence is a *diagonalization*—that is, the result of applying a predicate to its own quotation: the word is of course chosen in allusion to Cantor's demonstration that, in any list of real numbers, the real number obtained 'by going down the diagonal' and systematically altering it is not in the list. Observe

[1] The predicates discussed in the first four sections of this chapter are all assumed to be singulary.

‘$p.p$ is choleric’	‘Jones’	‘Jones is choleric’
‘$\epsilon.\epsilon$ is a monosyllable’	“Jones”	“Jones’ is a monosyllable’
‘$\zeta.\zeta$ is the quotation of a name’	‘“Jones”’	‘“Jones” is the quotation of a name’
⋮	⋮	⋮
‘$\eta.\eta$ contains an archaism’	“$p.p$ is choleric”	“$p.p$ is choleric’ contains an archaism’
‘$\theta.\theta$ contains just one pair of quotes’	‘“$p.p$ is choleric”’	‘“$p.p$ is choleric” contains just one pair of quotes’
⋮	⋮	⋮

Fig. 2: results of application of predicates to subjects.

‘$\epsilon.\epsilon$ is a monosyllable’	‘Jones’	“Jones’ is a monosyllable’
‘$\zeta.\zeta$ is the quotation of a name’	“Jones”	‘“Jones” is the quotation of a name’
⋮	⋮	⋮
‘$\eta.\eta$ contains an archaism’	‘$p.p$ is choleric’	“$p.p$ is choleric’ contains an archaism’
‘$\theta.\theta$ contains just one pair of quotes’	“$p.p$ is choleric”	‘“$p.p$ is choleric” contains just one pair of quotes’
⋮	⋮	⋮

Fig. 3: results of application of predicates to *the quotations of* subjects.

that the diagonalization of '$\eta.\eta$ contains an archaism' is false, because the predicate contains no archaism.

A few more examples: the diagonalization of '$\eta.\eta$ contains no archaism' is

"$\eta.\eta$ contains no archaism' contains no archaism'

and it is true; the diagonalization of '$\pi.\pi$ is a predicate' is

"$\pi.\pi$ is a predicate' is a predicate'

and it is true; the diagonalization of '$\zeta.\zeta$ is a subject' is

"$\zeta.\zeta$ is a subject' is a subject'

and it is false; the diagonalization of '$p.p$ is choleric' is

"$p.p$ is choleric' is choleric'

and it is "a category-mistake. It represents the facts [about the predicate '$p.p$ is choleric'] as if they belonged to one logical type or category ..., when they actually belong to another." (*Ryle 1949*, ch. 1, sect. 2.)

Now sentences have various linguistic properties, such as being interrogative, having the verb in the subjunctive mood, being in the past tense, containing an archaism, having exactly seven words: so consider the following predicate θ_1:

'$\pi.\pi$ is a predicate whose diagonalization contains an archaism'.

Since 'choleric' is—for our purposes—an archaism, θ_1 is true of '$p.p$ is choleric', but it is false of both '$\eta.\eta$ contains an archaism' and '$\eta.\eta$ contains no archaism'. Is θ_1 true of itself? Well, what is θ_1's diagonalization? It is the result of applying θ_1 to its own quotation, that is, the sentence

"$\pi.\pi$ is a predicate whose diagonalization contains an archaism' is a predicate whose diagonalization contains an archaism'.

Clearly, that sentence is true if, and only if, this one is:

'θ_1 is a predicate whose diagonalization contains an archaism'.

Since θ_1 *is* a predicate, the last sentence is true if, and only if, this one is:

'θ_1's diagonalization contains an archaism'.

And that one is true if, and only if,

θ_1's diagonalization contains an archaism.

To sum up, then,

θ_1's diagonalization is true
if, and only if,
θ_1's diagonalization contains an archaism.

And so we see that θ_1 is not true of itself, for θ_1's diagonalization is not true, since it contains no archaism—as is obvious from direct inspection of it.

VII.2 Let S be θ_1's diagonalization, that is, the sentence

"$\pi.\pi$ is a predicate whose diagonalization contains an archaism' is a predicate whose diagonalization contains an archaism'.

What does S say? Or rather, since it says what it says and you can see what it says, what does it *not* say? *One thing it most certainly does not say is that it itself contains an archaism.* And this is true even though S is analytically (i.e. *ex vi terminorum*) equivalent to the sentence

'θ_1's diagonalization contains an archaism'

and so to

'S contains an archaism'.

It is important to make this point in opposition to the constantly repeated claim that the Gödel sentence says that it itself is unprovable:[1] this claim seems to spring from an inadequate theory of saying and—what is more disturbing—misleads people into thinking that paradox and antinomy arise only where we have sentences that say things of themselves. For example, Cargile considers the "assumption ... (2) What the sentence: (A) A is not true: says is that the sentence A is not true" and proceeds: "My main concern will be with explaining why (2) is false, and with setting out the true answer to the question as to what, if anything, it is that the sentence A says" (*Cargile*, p. 226). The fact is that paradox may and does arise even where it is merely the case that a certain sentence is true iff it itself has a certain property—and that

[1] Gödel: "We therefore have before us a proposition that says about itself that it is not provable" (*1931*, p. 149); Quine: "(2) says that (2) is not a theorem" (*1951*, p. 308).

Both argue like this: a certain formula states that a certain result is not provable; but that formula actually *is* that result; so that formula states that that formula is not provable. (Gödel further argues, not unreasonably: so that formula says about itself that it is not provable.) But the argument seems no more valid than this one: Oedipus was loudly maintaining that Laius' son is a fool; but Oedipus actually *is* Laius' son; so Oedipus was loudly maintaining that Oedipus is a fool. Gödel's uneasy awareness of the invalidity of his procedure is given expression in his statement of the second premise: "*Only subsequently (and so to speak by chance) does it turn out* that this formula is precisely the one by which the proposition itself was expressed" (p. 151, my italics).

is far from its *saying* that it itself has that property.

This is not to deny that there are sentences that say things of themselves—perhaps 'This sentence contains an archaism' is one such. But any theory that only purports to solve the paradoxes generated by self-sayers is, to that extent, of limited interest.

The distinction between *S* and 'This sentence contains an archaism' can be drawn in another way: let us say that a sentence is *predicatively analyzable* just in case there are a predicate and appropriately many subjects such that the sentence is the result of applying the predicate to the subjects, and the subjects all denote, and, in the case of each, what it denotes can be determined without first applying the predicate to them. Then we see that *S* is predicatively analyzable, since it is the result of applying θ_1 to θ_1's own quotation, and θ_1's own quotation denotes, and what it denotes can be determined without first applying θ_1 to it. On the other hand, 'This sentence contains an archaism' is not predicatively analyzable; for, if it is a result of application at all, the only plausible candidates for predicate and subject are '$\eta.\eta$ contains an archaism' and 'This sentence'—yet what 'This sentence' denotes, if it denotes at all, cannot be determined without first applying the predicate to it. (I do not say that 'This sentence contains an archaism' is not straight-forwardly false, nor even that the noun-phrase 'This sentence' that occurs in it doesn't denote.) Solutions of the Liar paradox relying upon the fact that the Liar sentence is not predicatively analyzable include the famous one of Ryle (*1951*; cf. *Wittgenstein 1967*, §691) and that of Kneale (*1972*; *1971*, pp. 330–1); but my point is that these solutions can be of only limited interest.

Of course, the fact that 'This sentence contains an archaism' is not predicatively analyzable might be explained by denying that the only plausible candidates for predicate and subject are the ones mentioned. Notoriously, Frege did not think that 'Some sentence contains an archaism' had 'Some sentence' as subject, and Russell did not think that 'The first sentence in the Bible contains an archaism' had 'The first sentence in the Bible' as subject: ought we not perhaps to say that 'This sentence contains an archaism' is the result of applying the *second-level* predicate 'ξ. This thing ξ' to the *second-level* subject '$\eta.\eta$ (is a sentence and) contains an archaism' (cf. *Frege 1903*, pp. 371–3)? If one does say this, however, one ought to admit that it is not predicatively analyzable even *at the second-level*: for it is itself within what Russell called the "range of significance" of the second-level subject and so the range of significance does not, as he would say, "form a well-defined totality" (*1908*, pp. 72–3, 78)—so what the second-level subject denotes cannot be determined without first applying the second-level predicate to it. This explanation incidentally demonstrates that a link can quite easily be forged between this concept of a sentence's being predicatively analyzable and Russell's concept of a propositional function's being predicative (ib., p. 78): there is, however, a still closer connexion between the present concept and Poincaré's concept of a classification's being predicative (*1912*, pp. 46–8).

It is perhaps worth remarking that no-one who is impressed by the later work of Wittgenstein in the philosophy of language will be moved by the suggestion that all sentences that have a use in our language *must* be predicatively analyzable at some level or another, however much such a principle would have appealed to Frege, Russell or the young Wittgenstein (nor, *a fortiori*, by Buridan's 'Law': cf. *Geach 1980*).

VII.3 But where *does* paradox arise? We have seen that *S* is false—and there's no paradox in that. But just as sentences can have grammatical properties they seem also to be able to have semantical properties—being about Paris, mentioning Napoleon, being true, meaning the same as 'Je est un autre'.

So consider the predicate θ_2:

'$\pi.\pi$ is a predicate whose diagonalization is false'.

We see easily enough, as before, that θ_2's diagonalization is true iff it—the diagonalization—is false. The paradox, then, is that it must be both true *and* false: "This contradiction comes like a thunderbolt from a clear sky. How could we be prepared for anything like this in exact logic! Who can go surety for it that we shall not again suddenly encounter a contradiction as we go on? The possibility of such a thing points to a mistake in the original design." (Frege was not, of course, speaking of this paradox: *1895*, p. 439.)

Or consider the predicate θ_3:

'$\pi.\pi$ is a predicate whose diagonalization is true only if the Man in the Iron Mask was the Duc de Vermandois'.

θ_3's diagonalization is true iff it is true only if the Man in the Iron Mask was the Duc de Vermandois; but then it isn't false; so it's true; so the Man in the Iron Mask was the Duc de Vermandois—a rapid solution to a long-standing historical mystery! To this kind of paradox—constructed according to a recipe of Curry (*1942*; cf. *Geach 1954*)—belongs the most famous of all, the Liar: for if all Cretans are liars in that whatever they utter is false, then no Cretan *can utter* the diagonalization of θ_4—

'$\pi.\pi$ is a predicate whose diagonalization is uttered by a Cretan'.

"The point about the Epimenides, as was noted by Church, is not that when we examine the truth value of a Cretan's assertion that nothing true is ever asserted by a Cretan we are led to contradictory conclusions, for we are not; the paradox is rather that such examination makes it seem possible to settle an empirical question on logical grounds." (*Prior 1958*, p. 261.)

Yet a third form of paradoxicalness arises from θ_5:

'$\pi.\pi$ is a predicate whose diagonalization is true'.

This time we are forced to the innocuous conclusion that θ_5's diagonalization is true iff it is true. And the paradox is this: it looks as if one ought to be able to settle the question whether it is true *a priori*, yet one can't.

Next consider θ_6:

'$\pi.\pi$ is a predicate whose diagonalization is either false or else, if true, not known to be true'.

As usual, θ_6's diagonalization is true iff it is either false or else, if true, not known to be true; so it cannot be false; so it must be true; so it is not known to be true. But how can it not be known to be true given that we've just proved that it must be true? (The 'Paradox of the Knower': see *Kaplan & Montague*.)

Finally, we can capture the flavour of Gödel's thought by adapting θ_6. Let Σ be any particular set of sentences, and let θ_7 be

$\ulcorner\pi.\pi$ is a predicate whose diagonalization is either false or else, if true, such that its truth is not entailed by that of the members of $\Sigma\urcorner$.

Obviously, θ_7's diagonalization must be true; so its truth is not entailed by that of the members of Σ; so *whatever set of sentences one may choose* one can construct a sentence whose truth is not entailed by that of the members of the set. So there is no set of all true sentences! There is not even a set comprising all truths about application, quotation, truth and entailment!

However, this gives only the *flavour* of Gödel's thought, since, in view of all the paradoxes, we certainly cannot rely on the reasoning involved here: Gödel's real contribution was to demonstrate that we don't have to, but can rely on much less infirm reasoning to reach the conclusion, not that there is no set of all true sentences, but that there is none for which ⌜*S.S* is one of its members⌝ is effectively confirmable—the stroke of genius was to connect the concepts of application, quotation, truth and entailment with the concept of effectiveness (more accurately, less anachronistically, that of primitive recursiveness).

VII.4 The concept of quotation is the one upon which suspicion of responsibility for the paradoxes naturally first focuses: the feeling is 'Paradoxes? Of course—too many quotation marks!' The other notions, application, truth and entailment, are at the very centre of our conceptual universe, whereas quotation seems utterly peripheral: if there is a "mistake in the original design", that is where we seek it.[1]

But we should observe that essentially the same paradoxes are derivable using other concepts, such as—for instance—that of the *structural-description of* a predicate (*Tarski 1933*, p. 156), which is illustrated as follows:

—the structural-description of '*p.p* flies' is the following subject:

'the expression of length 9 whose terms are
'*p*', '.', '*p*', space, 'f', 'l', 'i', 'e', 's'';

—the structural-description of '$\eta.\eta$ contains an archaism' is the following subject:

'the expression of length 24 whose terms are
'η', '.', 'η', space, 'c', ..., 'i', 's', 'm''.

The structural-description of a predicate is thus a subject that denotes the predicate, just as the quotation of a predicate is a subject that denotes the predicate. Then the s-*diagonalization* of a predicate is the sentence that results from applying it to its own structural-description; and if we consider θ_8

'$\pi.\pi$ is a predicate whose s-diagonalization contains an archaism'

we see easily enough that

θ_8's s-diagonalization is true
if, and only if,
θ_8's s-diagonalization contains an archaism.

[1] But it only *seems* so: one of the first things you teach your child is to say 'Please', and you do so by saying 'Say 'Please'' (cf. *Wittgenstein 1953*, I §16; quotation is illuminatingly discussed in *Davidson 1979*).

In fact it is obvious that given *any* function whose arguments are predicates and whose value for any argument is a subject that denotes the argument, we can carry through the construction. Given such a function *f*, the *f-diagonalization of* a predicate θ is the sentence that results from applying θ to the subject that is the value of *f* for the argument θ; then consider θ_9

⌜$\pi.\pi$ is a predicate whose *f*-diagonalization contains an archaism⌝,

note that θ_9 is an argument of *f*, and deduce that

θ_9's *f*-diagonalization is true
if, and only if,
θ_9's *f*-diagonalization contains an archaism.

So the condition that there exists such a function is sufficient to carry through the construction and therefore sufficient to derive the paradoxes (in the presence of certain other conditions, of course): it is illuminating to divide this condition into two others, one of which can clearly be seen to hold. Suppose *g* is an injective function whose arguments are predicates, and *h* a function whose arguments are values of *g* and each of whose values is a subject that denotes *h*'s argument: then one can carry through the construction. (An *injective* function is one that, for any two distinct arguments, has two distinct values.) For we can define the *hg-diagonalization of* a predicate θ to be the sentence that results from applying θ to the subject that is the value of *h* for the value of *g* for θ.

Now, it is an important fact that we have a uniform effective procedure for associating with each *number* a subject that denotes it—viz. its numeral, in say the conventional Hindu-Arabic denary notation (this is not, as it were, a mere 'mathematical contingency': to have a grasp of what it is to be a number involves understanding this fact). So we have a function *h* whose arguments are numbers and each of whose values is a subject that denotes its argument. It follows, then, from the argument of the preceding paragraph that *the existence of an injective function whose arguments are predicates and whose values are numbers is a sufficient condition for carrying through the construction and deriving the paradoxes.*

Hence, on the one hand, it would seem that *there can be no such function*—for the impossible cannot follow from the possible (and one doesn't need to carry through the whole construction to see that the impossible would follow from the possibility of such a function *g*—one need only ask oneself what the value of *g* could be for the argument ⌜*n.n* is the value of *g* for some predicate that is not true of *n*⌝—which is 'Cantor's argument' in II.2). Yet, on the other hand, it would seem that *there must be such a function*—for each predicate has a quotation, or a structural-description, which denotes it, and which involves only the finitely many signs of the Greek and English alphabets (including punctuation signs)—so surely we can associate with each predicate a number just as we associated with each predicate-form its Gödel number? (This point was first made by J. Richard and J. König: see *Richard* and *König* and cf. VI.1, fn.)

VII.5 We now retreat from the deep waters of the semantics of natural language[1] to the relatively shallow waters of the 'semantics' of the formal language. We know that
— there is an injective function whose arguments are predicate-*forms* and whose values are numbers—to wit, in a self-explanatory notation, $P \rightarrow$ the Gödel number of P; and
— there is a function whose arguments are numbers and each of whose values is a subject-*form* that is standardly assigned the argument—to wit, $m \rightarrow$ the formal numeral for m.
So we have machinery enough to reconstruct a lot of the material of the preceding sections in the formal language.

We start by writing

$$\text{'}\mathbf{diag}\text{' for 'x.}\mathbf{ap}_1[\text{x},\mathbf{fn}[\text{x}]]\text{'}$$

and calling, for any singular predicate-form P, the expression whose Gödel number is $|\mathbf{diag}[*P*]|$ the *diagonalization of P*—why? Well, since $\mathbf{fn}[*P*]=**P**$ and $\mathbf{ap}_1[*P*,**P**]=*P[*P*]*$ are standardly assigned $\mathbb{T}$, so is $\mathbf{diag}[*P*]=*P[*P*]*$, and therefore the expression with Gödel number $|\mathbf{diag}[*P*]|$ is that with Gödel number $|*P[*P*]*|$, which is $P[*P*]$, which is the result of applying P to $*P*$, which is the result of applying P to the formal numeral for its own Gödel number.

To illustrate, suppose it chances that u, = and . are the first three letters, so that 21310031310314 is the Gödel number of u.u=u; then $\overline{21310031310314}=\overline{21310031310314}$ is its diagonalization. Again, $\exists$y.(*x.$\exists$y.(x+y)<y*+y)<y is that of x.$\exists$y.(x+y)<y.

Now, for any singular predicate-form P, the diagonalization of $\alpha.P[\mathbf{diag}[\alpha]]$ is *Carnap's fixed-point*[2] *for P*, or C_P (α being the

[1] They are further investigated in, e.g., *Martin*.

[2] A *fixed-* or *invariant*-point of a function is something that is at once both argument to and value of it; thus, for example, the function $|\text{xy}.(\overline{9}\times\text{x})=(\text{y}^{\overline{2}})|$ has two fixed-points, 0 and 9, but the function $|\text{xy}.(\overline{9}\times\text{x})=(\text{y}'^{\overline{2}})|$ has none.

prefix of P)—so called in view of Gödel's generous attribution (*1934*, p. 363 fn.). Thus the fixed-point for

$$y.\forall z.(z+\overline{3})<(y^z)$$

is the diagonalization of

$$y.\forall z.(z+\overline{3})<(\mathbf{diag}[y]^z),$$

which is

$$\forall z.(z+\overline{3})<(\mathbf{diag}[{}^*y.\forall z.(z+\overline{3})<(\mathbf{diag}[y]^z)^*]^z).$$

THEOREM VII.5.1. **CARNAP'S FIXED-POINT LEMMA.** *For any singulary predicate-form P,*

$$(C_P \equiv P[{}^*C_P{}^*])$$

is standardly assigned $\mathbb{T}$*—and, indeed, formally deducible from* Δ*-forms that are standardly assigned* $\mathbb{T}$.

PROOF. Let Q be $\alpha.P[\mathbf{diag}[\alpha]]$, α being the prefix of P, so that C_P is the diagonalization of Q.

Now the result of applying $\alpha.P[\mathbf{diag}[\alpha]]$ to a formal numeral μ is either the very same sentence-form as, or is at least congruent to, the result of applying P to $\mathbf{diag}[\mu]$. Thus C_P is at least congruent to $P[\mathbf{diag}[{}^*Q^*]]$, and so

(A) $$\vdash (C_P \equiv P[\mathbf{diag}[{}^*Q^*]]).$$

On the other hand, C_P is the diagonalization of Q—i.e. is the expression whose Gödel number is $|\mathbf{diag}[{}^*Q^*]|$—and so the Gödel number of C_P is $|\mathbf{diag}[{}^*Q^*]|$, whence ${}^*C_P{}^* = \mathbf{diag}[{}^*Q^*]$ is standardly assigned $\mathbb{T}$. Since $\mathbf{ap}_1$ and $\mathbf{fn}$ are Δ-forms, so are **diag** and this sentence-form, and thus

(B) $$S \vdash {}^*C_P{}^* = \mathbf{diag}[{}^*Q^*],$$

S being the set of Δ-forms that are standardly assigned $\mathbb{T}$.

The result follows from (A) and (B).

Q.E.D.

So now we can reconstruct formally such cases of 'self-reference' as Wittgenstein's saying 'What I'm saying is dreadfully muddled': letting M be a singulary predicate-form, take *Witt* to be Carnap's fixed-point for it—then

$$(Witt \equiv M[{}^*Witt^*])$$

is standardly assigned $\mathbb{T}$. Thus also with 'Only a few people understand what I'm saying', 'No-one knows that what I'm saying is true', etc., etc.

In trying to attenuate the influence of self-reference in the generation of the paradoxes, people often consider instead cross-reference: thus Buridan has us think about "The posited case … that Socrates says 'What Plato is saying is false', and nothing else, and Plato on the other hand says 'What Socrates is saying is true', and nothing else" (*1489*, c. viii, soph. ix). This actually exhibits no new features: letting T and F be singulary predicate-forms, take *Plat* to be Carnap's fixed-point for x.T[$\mathbf{ap}_1$[**F**, **fn**[x]]] and *Socr* to be *F*[**Plat**]—then the following are standardly assigned the same:

$$Plat$$
$$T[\mathbf{ap}_1[{*}F{*},\mathbf{fn}[{*}Plat{*}]]]$$
$$T[\mathbf{ap}_1[{*}F{*},{**}Plat{**}]]$$
$$T[{*}F[{*}Plat{*}]{*}]$$
$$T[{*}Socr{*}]$$

and so both

$$(Socr \equiv F[{*}Plat{*}]) \quad \text{and} \quad (Plat \equiv T[{*}Socr{*}])$$

are standardly assigned 𝕋.

VII.6 Obviously enough, the procedure of constructing Carnap's fixed-point for a form is a uniform effective one, so that—given Church's Thesis—the extension of '*mn.m* is the Gödel number of a singulary predicate-form *P* and *n* that of Carnap's fixed-point for *P*' is recursive. However, we don't need to appeal to Church's Thesis, for we shall now describe a singulary Δ-descriptor-form **carn** such that xy.(**Prdfm**[$\bar{1}$, x] ∧ y = **carn**[x]) represents the predicate. At the same time, we take the opportunity to extend Carnap's Lemma along lines explored by Montague (*1962*, sect. 1; cf. also *Feferman 1962*, Theorem 2.5, p. 271).

Write

'ι' for 'v.℩w < bd[v].(sz[w] = $\bar{1}$ ∧ pt[$\bar{1}$, w] = v)'

'$\overleftarrow{\mathbf{1}}$' for 'u.℩v < u.∃w < u.(u = (v⌢w) ∧ sz[v] = $\bar{1}$)'

'$\overrightarrow{\mathbf{2}}$' for 'u.℩w < u.∃v < u.(u = (v⌢w) ∧ sz[v] = $\bar{1}$)'

'**r**' for 'x.℩y < x.(**Prdfm**[y, x] ∨ **Dscfm**[y, x])'

'**px**' for 'x.℩y < x.∃z < x.(x = (y⌢z) ∧ sz[y] = **r**[x])'

'𝔨' for '**ap**[(ι[x]⌢ι[y])]'

'𝔮' for '($\overrightarrow{\mathbf{2}}$[**px**[x]]⌢*.*⌢**ap**[(ι[x]⌢ι[y]⌢$\overrightarrow{\mathbf{2}}$[**px**[x]])])'

'**pap**' for 'xy.℩z < (𝔨 + 𝔮)'.(($\bar{1}$ = **r**[x] ∧ z = 𝔨) ∨ ($\bar{1}$ < **r**[x] ∧ z = 𝔮))'

'𝔴' for '**pap**[x, $\mathbf{ap}_1$[y, $\overleftarrow{\mathbf{1}}$[**px**[x]]]]' 'ᴧ' for '$(\overleftarrow{1} \,[\mathbf{px}[x]]\!\,^\frown\!\mathbf{pap}[x,\mathbf{ap}_1[y, \overleftarrow{1}\,[\mathbf{px}[x]]]])$'

'**comp**' for 'xy.ɿz $<(\mathbf{w}+\mathbf{v})'.((\overline{1}=\mathbf{r}[x] \wedge z=\mathbf{w}) \vee (\overline{1}<\mathbf{r}[x] \wedge z=\mathbf{v}))$'

'**carn**' for 'x.**diag**[**comp**[x,*****diag*****]]'

'**diagg**' for 'x.**pap**[x,**fn**[x]]'

'**mont**' for 'x.**diagg**[**comp**[x,*****diagg*****]]'.

So **pap**, **comp**, **carn**, **diagg** and **mont** are all Δ-forms.

To grasp the significance of these definitions, suppose f is a predicate- or descriptor-form whose prefix is, say, wxyz: then

$$\overleftarrow{1}\,[\mathbf{px}[*f*]] = *w* \qquad\qquad \overrightarrow{2}\,[\mathbf{px}[*f*]] = *xyz*$$
$$\mathbf{pap}[*f*,*(w+\overline{3})*] = *xyz.f[(w+\overline{3}),x,y,z]*$$

and $\qquad\mathbf{comp}[*f*,*x.(x+\overline{3})*] = *wxyz.f[(w+\overline{3}),x,y,z]*$

are standardly assigned ⊤. So, for any such f and any expression e, we call the expression with Gödel number $|\mathbf{pap}[*f*,*e*]|$ the *result of partially applying f to e*; and, for any such f and any singulary descriptor-form e, we call the expression with Gödel number $|\mathbf{comp}[*f*,*e*]|$ the *composition of f with e*. Furthermore,

$$\mathbf{diagg}[*f*] = *xyz.f[*f*,x,y,z]*$$

and

$$\mathbf{mont}[*f*] = *xyz.f[\mathbf{diagg}[*wxyz.f[\mathbf{diagg}[w],x,y,z]*],x,y,z]*$$

are standardly assigned ⊤. For any such f, we call the expressions with Gödel numbers $|\mathbf{diagg}[*f*]|$ and $|\mathbf{mont}[*f*]|$ respectively the *diagonalization of f* and *Montague's fixed-point for f*, or M_f. Thus the diagonalization of f is the result of partially applying it to the formal numeral for its own Gödel number, and Montague's fixed-point for it is the diagonalization of the composition of f with **diagg**. (Notice that Montague's and Carnap's fixed-points for a singulary predicate-form are different, being the diagonalization of the composition of the form with, respectively, **diagg** and **diag**.)

We have, what is proved as the last theorem was,

THEOREM VII.6.1. **MONTAGUE'S FIXED-POINT LEMMA.** *Suppose P is a singulary predicate-form, Q an n-ary one (n>1), d a singulary descriptor-form, e an n-ary one (n>1) and $a_2,\ldots,a_n$ are variables. Then*

$$(M_P \equiv P[*M_P*])$$
$$\forall a_2.\ldots.\forall a_n.(M_Q[a_2,\ldots,a_n] \equiv Q[*M_Q*,a_2,\ldots,a_n])$$
$$M_d = d[*M_d*]$$
$$\forall a_2.\ldots.\forall a_n.M_e[a_2,\ldots,a_n] = e[*M_e*,a_2,\ldots,a_n]$$

are all formally deducible from Δ-forms that are standardly assigned ⊤.

For an example of the application of Montague's Lemma, consider the *casus* that Russell says to Bradley 'What you're saying is much sillier than what I'm saying', and nothing else, while Bradley says to Russell 'What I'm saying is a good deal more interesting than what you're saying', and nothing else. If S and I are binary predicate-forms and P is

$$\mathrm{zyx.}\begin{pmatrix}(\mathrm{x}={*I*} \wedge S[\mathbf{ap}_2[\mathrm{z},\mathbf{fn}[\mathrm{x}],\mathbf{fn}[\mathrm{y}]],\mathbf{ap}_2[\mathrm{z},\mathbf{fn}[\mathrm{y}],\mathbf{fn}[\mathrm{x}]]])\\ \vee\\ (\mathrm{x}={*S*} \wedge I[\mathbf{ap}_2[\mathrm{z},\mathbf{fn}[\mathrm{x}],\mathbf{fn}[\mathrm{y}]],\mathbf{ap}_2[\mathrm{z},\mathbf{fn}[\mathrm{y}],\mathbf{fn}[\mathrm{x}]]])\end{pmatrix}$$

then, by the Lemma, $\forall\mathrm{y}.\forall\mathrm{x}.(\mathrm{M}_P[\mathrm{y},\mathrm{x}] \equiv P[{*\mathrm{M}_P*},\mathrm{y},\mathrm{x}])$ is standardly assigned $\mathbb{T}$, so that, where *Russ* is $\mathrm{M}_P[{*S*},{*I*}]$ and *Brad* is $\mathrm{M}_P[{*I*},{*S*}]$,

$$(\mathit{Russ} \equiv S[{*\mathit{Brad}*},{*\mathit{Russ}*}]) \quad \text{and} \quad (\mathit{Brad} \equiv I[{*\mathit{Brad}*},{*\mathit{Russ}*}])$$

are both standardly assigned $\mathbb{T}$.

Or consider the policewoman and the man she has in charge (cf. *Cohen*): each speaks exactly once per day; on each non-initial day she says 'What he says is always more unreliable than what I said yesterday'; and he oscillates between saying 'What she says is sometimes more accurate than what I'll say tomorrow' and saying 'What I say is never more unreliable than what she said the day before'. It is a good exercise to construct, from a pair U, A of binary predicate-forms, a pair ♂, ♀ of singulary ones such that

$$\forall\mathrm{x}.(♀[\mathrm{x}'] \;\equiv\; \forall\mathrm{y}.U[\mathbf{ap}_1[{*♂*},\mathbf{fn}[\mathrm{y}]],\mathbf{ap}_1[{*♀*},\mathbf{fn}[\mathrm{x}]]]),$$

$$\forall\mathrm{x}.(\mathrm{O}[\mathrm{x}] \supset$$
$$(♂[\mathrm{x}] \;\equiv\; \exists\mathrm{y}.A[\mathbf{ap}_1[{*♀*},\mathbf{fn}[\mathrm{y}]],\mathbf{ap}_1[{*♂*},\mathbf{fn}[\mathrm{x}']]])),$$

$$\forall\mathrm{x}.({\sim}\mathrm{O}[\mathrm{x}] \supset$$
$$(♂[\mathrm{x}] \equiv {\sim}\exists\mathrm{y}.U[\mathbf{ap}_1[{*♂*},\mathbf{fn}[\mathrm{y}']],\mathbf{ap}_1[{*♀*},\mathbf{fn}[\mathrm{y}]]]))$$

are standardly assigned $\mathbb{T}$ (O being $\mathrm{x}.\exists\mathrm{y}.\mathrm{x}=(\mathrm{y}+\mathrm{y})'$).

Montague's Lemma also has immediate significance for recursion theory. Suppose, for example, we wish to Σ-represent '*m.m* is a beth-number': it is obvious from the recursive definition of the predicate that a sufficient condition that B represent it is that

$$\forall\mathrm{x}.(B[\mathrm{x}] \equiv (\mathrm{x}=\bar{0} \vee \exists\mathrm{y}.(B[\mathrm{y}] \wedge \mathrm{x}=(\bar{2}^{\mathrm{y}}))))$$

be standardly assigned $\mathbb{T}$, so the question is, Is there such a form B? Well, let P be

$$\mathrm{zx.}(\mathrm{x}=\bar{0} \vee \exists\mathrm{y}.(\mathbf{\Sigma pr}[\mathbf{ap}_1[\mathrm{z},\mathbf{fn}[\mathrm{y}]]] \wedge \mathrm{x}=(\bar{2}^{\mathrm{y}})))$$

so that, by the Lemma,

$$\forall\mathrm{x}.(\mathrm{M}_P[\mathrm{x}] \equiv (\mathrm{x}=\bar{0} \vee \exists\mathrm{y}.(\mathbf{\Sigma pr}[\mathbf{ap}_1[{*\mathrm{M}_P*},\mathbf{fn}[\mathrm{y}]]] \wedge \mathrm{x}=(\bar{2}^{\mathrm{y}}))))$$

is standardly assigned $\mathbb{T}$. Now—this is the crucial point—P is a

Σ-form and therefore so is M_P, whence, by Corollary VI.5.3,

$$\forall y.(\mathbf{\Sigma pr}[\mathbf{ap}_1[{}^*M_P{}^*,\mathbf{fn}[y]]] \equiv M_P[y])$$

is standardly assigned $\mathbb{T}$, and thus so is

$$\forall x.(M_P[x] \equiv (x=\bar{0} \vee \exists y.(M_P[y] \wedge x=(\bar{2}^y))))$$.

Hence M_P is a Σ-representation of the predicate.

Again, to Σ-represent '*n.n* is the Gödel number of a simple form' (as in VI.2), we need only find a singulary Σ-predicate-form S such that

$$\forall x.(S[x] \equiv (Q[x] \vee \exists y.(S[y] \wedge x=\mathbf{ngn}[y]) \vee \exists y.\exists z.(S[y] \wedge S[z] \wedge x=\mathbf{cnjn}[y,z]) \vee \exists y.\exists z.(S[y] \wedge S[z] \wedge x=\mathbf{dsjn}[y,z])))$$

is standardly assigned $\mathbb{T}$—and, because the appropriate form P is a Σ-form and hence so is M_P, that is easily done.

The upshot, which is due to Kleene (cf. *1952*, §66) is:

COROLLARY VII.6.2. **THE RECURSION THEOREM.** *Suppose Θ is a form of type $((i),i)$, and let P be* $zx.\Theta[x.\mathbf{\Sigma pr}[\mathbf{ap}_1[z,\mathbf{fn}[x]]],x]$: *if P is a Σ-form, then*

$$\forall x.(M_P[x] \equiv \Theta[M_P,x])$$

is standardly assigned $\mathbb{T}$.

The language of the supposition is simply explained in *Hilbert & Ackermann*, ch. IV, but enough can be gathered from the illustrative examples, in which Θ is

$$\zeta x.(x=\bar{0} \vee \exists y.(\zeta y \wedge x=(\bar{2}^y)))$$

and

$$\zeta x.(Q[x] \vee \exists y.(\zeta y \wedge x=\mathbf{ngn}[y]) \vee \ldots \vee \exists y.\exists z.(\zeta y \wedge \zeta z \wedge x=\mathbf{dsjn}[y,z])))$$.

Notice that the condition on Θ for its 'recursion equation' $\forall x.(\zeta x \equiv \Theta[\zeta,x])$ to be soluble, though sufficient, is not necessary: for example, $\zeta x.\sim\zeta x'$ doesn't meet the condition but its equation has two solutions—the set of odd numbers and the set of even numbers. (On the other hand, $\zeta x.\sim\zeta x$ doesn't meet the condition either but *its* equation has no solutions!)

VII.7 Consider a singulary descriptor-form d; by definition,

$${}^*M_d{}^* = \mathbf{mont}[{}^*d^*]$$

is standardly assigned $\mathbb{T}$ and, by Montague's Lemma, so is

$$M_d = d[{}^*M_d{}^*]$$

whence so is

$$M_d = d[\mathbf{mont}[{}^*d^*]];$$

but, unless the variable in d's prefix doesn't occur free in its matrix,

$$*\mathrm{M}_d* = *d[\mathbf{mont}[*d*]]*$$

is not standardly assigned $\mathbb{T}$,[1] and hence nor is

$$\mathbf{mont}[*d*] = *d[\mathbf{mont}[*d*]]*;$$

consequently,

$$\forall \mathrm{x}.\mathbf{mont}[\mathrm{x}] = \mathbf{pap}[\mathrm{x}, \mathbf{ap}_1[*\mathbf{mont}*, \mathbf{fn}[\mathrm{x}]]]$$

is not standardly assigned $\mathbb{T}$.

But now, following *Jeroslow*, write

'**jer**' for 'Montague's fixed-point for $\mathrm{yx}.\mathbf{pap}[\mathrm{x}, \mathbf{ap}_1[\mathrm{y}, \mathbf{fn}[\mathrm{x}]]]$'

and, for any predicate- or descriptor-form f, call the expression whose Gödel number is $|\mathbf{jer}[*f*]|$ *Jeroslow's fixed-point for* f, or J_f. Then, according to Montague's Lemma,

$$\forall \mathrm{x}.\mathbf{jer}[\mathrm{x}] = \mathbf{pap}[\mathrm{x}, \mathbf{ap}_1[*\mathbf{jer}*, \mathbf{fn}[\mathrm{x}]]]$$

is standardly assigned $\mathbb{T}$ and hence, for any singulary descriptor-form d, so is

$$\mathbf{jer}[*d*] = *d[\mathbf{jer}[*d*]]*$$

whence so is

$$*\mathrm{J}_d* = *d[\mathbf{jer}[*d*]]*$$

and thus also

$$\mathrm{J}_d = d[\mathbf{jer}[*d*]]$$

and thus also

$$\mathrm{J}_d = d[*\mathrm{J}_d*].$$

This, then, is the prettiest fixed-point result of all:

THEOREM VII.7.1. **JEROSLOW'S FIXED-POINT LEMMA.**

$$\forall \mathrm{x}.\mathbf{jer}[\mathrm{x}] = \mathbf{pap}[\mathrm{x}, \mathbf{ap}_1[*\mathbf{jer}*, \mathbf{fn}[\mathrm{x}]]]$$

is formally deducible from Δ*-forms that are standardly assigned* $\mathbb{T}$.

[1] For if the variable, say α, occurs free in its matrix, then because

$$*\alpha.d[\mathbf{diagg}[\alpha]]* \quad , \quad \mathbf{comp}[*d*, *\mathbf{diagg}*]$$

are different subject-forms (the first being a formal numeral and the second not)

$$d[\mathbf{diagg}[*\alpha.d[\mathbf{diagg}[\alpha]]*]] \quad , \quad d[\mathbf{diagg}[\mathbf{comp}[*d*, *\mathbf{diagg}*]]]$$

are also different subject-forms, so that

$$\mathrm{M}_d \quad , \quad d[\mathbf{mont}[*d*]]$$

are different subject-forms, and thus have different Gödel numbers.

In fact, for *no* pair s, t of *different* subject-forms is $*s* = *t*$ standardly assigned $\mathbb{T}$: it is only an illusion, though frequently a compelling one, that there is a singulary descriptor-form d for which $d[s] = *s*$ is standardly assigned $\mathbb{T}$ for every subject-form s, or even for every Δ-subject-form s. (On the other hand, there is one—viz. **fn**—for which that is true for every *formal numeral* s.)

VIII
Gödel's Theorems, and their Relatives

VIII.1 The search for a reasonable axiomatization of the first-order truths involving only the concepts *natural number*, *less than*, *sum of*, *product of* and *power of* raised, or was recast as, the question whether there is a reasonable set of grounded forms that is both sound and complete. The only natural candidate that has been proposed is Peano's Arithmetic **P**. But, as foretokened in II.4, despite appearances, it does not fill the bill: although sound—or so we assume—it is not complete. This we now prove.

Since for the moment we are discussing **P** alone, let us mean by a *Deduction* a formal deduction from **P**, and by being *Deducible* being formally deducible from **P**; analogously, let us abbreviate '$\mathbf{Fmddn_P}$' to '**Ddn**' and '$\mathbf{Fmdbl_P}$' to '**Dbl**'.

THEOREM VIII.1.1. **P** *is not complete.*

PROOF. In the first place, if a form *X* is Deducible, then **Dbl**[**X**] is—by the results in VI.7—standardly assigned $\mathbb{T}$, and thus—by Theorem III.1.2—Deducible: hence

1— for any form *X*, if *X* is Deducible so is **Dbl**[**X**].

Then let G be Carnap's fixed-point for x. ~**Dbl**[x], so that—by his Lemma—(G ≡ ~**Dbl**[*G*]) is Deducible, and hence

2— if **Dbl**[*G*] is Deducible so is ~G; and

3— if ~**Dbl**[*G*] is Deducible so is G.

Finally, using again the results in VI.7,

4— for any form *X*, if *X* is not Deducible then ~**Dbl**[**X**] is standardly assigned $\mathbb{T}$.

Now **P** is sound, so it is not the case that both some form and its negation are Deducible, and so—by 1 and 2—G is not Deducible; then by 3 ~**Dbl**[*G*] is not Deducible and by 4 ~**Dbl**[*G*] is standardly assigned $\mathbb{T}$.

Q.E.D.

Instead of saying that ~**Dbl**[*G*] is un-Deducible though standardly assigned 𝕋, or equivalently that G is, it is illuminating to state the matter in another way by letting **UnDbldiag** be x. ~**Dbl**[**diag**[x]], whose diagonalization G is: for then we can say that **UnDbldiag** has an un-Deducible diagonalization—it has a diagonalization that is un-Deducible though standardly assigned 𝕋. The analogy with the predicate

'$\pi.\pi$ is a singulary predicate with an untrue diagonalization'

leaps to the eye, to use Gödel's phrase: for the predicate has a diagonalization that is—apparently—untrue though true.

A corollary of the theorem is of course that **P** doesn't have the ∨-, ∃- or ∀-properties: in fact, letting *P* be y. ~**Ddn**[y, *G*], we see that

— (∀*P* ∨ ~∀*P*) is Deducible though neither of its immediate descendants is;

— ∃y.(∀*P* ∨ ~*P*[y]) is Deducible though none of its immediate descendants is; and

— ∀*P* is not Deducible though every one of its immediate descendants is.

VIII.2 We have been assuming **P**'s soundness: so constructivists—those cherubim who keep the way to Cantor's paradise—will be unimpressed by the outcome; they say that we are unable to understand even the statement of the theorem as we can have no proper grasp of the predicate '*X*.*X* is standardly assigned 𝕋', which involves infinitistic, 'verification-transcendent', notions. For this, or a closely related, reason Gödel chose to replace the assumption of soundness "by a purely formal and much weaker one" (*1931* p. 151), enabling him to salvage the following constructive result:

THEOREM VIII.2.1. **P** *doesn't have the ∀-property if it is consistent.*

PROOF. 1, 2 and 3 are constructively acceptable, and one can replace 4 by the constructively acceptable

4′— for any form *X*, if *X* is not Deducible then, for every number *n*, ~**Ddn**[$\bar{n}$, **X**] is Deducible.

Then if **P** is consistent—that is, if it is not the case that both some form and its negation are Deducible—then, as before, G is not Deducible; hence by 3 ~**Dbl**[*G*] is not Deducible and so nor is ∀y. ~**Ddn**[y, *G*]; but by 4′, for every number *n*, ~**Ddn**[$\bar{n}$, *G*] is Deducible.

Q.E.D.

It may be wondered whether 1 and 4′ are, as claimed, really constructively acceptable: do not the only proofs we have given of them (by way of the results of VI.7 and Theorem III.1.2) involve infinitistic notions? They do: but note that they can be held to be concerned only with Δ-forms and, for such forms, the constructively acceptable condition of being Σ-provable can replace the unacceptable condition of being standardly assigned 𝕋; thus the role of the appropriate result from VI.7 can be taken by

— for all numbers *n* and forms *X*, **Ddn**[$\bar{n}$, **X**] is Σ-provable if *n* is the Gödel number of a Deduction of *X* and ~**Ddn**[$\bar{n}$, **X**] is Σ-provable otherwise,

and that of Theorem III.1.2 by

— all Σ-provable forms are Deducible.

VIII.3 Hilbert's Programme, as will be briefly explained in section VIII.7, required that one be able to give what he called a finitary proof of the consistency of finitary mathematics. If one were to identify finitary mathematics with some part of what is 'formalized in' **P**, then the programme would demand that **P** be consistent and that that fact be finitarily provable. So the expectation would be that ~∃x.(**Dbl**[x] ∧ **Dbl**[**ngn**[x]]) were Deducible. However, as Gödel and von Neumann independently showed, it is not.

THEOREM VIII.3.1. ~∃x.(**Dbl**[x] ∧ **Dbl**[**ngn**[x]]) *is not Deducible if* **P** *is consistent.*

PROOF. The initial move in the proof of Theorem VIII.2.1 could have been represented as the inferring that

— if **P** is consistent, then G is not Deducible

from the facts that

— for any form *X*, if *X* is Deducible so is **Dbl**[**X**];

— (**Dbl**[*G*] ⊃ ~G) is Deducible;

— for any forms *X*, *Y*, if (*X* ⊃ *Y*) is Deducible then *Y* is if *X* is.

That inference is, of course, purely logical, and the form

(~∃x.(**Dbl**[x] ∧ **Dbl**[**ngn**[x]]) ⊃ ~**Dbl**[*G*])

is formally deducible from the (set of) forms

∀x.(**Dbl**[x] ⊃ **Dbl**[$\mathbf{ap}_1$[***Dbl***, **fn**[x]]])

Dbl[**hk**[$\mathbf{ap}_1$[***Dbl***, **fn**[*G*]], **ngn**[*G*]]]

∀x.∀y.(**Dbl**[**hk**[x, y]] ⊃ **Dbl**[x] ⊃ **Dbl**[y]).

These three forms are all Deducible: the first and last unobviously (see section VIII.8) and the second fairly obviously (by the first two premises of the inference above, **Dbl**[*(**Dbl**[*G*] ⊃ ∼G)*] is Deducible). Consequently, ∼∃x.(**Dbl**[x] ∧ **Dbl**[**ngn**[x]]) is not Deducible unless ∼**Dbl**[*G*] is—which it isn't if **P** is consistent.

Q.E.D.

The above proof is in essence Löb's version of Gödel's; a much simpler, but quite different, proof was later given by Feferman (*Löb*; *Feferman 1960*, Theorem 5.6):

Proof. Note that

(∼∃x.(**Dbl**[x] ∧ **Dbl**[**ngn**[x]]) ⊃ G)

is formally deducible from the (set of) forms

(∼G ⊃ **Dbl**[**ngn**[*G*]])
(∼**Dbl**[*G*] ⊃ G).

These two forms are both Deducible: the first unobviously (see section VIII.8) and the second obviously (Carnap's Lemma).

Q.E.D.

Löb's real contribution was to extend the theorem as follows:

Theorem VIII.3.2. *For any sentence-form X: X is Deducible if* (**Dbl**[*X*] ⊃ X) *is*.

Proof. Consider a sentence-form X—let L be Carnap's fixed-point for x.**Dbl**[**hk**[x, *X*]].

Then by Carnap's Lemma (L ⊃ **Dbl**[**hk**[*L*, *X*]]) is Deducible; but so is (**Dbl**[**hk**[*L*, *X*]] ⊃ **Dbl**[*L*] ⊃ **Dbl**[*X*]), (see section VIII.8); thus so is (L ⊃ **Dbl**[*L*] ⊃ **Dbl**[*X*]).

Now, as we shall see in section VIII.8, (L ⊃ **Dbl**[*L*]) is Deducible; hence so is (L ⊃ **Dbl**[*X*]).

So suppose (**Dbl**[*X*] ⊃ X) were Deducible; then so would be (L ⊃ X); and then **Dbl**[*(L ⊃ X)*] would be; and then **Dbl**[**hk**[*L*, *X*]] would be; and then by Carnap's Lemma L would be; so that—as (L ⊃ X) would also be—X would be.

Q.E.D.

This is a genuine extension of Theorem VIII.3.1 because by it $\bar{0} = \bar{1}$ would be Deducible, if (**Dbl**[*$\bar{0} = \bar{1}$*] ⊃ $\bar{0} = \bar{1}$) were, and so if ∼**Dbl**[*$\bar{0} = \bar{1}$*] were, and so if ∼∃x.(**Dbl**[x] ∧ **Dbl**[**ngn**[x]]) were. Leon Henkin's problem, to which Löb was addressing himself, was: what is the status of Carnap's fixed-point for **Dbl**?—by Löb's result it is Deducible, because by Carnap's Lemma (**Dbl**[*it*] ⊃ it) is Deducible (cf. θ_5 in section VII.3).

VIII.4 We accept, if we accept its soundness, that **P** hasn't got the ∨-property—indeed, that much is entailed even by the fact that all Deducible Σ-forms are standardly assigned $\mathbb{T}$ (as G is not Deducible, **Dbl**[*G*] is a Σ-form that is not standardly assigned $\mathbb{T}$; hence **Dbl**[*G*] is not Deducible; but nor is ∼**Dbl**[*G*]). Gödel, however, mentions the following corollary of Theorem VIII.3.1, which is acceptable even to the constructivist:

THEOREM VIII.4.1. **P** *doesn't have the* ∨*-property if it is consistent and* ∃x.(**Dbl**[x] ∧ **Dbl**[**ngn**[x]]) *is not Deducible.*

Later Rosser showed how, using a curious and still improperly understood trick, to dispense with the second conjunct (*Rosser*; I give the more suggestive proof of Feferman—cf. *1960*, p. 37):

THEOREM VIII.4.2. **P** *doesn't have the* ∨*-property if it is consistent.*

PROOF. The trick is to consider, not Deductions, but Rosser-deductions—a *Rosser-deduction* being a Deduction of a form than which there are no un-'longer'[1] Deductions of both some un-'longer' form and its negation—and not Deducibility but Rosser-deducibility: **Rdbl** is x.∃y.**Rddn**[y,x], where **Rddn** is

yx.(**Ddn**[y,x] ∧
∼∃w<x'.(∃z<y'.**Ddn**[z,w] ∧ ∃z<y'.**Ddn**[z,**ngn**[w]])).

Now suppose **P** is consistent; then clearly the Rosser-deductions *are* the Deductions, and so the Rosser-deducible forms are the Deducible ones; thus

1°— for any form *X*, if *X* is Rosser-deducible so is **Rdbl**[**X**].

Letting R be Carnap's fixed-point for x.∼**Rdbl**[x], we have

2°— if **Rdbl**[*R*] is Rosser-deducible so is ∼R; and

3°— if ∼**Rdbl**[*R*] is Rosser-deducible so is R.

Finally, we shall see shortly that

4°— ∼∃x.(**Rdbl**[x] ∧ **Rdbl**[**ngn**[x]]) is Rosser-deducible.

So, since it is not the case that both some form and its negation are Rosser-deducible, by 1° and 2°, R is not Rosser-deducible; thus by 3° ∼**Rdbl**[*R*] is not and so by 4° **Rdbl**[*∼R*] is not whence by 1° again ∼R is not: hence, although (R ∨ ∼R) is Deducible, neither of its immediate descendants is.

[1] The ordering of Deductions by size of Gödel number—'length, in Mostowski's sense'—is used again in Mostowski's Speed-up Theorem: as pointed out at the end of IX.5, its connectedness prevents it from corresponding to any natural ordering of proofs by length or complexity; unfortunately, it is precisely on the connectedness that the successful demonstration of 4° in the text turns.

To finish off, we need to establish 4°: but clearly

$$\forall x.\forall y.(\mathbf{Rddn}[y,x] \supset \sim\exists z<y'.\mathbf{Rddn}[z,\mathbf{ngn}[x]])$$

is Deducible and—as $\forall x.x<\mathbf{ngn}[x]$ obviously is—so is

$$\forall x.\forall z.(\mathbf{Rddn}[z,\mathbf{ngn}[x]] \supset \sim\exists y<z'.\mathbf{Rddn}[y,x]);$$

thus

$$\forall x.\forall y.\forall z.((z<y' \vee y<z') \supset \sim(\mathbf{Rddn}[y,x] \wedge \mathbf{Rddn}[z,\mathbf{ngn}[x]]))$$

is Deducible, and hence also

$$\forall x.\forall y.\forall z.\sim(\mathbf{Rddn}[y,x] \wedge \mathbf{Rddn}[z,\mathbf{ngn}[x]]).$$

Q.E.D.

Notice incidentally that

$$(\sim\exists x.(\mathbf{Dbl}[x] \wedge \mathbf{Dbl}[\mathbf{ngn}[x]]) \equiv \forall x.(\mathbf{Dbl}[x] \equiv \mathbf{Rdbl}[x]))$$

is Deducible so that, in view of Theorem VIII.3.1,

$$\forall x.(\mathbf{Dbl}[x] \equiv \mathbf{Rdbl}[x])$$

is not Deducible; more particularly, we can see that

$$(\mathbf{Dbl}[{*}\sim R{*}] \supset \mathbf{Rdbl}[{*}\sim R{*}])$$

is not Deducible (by mimicking Feferman's proof of Theorem VIII.3.1, with **Rdbl** in place of **Dbl**).

VIII.5 We have now found at least half-a-dozen witnesses to **P**'s incompleteness, amongst them G, $\sim\exists x.(\mathbf{Dbl}[x] \wedge \mathbf{Dbl}[\mathbf{ngn}[x]])$ and R; Löb's result, Theorem VIII.3.2, is a potent source of others. Thus it is easy to confirm that, *inter alia*,

— *these are Deducible, and so standardly assigned* $\mathbb{T}$*:*

$(G \vee \mathbf{Dbl}[{*}G{*}])$ $(G \vee \mathbf{Dbl}[{*}\sim G{*}])$ $(\sim G \vee \sim\mathbf{Dbl}[{*}G{*}])$

— *these are not Deducible, though standardly assigned* $\mathbb{T}$*:*

G

$\sim\mathbf{Dbl}[{*}G{*}]$ $\sim\mathbf{Dbl}[{*}\sim G{*}]$

$(G \vee \sim\mathbf{Dbl}[{*}G{*}])$ $(G \vee \sim\mathbf{Dbl}[{*}\sim G{*}])$ $(\sim G \vee \sim\mathbf{Dbl}[{*}\sim G{*}])$

Nevertheless, many people who are competent to assess these results have been somewhat unimpressed by them because the sentences that standardly fit the witnesses are not, or not obviously, expressive of anything arithmetically interesting. Coupled with a careful account of what it is to be arithmetically interesting this could be a formidable criticism, which would lead one to treat the Gödelian incompletenesses as local, and trivial, though inexplicable, eccentricities, in the way that the paradoxes of VII.3 are commonly treated.

However, since 1977 more and more witnesses have been discovered that are not nearly so vulnerable to this criticism. Many of the most interesting—especially those due to Friedman, who has made particularly stringent demands—are too complicated to explain, but there is at least one exception, whose study makes a charming diversion that I am utterly unable to resist: that it is standardly assigned $\mathbb{T}$ was—in effect—established by Goodstein, and that it is not Deducible by Kirby and Paris (cf. *Harrington et al.*, *Kirby & Paris*, *Cichon*).

To explain Goodstein's Theorem, recall that every number can be written in binary notation, and call the appropriate sequence of the numbers 0 and 1 its *binary representative*; now we can define the *pure binary representative*, $\underset{**}{m}$, *of* a number m as follows:

— $\underset{**}{0}$ is 0;

— if the binary representative of m is say $\langle d_1, d_2, \ldots, d_k\rangle$, then

$$\underset{**}{m} \text{ is } \langle \underbrace{\underset{**}{k-1}, \ldots, \underset{**}{k-1}}_{d_1}, \underbrace{\underset{**}{k-2}, \ldots, \underset{**}{k-2}}_{d_2}, \ldots, \underbrace{\underset{**}{0}, \ldots, \underset{**}{0}}_{d_k} \rangle .$$

For example, here are the representatives—binary in the centre, pure binary at right—of a few numbers:

0	0	0
1	$\langle 1\rangle$	$\langle 0\rangle$
2	$\langle 1,0\rangle$	$\langle\langle 0\rangle\rangle$
3	$\langle 1,1\rangle$	$\langle\langle 0\rangle,0\rangle$
4	$\langle 1,0,0\rangle$	$\langle\langle\langle 0\rangle\rangle\rangle$
11	$\langle 1,0,1,1\rangle$	$\langle\langle\langle 0\rangle,0\rangle,\langle 0\rangle,0\rangle$

To write a number in binary notation is to write it to the base 2: now one can write it to any other positive base n, and it has an n-ary representative and a pure n-ary representative—for example, the pure ternary representative of 11 is $\langle\langle 0,0\rangle,0,0\rangle$ and its pure denary representative is $\langle\langle 0\rangle,0\rangle$. Let rep be a binary Δ-descriptor-form such that uvw.rep[u, v] = w represents

'*nmk*.*k* is the code-number of *m* if *n* is zero but otherwise that of the pure *n*-ary representative of *m*'.

By the Recursion Theorem, there is a quaternary Σ-predicate-form Gn such that

$$\forall z.\forall u.\forall x.\forall v.(\mathrm{Gn}[z,u,x,v] \equiv ((x=\bar{0} \wedge v=z) \vee$$
$$\exists y.\exists w.(\mathrm{Gn}[z,u,y,w] \wedge x=y' \wedge \mathrm{rep}[(u+x),v']=\mathrm{rep}[(u+y),w])))$$

is standardly assigned $\mathbb{T}$. Obviously, |Gn| is a recursive function—consider a special case, writing ⌜g_n⌝ for ⌜$\imath$v.Gn[$\overline{11}, \bar{3}, \bar{n}$, v]⌝ for any number n, so that the forms

$$g_0 = \overline{11}$$
$$(g_n \neq \overline{0} \supset g_{n+1} = \imath v.\text{rep}[\overline{n+4}, v'] = \text{rep}[\overline{n+3}, g_n])$$

are standardly assigned 𝕋, and thus

if n is	then $\lvert g_n \rvert$ is	
0	11	i.e. 1.3^2+2
1	$-1+1.4^2+2$	i.e. 1.4^2+1
2	$-1+1.5^2+1$	i.e. 1.5^2
3	$-1+1.6^2$	i.e. $5.6+5$
8	$-1+5.11$	i.e. $4.11+10$
38	$-1+3.41$	i.e. $2.41+40$
158	$-1+1.161$	i.e. 160
318	$-1+1$	i.e. 0

This example shows that the values of $\lvert xv.\text{Gn}[\overline{11}, \overline{3}, x, v]\rvert$ first grow, erratically and slowly, to a maximum and then shrink steadily to zero: is the same true of all such functions? The example is in a crucial respect atypical—since 11 is not sufficiently much larger than 3, exponentiation plays no essential role; a more typical case is that of $\lvert xv.\text{Gn}[\overline{28}, \overline{3}, x, v]\rvert$, whose values begin by growing explosively: in the general case the question is whether subtraction decreases the values fast enough to compensate for the increase by exponentiation.

The answer is affirmative: Goodstein proved that which is expressed by what standardly fits $\forall z.\forall u < z.\exists x.\text{Gn}[z, u, x, \overline{0}]$; so the form is standardly assigned 𝕋; but Kirby and Paris showed that it is not Deducible. A sketchy outline of a proof follows.

Corresponding to any binary predicate-form α such that $\lvert\alpha\rvert$ is a well-ordering of the natural numbers[1] there is a principle, the principle of α-induction, stating that *a 'determinate' predicate that is true of any number of all of whose predecessors (in the ordering* $\lvert\alpha\rvert$*) it is true, is true of every number*. Furthermore, if α is sufficiently simple, the principle is a consequence of the ordinary one.

By way of illustration, consider $\underline{\text{L}}$ in II.5, a particularly simple case: the natural numbers are well-ordered by $\lvert\underline{\text{L}}\rvert$ as follows:

$$1, 3, 5, 7, 9, \ldots \quad \ldots \quad 0, 2, 4, 6, 8, \ldots$$

and the principle of $\underline{\text{L}}$-induction is a consequence of the ordinary

[1] In Cantor's terms, α is the 'order of precedence' that rules over the natural numbers, and $\lvert\alpha\rvert$ is the resulting 'well-ordered aggregate'; the 'order-type' of the latter is thus an 'ordinal number': $\omega.2$ is the ordinal number of $\lvert\underline{\text{L}}\rvert$, and the least ε-number that of $\lvert\varepsilon_0\rvert$—cf. *Cantor*, esp. §§7, 8, 20.

one because a predicate that is true of any number of all of whose |L̲|-predecessors it is true is true, first, of every odd number and then, secondly and consequently, of every even number, and so is true of every number. It is now easy to see that, for any singulary predicate-form *P*,

$$(\forall x.(\forall y.(\underline{L}[y,x] \supset P[y]) \supset P[x]) \supset \forall P)$$

is Deducible.

However, of rather less simple such forms, these things aren't true, and the simplest of which they aren't is known as 'ε_0': although $|\varepsilon_0|$ is a well-ordering of the natural numbers, the principle of ε_0-induction is not a consequence of the ordinary one; in fact, there is a Δ-form *P* such that

$$((\forall x.(\forall y.(\varepsilon_0[y,x] \supset P[y]) \supset P[x]) \supset \forall P) \supset \sim\exists x.(\mathbf{Dbl}[x] \wedge \mathbf{Dbl}[\mathbf{ngn}[x]]))$$

is Deducible—a famous result of Gentzen, carefully explained in *Takeuti*, §§11–13.

Now Goodstein devised Gn so that (a) for any numbers *m*, *n* the function $|xv.\mathrm{Gn}[\overline{m},\overline{n},x,v]|$ corresponds in a specified way to a well-ordering simpler than $|\varepsilon_0|$, and (b) to any such well-ordering there corresponds in just that way one of those functions. Hence the easy and natural proof of Goodstein's Theorem uses the principle of ε_0-induction; and hence also $\forall z.\forall u<z.\exists x.\mathrm{Gn}[z,u,x,\overline{0}]$ is not Deducible—for, if it were, that principle would be a consequence of the ordinary one.

This deflects the full force of the criticism that the known witnesses to **P**'s incompleteness 'say nothing arithmetically interesting', but there remains a difficulty: the considerations of Wittgenstein on proof and the theorem proved ("the proof is part of the grammar of the proposition": *1969*, p. 369 f.; *1978*, p. 158 f.) suggest that the critics should not be satisfied with a witness unless the proof that it is one involves only arithmetical concepts. It is sometimes said that a debate about whether or not such concepts as the principle of ε_0-induction are arithmetical must be sterile and 'purely verbal'—as if there were no such thing as an extra-mathematical reason to be advanced for or against: the absurdity of this position is most clearly seen when one considers such powerfully argued claims as those of Isaacson—that none of the known witnesses can be seen to be so by purely arithmetical means; that "a truth expressible in the language of arithmetic may be such that it is not a truth of arithmetic"; and even that "Peano arithmetic may be seen as complete for finite mathematics"!

(*Isaacson*, pp. 147, 163, 148)

Two final points. First, one result of the explosion of activity since 1977 has been the re-vamping of the classic techniques of I.3 and II.5 and their application in the present case: a direct mathematical construction can now be given of a non-standard model of **P** that assigns $\mathbb{F}$ to $\forall z.\forall u < z.\exists x.\mathrm{Gn}[z, u, x, \overline{0}]$ (cf. *Kochen & Kripke*). Second, a remark about forms of type $\forall$ that are not Deducible although all their immediate descendants are (the present form is one, since its immediate descendants are all Σ-forms): for any such form, *there can be no discernible pattern or uniformity running through the Deductions of its immediate descendants*—because any such pattern could be turned into a Deduction of the form itself. It would be nice to be able to tighten up this claim by introducing a way of comparing Deductions in point of length and then saying:

> A form of type $\forall$ is Deducible if all its immediate descendants are, and they have Deductions of bounded length (in the sense that there is one than which none is longer).

This, however, is not known to be true, though a tantalizingly similar result was established by Parikh (*1973*).

VIII.6 **P**, then, is not complete: a first reaction is that it is incomplete in just the easily reparable way that **S** is—i.e. that a sufficiently carefully selected sentence-form, or set of them, added to **P** would result in a complete extension of it: but second thoughts show that such a reaction is not sensitive to the extreme *generality* of the method of the incompleteness proof—the generality that is the really significant aspect of Gödel's achievement. The incompleteness is in a precise sense irreparable:

THEOREM VIII.6.1. *Consider an extension of* **R** *for which* ⌜*n.n is the Gödel number of one of its members*⌝ *is Σ-representable: if it is sound, it is not complete.*

PROOF. Suppose S is the extension and P a Σ-representation of the predicate; let G be Carnap's fixed-point for $x.\sim\mathbf{Fmdbl}_P[x]$: then, as in Theorem VIII.1.1,

1— for any form X, if X is formally deducible from S so is $\mathbf{Fmdbl}_P[{*X*}]$;

2— if $\mathbf{Fmdbl}_P[{*G*}]$ is formally deducible from S so is $\sim G$;

3— if $\sim\mathbf{Fmdbl}_P[{*G*}]$ is formally deducible from S so is G; and

4— for any form X, if X is not formally deducible from S then $\sim\mathbf{Fmdbl}_P[{*X*}]$ is standardly assigned $\mathbb{T}$.

Hence, if S is sound, $\sim\mathbf{Fmdbl}_P[{*}G{*}]$ is not formally deducible from it although it is standardly assigned $\mathbb{T}$.

Q.E.D.

In just the same way one can generalize Theorem VIII.2.1 to obtain the following, which is as close as it is possible to get to Gödel's "general result about the existence of undecidable propositions", Theorem VI (*1931*, p. 173):

THEOREM VIII.6.2. **GÖDEL'S FIRST THEOREM.** *Consider an extension of* **R** *for which* ⌜*n.n is the Gödel number of one of its members*⌝ *is* Σ*-representable: if it is consistent, it doesn't have the* $\forall$*-property.*

And one can write down the appropriate generalizations of Theorem VIII.3.1—'**GÖDEL'S SECOND THEOREM**', VIII.3.2—'**LÖB'S THEOREM**', VIII.4.1 and VIII.4.2—'**ROSSER'S THEOREM**'. Actually, there are different generalizations of VIII.3.1 corresponding to different proofs; for instance, that corresponding to our first proof would be:

THEOREM VIII.6.3. *Consider an extension of* **R** *for which* ⌜*n.n is the Gödel number of one of its members*⌝ *has a* Σ*-representation* P *such that the two forms*

$$\forall x.\forall y.(\mathbf{Fmdbl}_P[\mathbf{hk}[x,y]] \supset \mathbf{Fmdbl}_P[x] \supset \mathbf{Fmdbl}_P[y])$$
$$\forall x.(\mathbf{Fmdbl}_P[x] \supset \mathbf{Fmdbl}_P[\mathbf{ap}_1[{*}\mathbf{Fmdbl}_P{*},\mathbf{fn}[x]]])$$

are formally deducible from it (the extension): if it is consistent, $\sim\exists x.(\mathbf{Fmdbl}_P[x] \wedge \mathbf{Fmdbl}_P[\mathbf{ngn}[x]])$ *is not formally deducible from it.*

Note, incidentally, the following somewhat more easily appraised consequence of this theorem:

COROLLARY VIII.6.4. *Consider an extension of* **P** *for which* ⌜*n.n is the Gödel number of one of its members*⌝ *has a* Σ*-representation* P *such that the form*

$$\forall x.(\mathbf{\Sigma fm}[x] \supset \mathbf{Dbl}[x] \supset \mathbf{Fmdbl}_P[x])$$

is formally deducible from it (the extension): if it is consistent, $\sim\exists x.(\mathbf{Fmdbl}_P[x] \wedge \mathbf{Fmdbl}_P[\mathbf{ngn}[x]])$ *is not formally deducible from it.*

PROOF. As we shall see in VIII.8, the first form mentioned in the theorem is Deducible, and so formally deducible from the extension under consideration. As to the second form mentioned: the results of VIII.8 assure us that $\forall x.(\mathbf{\Sigma pr}[x] \supset \mathbf{Dbl}[x])$ and $\forall x.(\mathbf{\Sigma pr}[\mathbf{ap}_1[{*}\mathbf{Fmdbl}_P{*},\mathbf{fn}[x]]] \equiv \mathbf{Fmdbl}_P[x])$ are Deducible; it is obvious, too, that $\forall x.\mathbf{\Sigma fm}[\mathbf{ap}_1[{*}\mathbf{Fmdbl}_P{*},\mathbf{fn}[x]]]$ is; hence all three are formally deducible from the extension; but so, *ex hypothesi*, is $\forall x.(\mathbf{\Sigma fm}[x] \supset \mathbf{Dbl}[x] \supset \mathbf{Fmdbl}_P[x])$, and therefore so is $\forall x.(\mathbf{Fmdbl}_P[x] \supset \mathbf{Fmdbl}_P[\mathbf{ap}_1[{}^*\mathbf{Fmdbl}_P{}^*, \mathbf{fn}[x]]])$.

Q.E.D.

VIII.7 Frege hoped "to have made it probable that the laws of arithmetic are analytic judgements and consequently a priori. Arithmetic thus becomes simply a development of logic, and every proposition of arithmetic a law of logic ..." The implicit doubt, he went on, could be removed "by producing a chain of deductions with no link missing, such that no step in it is taken which does not conform to some one of a small number of principles of inference recognized as purely logical"; he was confident that we shall "succeed in compiling with certainty a complete set of axioms ... such that from them alone we can derive, by means of the laws of logic, every proof in mathematics"; and he spoke of his concept writing—*Begriffsschrift*—that was "to be operated like a calculus by means of a small number of standard moves, so that no step is permitted which does not conform to the rules which are laid down once and for all". Nine years later, he believed he had "essentially attained [this] ideal of a strictly scientific method in mathematics", and again explained the ground for his anti-Kantian conclusion: "Because there are no gaps in the chains of inference, every 'axiom', every 'assumption', 'hypothesis', or whatever you wish to call it, upon which a proof is based is brought to light; and in this way we gain a basis upon which to judge the epistemological nature of the law that is proved" (*1884*, §§ 87, 90; *1893*, pp. vi, vii).

This enormously influential vision is in all essential respects that of a *formal system* for the generation of mathematical truth. It differs, indeed, in that it satisfies "the basic principle that every correctly-formed name is to denote something" (*1893*, p. xii), whereas a formal system is commonly understood to want no truck with any semantical notion (such as that of denotation). Frege's view was that a formal system in abstraction from semantical notions had no more epistemological significance than a configuration of chess pieces, and he acidly remarked: "Where people are satisfied with such superficialities, of course there is no basis for any deeper understanding" (ib., p. xiii). Even Hilbert, called a formalist because he made so much of the notion of a formal system, was not one in this sense: "contentual logical inference is indispensable ... mathematics has at its disposal a content secured independently of all logic ... we use the signs +, =, >, and others, which serve to communicate assertions" (*1925*, pp. 376–7). What makes Frege's system formal is not that it is an *uninterpreted* calculus, but that it is a calculus: so that the interpretation is in effect disengaged and plays no essential role in moving from one 'assertion' to the next.

By the time of our interest, the formal system had become widely accepted as the standard of epistemological probity in mathematics, for the reasons Frege gives. There were a few dissenters—in particular the intuitionists, for whom the discipline is essentially a languageless activity of the mind (cf. e.g. *Brouwer*, p. 460 fn. 8)—but by and large it was felt to embody the ideal of rational deduction from first principles. And by 1930 "enough progress had been made on the constructive side for the process of formalization itself to be a possible object of critical study; and in a terse but incisive paper, distinguished alike by astonishing originality, profundity of conception, and mastery of intricate detail, Gödel carried metamathematics over at a single stride into its second and more reflective phase" (*Kneebone*, p. 229).

Gödel's methods show that the ideal of the formal system is too constricting. In the first place, *arithmetic as a whole cannot be codified in a single formal system*. This may not be absolutely obvious, for the proofs of the results in VIII.6 all demand a detailed understanding of formal deducibility, and the ideal of the formal system does not demand that *particular* connexion between axioms and theorems: but it is clear enough even from Frege's description that the predicate ⌜*X.X* is generable in the calculus⌝ must be effectively confirmable, and therefore not co-extensive with '*X.X* is standardly assigned $\mathbb{T}$' (cf. IX.1). No Turing machine, no formal system, no effective procedure of any kind for generating forms, can possibly succeed in exactly generating those that are standardly assigned $\mathbb{T}$. And the reason—we can now see—is that the effective confirmability depends somehow upon a *fixed* set of rules, which opens the way to introspective reflexion on those very rules and their fixity. That is how the matter first presented itself, as Rudolf Carnap noted in his diary for 23 December 1929 after talking with Gödel in the early evening at the Arkadencafé in Vienna: "We admit as legitimate mathematics certain reflections on the grammar of a language that concerns the empirical. If one seeks to formalize such a mathematics, then with each formalization there are problems, which one can understand and express in ordinary language, but cannot express in the given formalized language. It follows ... that mathematics is inexhaustible: one must always again draw afresh from the 'fountain of intuition'" (*Wang 1987*, p. 50).

But there is more to it than that: Gödel emphasized that "for me the essential point of my result is not that one can somehow or other exceed every formal system (which already follows from the diagonal procedure) but rather that for every formal system there is a mathematical proposition that can be *expressed* within the system but *cannot be decided* by the axioms of the system" (*1931a*, p. 301). The argument of the last paragraph shows, of any single formal system, that it is incapable of exactly generating all mathematical truths; the new argument shows that it is incapable even of exactly generating all those mathematical truths *that are relevant to it*. Not only: no system can embrace arithmetic and algebra and geometry and ...; but also: no system can embrace arithmetic and no system can embrace algebra and no system can embrace geometry and ... (because each of the sub-disciplines 'contains' enough arithmetic to carry through the Gödelian argument).

Carnap spoke—initially, lyrically—of our having ever and again to "draw afresh from the 'fountain of intuition'" and Gödel famously came to affirm his faith in a special faculty, 'mathematical intuition', the proof of which is "the fact that the axioms force themselves upon us as being true" and to which "continued appeals ... are necessary ... for the solution of the problems of finitary number theory": the faculty is expressly compared to *perception of objects*, and he supposed Peano's axioms to "describe some well-determined reality" in which his own proposition "must be either true or false"; hence the fact that it cannot be decided by them "can only mean that these axioms do not contain a complete description of that reality"; however, they "can be supplemented without arbitrariness by new axioms which only unfold the content of" the concept of natural number (*1947*, pp. 271–2, 263–4; his remarks concern the concept of set and have been adapted to our purposes). According to this view, it is our intuition of that reality that guides us in our construction of formal systems and assures us of their 'soundness', and—subsequently—their 'incompleteness'. (It is, however, left mysterious what the *point* of constructing formal systems is at all, if, as it has been pungently put, "proof is, as it were, a mere cognitive auxiliary whereby finite, if ingenious, minds may sometimes gain access to infinitary states of affairs": *Wright 1986*, p. 4).

But the inexhaustibility of mathematics does not seem to *entail* the correctness of Gödel's vision, though no doubt the latter would explain the former. The issue obviously turns upon whether the axioms "force themselves upon us as being true": in particular, whether the principle of mathematical induction does so. We saw in I.2 the necessity for an unexplained reference to 'determinacy' in formulating this principle; and we should recall that it is the *only* ground we *ever* have for asserting a predicate to be true of *all* natural numbers, for making a universal generalization about them ("I want to say: once you've got the induction, it's all over"—*Wittgenstein 1969*, p. 407; cf. *Waismann*, ch. 8). That being so, it strikes me that Dummett was nearer the truth when he concluded that Gödel's discovery forces us "to recognize the meaning of 'natural number' as inherently vague", because "a central feature of it, which would be involved in any characterisation of the concept, is the validity of induction with respect to any well-defined property; and the concept of a well-defined property in turn exhibits a particular variety of inherent vagueness, namely indefinite extensibility"; it exhibits it because "for any definite characterisation of it, there is a natural extension of this characterisation, which yields a more inclusive concept"; hence finally "there is no ground for recourse to the conception of a mythical limit to the process of extension, a perfectly definite concept incapable of complete description but apprehended by an ineffable faculty of intuition, which guides us in replacing our necessarily incomplete descriptions by successively less incomplete ones" (*1963*, pp. 194–5, 198).

Most of the interest of Gödel's theorems for the philosophy of mathematics belongs to the first, but the second has some of its own, of a local and specialized nature. Let us recall that Frege failed in his stated aim, the demonstration of the analyticity of mathematics, not because the general notion of a formal system was seen to be worthless for the task, but because his *particular* formal system was flawed: it employed, as a primitive, a naïve concept of set, which did not survive Russell's famous criticism. Hilbert later attempted to use the general notion again, under the name 'proof theory' or 'metamathematics', in an attempt at "the definitive clarification of the *nature of the infinite*", in order to "endow mathematical method ... with definitive reliability" (*1925*, p. 370–1).

Holding that "the modes of inference employing the infinite must be replaced generally by finite processes that have precisely the same results" (ib.), the programme called for mathematical thought to be divided into two broad fields, base and superstructure, the finitary and the infinitary. Finitary language was held to be meaningful and finitary thought to be self-justifying, because somehow amounting to perception (pp. 376, 370); infinitary language was without meaning of its own and infinitary thought justified only instrumentally, as an aid to finitary thought (*1927*, p. 475). When is it in this way an aid? Well, "the science of mathematics ... is an apparatus that must always yield correct numerical equations when applied to integers", and so "there is a condition, a single but absolutely necessary one, to which the use of the method ... is subject, and that is the *proof of consistency*", which reduces to seeing that "$1 \neq 1$" is not a provable formula—"a task that fundamentally lies within the province of" the finitary, because "a formalized proof ... is a concrete and surveyable object" (*1925*, pp. 376, 383). Thus the self-justifying nature of finitary thought is essential: if it were flawed, finitary proofs of consistency would be valueless.

Now Gödel's Second Theorem shows us that in no reasonable extension of **P** could one formalize a proof of its own consistency, in the sense in which one *could* formalize proofs of the consistency of various of its subsystems, such as **Q** (cf. X.3, VIII.8 *ad fin.*); so no consistency proof could be any more *reliable* than the methods already formalized within the system. Gödel cautiously added that this result does not contradict Hilbert's viewpoint because there might exist finitary methods that cannot be formalized in the system (*1931*, p. 195; cf. also *1958*, pp. 133–5), and it has indeed been maintained that the principle of ε_0-induction is finitary despite being un-capturable in **P** (cf. VIII.5). But it is not credible that epistemological security is to be found in a conception of the finitary that could not be formalized. The point of the infinitary methods was held to be that they delivered *truths*—"correct numerical equations": if that cannot be guaranteed, and the methods themselves are meaningless, then the entire enterprise degenerates, as Brouwer scathingly remarked, into a mere "formula game", and we have no reason to believe that Hilbert's stated aim is achievable—"to describe the activity of our understanding, to make a protocol of the rules according to which our thinking actually proceeds" (*1927*, p. 475).

Thus metamathematics, proof theory, founded upon Hilbert's brilliant idea of treating the mathematical proof as just another mathematical object, was turned against itself by the youthful

Gödel. But that it was not laid in ruin the subsequent history of mathematical logic testifies.

As for the supposed implications of Gödel's method for the philosophy of mind, its alleged support for anti-mechanism, or for mechanism: the best comment is that with which Wittgenstein closes his greatest work—its existence "makes us think we have the means of solving the problems which trouble us; though problem and method pass one another by."

VIII.8 It was claimed in the proofs of Theorem VIII.3.1 that the following forms are Deducible:

$$\forall x.\forall y.(\mathbf{Dbl}[\mathbf{hk}[x,y]] \supset \mathbf{Dbl}[x] \supset \mathbf{Dbl}[y])$$
$$\forall x.(\mathbf{Dbl}[x] \supset \mathbf{Dbl}[\mathbf{ap}_1[{}^*\mathbf{Dbl}^*, \mathbf{fn}[x]]])$$
$$({\sim}G \supset \mathbf{Dbl}[\mathbf{ngn}[{}^*G^*]]).$$

(Other such claims were made in the proofs of Theorems VIII.3.2 and VIII.6.4.) These forms are certainly standardly assigned $\mathbb{T}$, but in view of **P**'s incompleteness their Deducibility does not follow. In a similar way, the mere fact that **Sntfm** represents what it does shows that $\forall x.(\mathbf{Sntfm}[x] \supset \mathbf{Sntfm}[\mathbf{ngn}[x]])$ is standardly assigned $\mathbb{T}$, but its Deducibility does not follow.

The key to the Deducibility claim is the words that open VI.4: "Following the definitions of the predicates, and using the techniques illustrated in VI.2 ..."—one needs to make use, not merely of the extensions of the predicates, but of their *senses*, as given by their definitions. Just as there is a scale of goodness of translation from the Russian, so also there is a scale of goodness of representations of predicates: thus $x.(\bar{1} < x \wedge x < \bar{4})$ is a better representation of '*n.n* is between 1 and 4' than $x.((x^2)+\bar{6})=(\bar{5} \times x)$ is; again, each of the representations given in Chapter V of '*n.n* is a beth-number' is better than that given in illustration of the Recursion Theorem; finally, **Dbl** is a better representation of '*n.n* is the Gödel number of a Deducible form' than **Rdbl** is. It is exceedingly difficult to say anything non-platitudinous in general about whatever criteria might be used as a basis for such judgements, but one simple fact clearly suffices to explain these particular examples: viz. that the representations have been reached "following the definitions of the predicates, and using the techniques illustrated in VI.2". Thus it is due to **Sntfm**'s being in this sense a good representation that one may be sure that $\forall x.(\mathbf{Sntfm}[x] \supset \mathbf{Sntfm}[\mathbf{ngn}[x]])$ is Deducible; and to **Rgtb**'s being so that one may be sure that, for any singulary predicate-form P, $\forall x.\forall y.(\mathbf{Fmdbl}_P[\mathbf{hk}[x,y]] \supset \mathbf{Fmdbl}_P[x] \supset \mathbf{Fmdbl}_P[y])$ is Deducible—so that $\forall x.\forall y.(\mathbf{Dbl}[\mathbf{hk}[x,y]] \supset \mathbf{Dbl}[x] \supset \mathbf{Dbl}[y])$ is Deducible.[1]

Now imagine written down, once again following the definitions of the predicates and using the techniques illustrated in VI.2, further Δ-representations as follows:

— $\mathbf{Typ}_{\mathsf{B}}$, of '*n.n* is the Gödel number of a form of type B';

⋮

— $\mathbf{Typ}_{\forall}$, of '*n.n* is the Gödel number of a form of type $\forall$';

— **Imdsc**, of '*mn.m* is the Gödel number of an immediate descendant of a form with Gödel number *n*'.

Then it is clear that the 'arithmetization' of Theorem III.2.1 is Deducible: that is, that the following form is Deducible—

$$\forall x.(\mathbf{\Sigma fm}[x] \supset ((\mathbf{Typ}_{\mathsf{R}}[x] \supset (\mathbf{\Sigma pr}[x] \equiv \mathbf{\Sigma pr}[\imath y.\mathbf{Imdsc}[y,x]])) \wedge ((\mathbf{Typ}_{\vee}[x] \vee \mathbf{Typ}_{\exists}[x]) \supset (\mathbf{\Sigma pr}[x] \equiv \exists y.(\mathbf{Imdsc}[y,x] \wedge \mathbf{\Sigma pr}[y]))) \wedge (\mathbf{Typ}_{\wedge}[x] \supset (\mathbf{\Sigma pr}[x] \equiv \forall y.(\mathbf{Imdsc}[y,x] \supset \mathbf{\Sigma pr}[y]))))).$$

A more or less direct consequence of this fact is the theorem below; since $\forall x.(\mathbf{\Sigma pr}[x] \supset \mathbf{Dbl}[x])$ is certainly Deducible (hint: Theorems III.2.1 + II.4.1 + II.3.3), it follows from it as a corollary that, since **Dbl** is a Σ-form,

$$\forall x.(\mathbf{Dbl}[x] \supset \mathbf{Dbl}[\mathbf{ap}_1[{}^*\mathbf{Dbl}^*, \mathbf{fn}[x]]])$$

is Deducible, and, since $\sim$G is a Σ-form,

$$(\sim \mathrm{G} \supset \mathbf{Dbl}[\mathbf{ngn}[{}^*\mathrm{G}^*]])$$

is Deducible. (The other claims made earlier follow similarly.)

THEOREM VIII.8.1. *For any Σ-sentence-form X,*

$$(\mathbf{\Sigma pr}[{}^*X^*] \equiv X)$$

is Deducible; and so, for any n-ary Σ-predicate-form P ($n>0$) and variables $\alpha_1, \ldots, \alpha_n$, is

$$\forall \alpha_1. \ldots .\forall \alpha_n.(\mathbf{\Sigma pr}[\mathbf{ap}_n[{}^*P^*, \mathbf{fn}[\alpha_1], \ldots, \mathbf{fn}[\alpha_n]]] \equiv P[\alpha_1, \ldots, \alpha_n]).$$

[1] This is a very much tighter criterion than the criterion of 'canonical representation' that has been proposed in various places by Kreisel (cf. e.g. *Kreisel 1965*, §3.222; *Kreisel & Lévy*, pp. 122–4). His criterion has the disadvantage that it does not discriminate in point of goodness between two representations P and Q for which $\forall x.(P[x] \equiv Q[x])$ is formally deducible from the set under consideration (cf. *Kreisel & Takeuti*, fn. 3). On the other hand it has the feature, which some will think an advantage, that it does not make reference to the definitions or senses of predicates.

PROOF. The *local* **Σpr**-*equivalence*,[1] or *LE, for* a sentence-form X is the sentence-form (**Σpr**[*X*] ≡ X); similarly, the *LEs for* a predicate-form are the sentence-forms mentioned in the statement of the theorem. What we want to show is that all LEs for Σ-forms are Deducible, which we do by showing that the English predicate

'k. all LEs for Σ-forms of degree less than $k+2$ are Deducible'

is true of all numbers (the *degree of* a Σ-predicate-form being that of the results of applying it to formal numerals); that follows from two lemmas.

Lemma 1. The predicate is true of 0.

Proof. Consider a Σ-form P of degree less than 2—perhaps a binary predicate-form such as

$$\mathrm{wx}.\overline{2}=\overline{3} \qquad \mathrm{yz.z'''}\neq\mathrm{y''} \qquad \mathrm{xy}.\overline{3}<\mathrm{x''} \qquad \mathrm{xy}.\sim\mathrm{x'}<\mathrm{y'}$$

Then it should be clear that the forms

$$\forall\mathrm{x}.(\mathbf{Typ_B}[\mathrm{x}]\supset(\mathbf{\Sigma pr}[\mathrm{x}]\equiv\mathbf{Tr_B}[\mathrm{x}]))$$
$$\forall\mathrm{u}.\forall\mathrm{v}.\mathbf{Typ_B}[\mathbf{ap_2}[{*P*},\mathbf{fn}[\mathrm{u}],\mathbf{fn}[\mathrm{v}]]]$$

are Deducible; from which it follows that

$$\forall\mathrm{u}.\forall\mathrm{v}.(\mathbf{\Sigma pr}[\mathbf{ap_2}[{*P*},\mathbf{fn}[\mathrm{u}],\mathbf{fn}[\mathrm{v}]]] \equiv \mathbf{Tr_B}[\mathbf{ap_2}[{*P*},\mathbf{fn}[\mathrm{u}],\mathbf{fn}[\mathrm{v}]]])$$

is Deducible. But it is easy to see that

$$\forall\mathrm{u}.\forall\mathrm{v}.(\mathbf{Tr_B}[\mathbf{ap_2}[{*P*},\mathbf{fn}[\mathrm{u}],\mathbf{fn}[\mathrm{v}]]]\equiv P[\mathrm{u},\mathrm{v}])$$

is Deducible; consequently, so is

$$\forall\mathrm{u}.\forall\mathrm{v}.(\mathbf{\Sigma pr}[\mathbf{ap_2}[{*P*},\mathbf{fn}[\mathrm{u}],\mathbf{fn}[\mathrm{v}]]]\equiv P[\mathrm{u},\mathrm{v}])$$

—and since one of the LEs for P is Deducible, all are.

Lemma 2. The predicate is true of the successor of any number of which it is true.

Proof. Suppose that, for a number k, all the LEs for Σ-forms of degree less than $k+2$ are Deducible, and consider a Σ-form P of degree $k+2$—perhaps a singulary predicate-form: it can be of any one of five kinds, determined by the type of the results of applying it to formal numerals—for instance, it might possibly be (type ∧)

[1] An 'equivalence' in unsubtle allusion to Tarski's "*equivalence of the form* (T)" (*1944*, §4, q.v.), and 'local' by way of contrast with '*global* **Σpr**-*equivalence*', used to describe the form in the preceding paragraph that is the 'arithmetization' of Theorem III.2.1, whose Deducibility is the source of that of the local equivalences and which is, what Tarski demands, "in a certain sense, a logical conjunction of all" of them (cf. also *Tarski 1933*, the fourth sentence of fn. 2 on p. 237).

$y.\forall x<y''.Q[x,y]$, or (type $\exists$) $u.\exists v.Q[u,v]$, for some binary predicate-form Q. Take it to be of the latter kind: then it should be clear that the forms

$$\forall x.(\mathbf{\Sigma fm}[x]\supset \mathbf{Typ}_{\exists}[x]\supset(\mathbf{\Sigma pr}[x]\equiv\exists y.(\mathbf{Imdsc}[y,x]\wedge\mathbf{\Sigma pr}[y])))$$

$$\forall u.(\mathbf{\Sigma fm}[\mathbf{ap}_1[{}^*P^*,\mathbf{fn}[u]]]\wedge \mathbf{Typ}_{\exists}[\mathbf{ap}_1[{}^*P^*,\mathbf{fn}[u]]])$$

$$\forall u.\forall y.(\mathbf{Imdsc}[y,\mathbf{ap}_1[{}^*P^*,\mathbf{fn}[u]]]\equiv\exists v.y=\mathbf{ap}_2[{}^*Q^*,\mathbf{fn}[u],\mathbf{fn}[v]])$$

are Deducible; from which it follows that

$$\forall u.(\mathbf{\Sigma pr}[\mathbf{ap}_1[{}^*P^*,\mathbf{fn}[u]]]\equiv\exists v.\mathbf{\Sigma pr}[\mathbf{ap}_2[{}^*Q^*,\mathbf{fn}[u],\mathbf{fn}[v]]])$$

is Deducible. But since Q is of lower degree than P, *ex hypothesi*,

$$\forall u.\forall v.(\mathbf{\Sigma pr}[\mathbf{ap}_2[{}^*Q^*,\mathbf{fn}[u],\mathbf{fn}[v]]]\equiv Q[u,v])$$

is Deducible; consequently, so is

$$\forall u.(\mathbf{\Sigma pr}[\mathbf{ap}_1[{}^*P^*,\mathbf{fn}[u]]]\equiv P[u])$$

—and since one of the LEs for P is Deducible, all are.

Q.E.D.

In conclusion it is worth cautioning against over-hasty claims to Deducibility. What is required for the 'arithmetization' of a metamathematical theorem to be Deducible is, roughly speaking, that it can be given a proof that involves no methods more advanced than mathematical induction: it was for that reason $\forall x.(\mathbf{\Sigma pr}[x]\supset\mathbf{Dbl}[x])$ was said to be 'certainly' Deducible. Some more examples:

—$\sim\mathbf{Fmdbl_Q}[{}^*\sim\exists x.(x\neq\bar{0}\wedge\forall y<x.y'<x)^*]$ by Theorem II.5.1;
—$\sim\exists x.(\mathbf{Fmdbl_Q}[x]\wedge\mathbf{Fmdbl_Q}[\mathbf{ngn}[x]])$ by the last;
—$\forall x.(\mathbf{\Sigma fm}[x]\supset\mathbf{Fmdbl_Q}[x]\supset\mathbf{\Sigma pr}[x])$ by Theorem X.3.2;

and two counterexamples:

—$\sim\exists x.(\mathbf{Fmdbl_P}[x]\wedge\mathbf{Fmdbl_P}[\mathbf{ngn}[x]])$ by Theorem VIII.3.1;
—$\forall x.(\mathbf{\Sigma fm}[x]\supset\mathbf{Fmdbl_P}[x]\supset\mathbf{\Sigma pr}[x])$ by the last.

It is obviously no easier to decide whether or not a metamathematical theorem can be given a proof that is convertible into a Deduction than it is to decide whether or not an arithmetical theorem like Dirichlet's (end of II.4) can be given such a proof.

IX
The Limits of Representability

IX.1 Gödel spoke of his argument being "closely related to the 'Liar' " (*1931*, p. 149), and he meant the Eubulidean Liar, the antinomy in which a man says that he is lying or that what he says is not true, so apparently providing a proposition that says about itself that it is not true. However that may be (cf. VII.2, esp. fn. 1), there is undoubtedly a close relation between it and the Epimenidean Liar, the antinomy in which he only says something *to the effect* that what he says is not true—something, say, that p, that has the property of being true just in case that it is not true that p also has that property (though saying, as St Paul quotes Epimenides the Cretan as saying, that the Cretans are always liars only half-fulfils this condition: cf. *Prior 1958*, p. 261). For, taking Tr to be a representation of

'$n.n$ is the Gödel number of a form that is standardly assigned $\mathbb{T}$',

let L be Carnap's fixed-point for $x.\sim Tr[x]$; then L has the property of being standardly assigned $\mathbb{T}$ just in case $\sim Tr[*L*]$ also has that property. So now we have relatives of the four components of Gödel's argument for Theorem VIII.1.1:

1— for any form X, if X is standardly assigned $\mathbb{T}$ so is $Tr[*X*]$;
2— if $Tr[*L*]$ is standardly assigned $\mathbb{T}$ so is $\sim L$;
3— if $\sim Tr[*L*]$ is standardly assigned $\mathbb{T}$ so is L; and
4— for any form X, if X is not standardly assigned $\mathbb{T}$ then $\sim Tr[*X*]$ is standardly assigned $\mathbb{T}$.

These four propositions are incompatible—which establishes the falsity of the assumption that the predicate mentioned is representable:

THEOREM IX.1.1. **TARSKI'S THEOREM.** *There is* no *representation of '$n.n$ is the Gödel number of a form that is standardly assigned* $\mathbb{T}$'.

This theorem is simply a version of that at the end of section II.2; another way to reach the same conclusion is to argue that, if there were a representation of the predicate, then there would also be one of

> '*n.n* is the Gödel number of a singulary predicate-form whose diagonalization is not standardly assigned 𝕋'

and then the diagonalization of *that* representation would both be and not be standardly assigned 𝕋: once again, we are reminded of Grelling's 'heterologicality' predicate

> '$\pi.\pi$ is a singulary predicate with an untrue diagonalization'

with its diagonalization that seems to both be and not be true.

Notice, too, that the theorem has Theorem VIII.6.1 as a corollary—for consider an extension *S* of **R** for which ⌜*n.n* is the Gödel number of one of its members⌝ is representable; then the predicate ⌜*n.n* is the Gödel number of a form that is formally deducible from *S*⌝ is also representable and so not co-extensive with any predicate that is not representable—such as the one mentioned in Tarski's Theorem; thus either there is a form that is formally deducible from *S* but not standardly assigned 𝕋 or else there is one that is standardly assigned 𝕋 but not formally deducible from *S*; that is, either *S* is not sound or *S* is not complete (*Tarski 1933*, p. 254).

It is worth mentioning here that Gödel was aware of both these things—both of Theorem IX.1.1 and of the fact that Theorem VIII.6.1 is a corollary thereto. In 1965 he added a footnote to *1934* that referred readers to Tarski's writings for "a closer examination" of them, and this appears to have given rise to the impression that he did not know them before Tarski made them public (*Tarski 1933*, pp. 247, 278). However, he had patiently explained both in a letter to Zermelo (*1931a*), and later said that "long before" completing his famous paper he "had found the *correct* solution of the semantic paradoxes in the fact that truth in a language cannot be defined in itself" (*1970*). Why didn't he make these points in the paper? Presumably partly for the reason that they are obvious to anyone who considers his sketch of the main idea of the proof (*1931*, pp. 147–51), but also for the same reason that he had for replacing the assumption of consistency by "a purely formal and much weaker one" (cf. VIII.2 *sup.*)—that is, to obtain results invulnerable to attack by those in the grip of what he thought of as the "prejudice, or whatever you may call it" against non-constructive notions such as that of truth (*1967*).

IX.2 Not only was Gödel aware of Tarski's Theorem and the corollary thereto but he even maintained, in *1961*, that the theorem "is the true reason for the existence of undecidable propositions in the formal systems containing arithmetic". Yet there is a famous footnote in the original paper that seems to be in tension with this: "the true reason for the incompleteness inherent in all formal systems of mathematics is that the formation of ever higher types can be continued into the transfinite [see *Hilbert 1925*, p. 389 f.], while in any formal system at most denumerably many of them are available. For it can be shown that the undecidable propositions constructed here become decidable whenever appropriate higher types are added ..." (p. 181; cf. *1932*, p. 237). It cannot of course be that there are *two* "true reasons" for a phenomenon, so either Gödel had changed his mind in the interim or he thought of himself as making essentially the same claim both times. The latter is more probably the case, for there is a close connexion between the two possible reasons, as we shall now see.

From the fact that the predicate

'*n.n* is the Gödel number of a form that is standardly assigned 𝕋'

is not representable we may reasonably infer that *the concept of being a first-order truth involving only the standard arithmetical concepts is not explicable in terms of those concepts using the devices of first-order predicate logic*; but we may certainly not infer that it is not explicable *at all*—especially in view of the fact that giving a rigorous recursive definition of a predicate co-extensive with the non-representable one, which he did before he had proved the above theorem, was Tarski's most notable achievement (*1933*, §3).

To locate exactly the amount of involvement of unfamiliar ideas, note this fact (expressed in a somewhat cumbersome fashion to make it easy to compare with Tarski's "normal definition" in his footnote to Definition 22 on p. 193):

A grounded form is standardly assigned 𝕋 if, and only if, we have that it is a member of every set that satisfies the following condition:

In order that something is a member of the set it is necessary and sufficient that it is a grounded form and either

— *it is of type* B, *and is standardly assigned 𝕋; or*

— *it is of type* R, *and its immediate descendant is a member; or*

— *it is of type* ∨ *or* ∃, *and at least one of its immediate descendants is a member; or finally*

— *it is of type* ∧ *or* ∀, *and every one of its immediate descendants is a member.*

(This is an easy consequence of the fact that the set of all grounded forms that are standardly assigned $\mathbb{T}$ satisfies the condition, and is a subset of any other set that does so—which can be proved by induction, as in Theorem III.3.1.) Now what we have here cannot be turned into a representation of the predicate

'*n*.*n* is the Gödel number of a grounded form that is standardly assigned $\mathbb{T}$'

because the quantification involved is over sets: if it could be restricted to being over finite sets then, as with the predicate discussed in V.1, we could attain a representation—but we know that that's impossible.

However, it can be turned into a *second-order* representation—one that uses the devices of *second-order* logic:[1]

$$\mathrm{x}.\forall\zeta.(\forall \mathrm{x}.(\zeta\mathrm{x} \equiv \Theta[\zeta,\mathrm{x}]) \supset \zeta\mathrm{x})$$

where Θ is the form

$$\begin{aligned}\zeta\mathrm{x}.(\mathbf{Grfm}[\mathrm{x}] \wedge ((\mathbf{Typ_B}[\mathrm{x}] \wedge \mathbf{Tr_B}[\mathrm{x}]) \vee \\ (\mathbf{Typ_R}[\mathrm{x}] \wedge \zeta\text{ɿ}\mathrm{y}.\mathbf{Imdsc}[\mathrm{y},\mathrm{x}]) \vee \\ ((\mathbf{Typ_\vee}[\mathrm{x}] \vee \mathbf{Typ_\exists}[\mathrm{x}]) \wedge \exists\mathrm{y}.(\mathbf{Imdsc}[\mathrm{y},\mathrm{x}] \wedge \zeta\mathrm{y})) \vee \\ ((\mathbf{Typ_\wedge}[\mathrm{x}] \vee \mathbf{Typ_\forall}[\mathrm{x}]) \wedge \forall\mathrm{y}.(\mathbf{Imdsc}[\mathrm{y},\mathrm{x}] \supset \zeta\mathrm{y}))))\end{aligned}$$

—that is, a form of type $((i), i)$, as in the discussion of the Recursion Theorem (—which, be it noted, does not supply a representation because $\mathrm{zx}.\Theta[\mathrm{x}.\mathbf{\Sigma pr}[\mathbf{ap}_1[\mathrm{z},\mathbf{fn}[\mathrm{x}]]],\mathrm{x}]$ is not a Σ-form).[2]

The two facts together, that there is no first-order representation and that there is a second-order one, Tarski was wont to summarize by saying that the language in which the representation is formulated has to be "essentially richer" than the object language (*1933*, pp. 271–3; *1944*, pp. 351–2). And the point Gödel was making in 1931 only adds to this that "the undecidable propositions constructed here become decidable" when we move to the richer language: which is of course true (G, for example, is standardly assigned $\mathbb{T}$).

Four notes : (1) On satisfaction. One who, as suggested, compares the condition given for a grounded form to be standardly assigned $\mathbb{T}$ with Tarski's "normal definition" may be struck by the absence of any use of the concept of satisfaction. The concept is simple

[1] Second-order logic is explained in *Hilbert & Ackermann*, ch. IV.

[2] Tarski also considered a second procedure "for the establishment of a materially correct way of using the semantical concepts in the metalanguage", but rejected it (*1936*, pp. 405–6; cf. *1933*, pp. 255–8, 273): it is pursued in *Friedman & Sheard* and, to a different end, in *Davidson 1985* (*passim*, but cf. esp. pp. 150, 172–3).

enough—a finite sequence of numbers *standardly satisfies* a predicate-form just in case the result of applying it to their formal numerals is standardly assigned $\mathbb{T}$ (so $\langle 2,5,3\rangle$ standardly satisfies $xyz.(x+(y^x))=(z^z)$).

The reason Tarski had to define satisfaction before defining truth for his formal language is *not* that "in general composite sentences are in no way compounds of simple *sentences*" (*1933*, p. 189), *nor* that there is no "way in which the truth or falsity of composite sentences depends on the truth or falsity of the simpler ones contained in them" (ib.), *but* that there is no way in which the truth or falsity of composite sentences depends on the truth or falsity of simpler ones. The first two things are equally true of our formal language, but the third is not—for what a grounded form not of type **B** is standardly assigned *does* depend on what its immediate descendants are standardly assigned.

: *(2) On simplicity.* The demand that the dependence be of composite sentences on simpler ones is also un-motivated: all that is strictly necessary is that the sentences—assumed to be infinitely many—can be exhaustively and exclusively partitioned into infinitely many sets $S_0, S_1, S_2, \ldots$ in such a way that (i) the truth or falsity of those in S_0 does not depend on that of any not in S_0, and (ii) for each number n, the truth or falsity of those in S_{n+1} depends on that of those in S_n—the sentences in S_n need not be simpler, in any pre-determined sense, than those in S_{n+1}, although it usually helps if they are. In what sense, to consider only the most famous dependence-claim of all, is 'It is not always false of *x* that *x* begat Charles II and that *x* was executed and that "if *y* begat Charles II, *y* is identical with *x*" is always true of *y*' simpler than 'the father of Charles II was executed'?

The demand could really only be motivated by some such desire as that for the 'theory' of truth to show "how the meanings of sentences depend upon the meanings of words" and so qualify as a 'theory' of meaning (*Davidson 1985*, *passim*, but cf. pp. 17, 23, 61); that this was in no way Tarski's desire is conclusively established in *Etchemendy* (§1), and we are left with the conclusion that he is being slightly careless at this point—because it shouldn't have mattered to him *how* his project of defining truth was accomplished, as long as it was. (His reference, early in the passage, to our finding expressions of rather varied kinds "from the point of view of logical structure" is not decisive for interpreting him: after all, *any* recursive construction of the set of expressions will *eo ipso* impose a 'logical structure' upon them.)

: (3) On convention **T**. Tarski notoriously insisted that an "adequate" representation *Tr* of

'*n.n* is the Gödel number of a grounded form that is standardly assigned $\mathbb{T}$'

would have to satisfy the condition that from it "follows", for every grounded form *X*, the 'local *Tr*-equivalence', $(Tr[{}^*X^*] \equiv X)$, for that form (cf. proof of Theorem VIII.8.1; *Tarski 1944*, §§4, 12; *1933*, pp. 187–8). Since, as we have seen, *Tr*, to be a representation at all, must be *second-order*, the concept of a form's "following from" the representation has to be explained as its being formally deducible, in the sense of second-order logic, from some particular, appropriate, set of forms. The set that most immediately suggests itself is $^2\mathbf{P}^+$, being $^2\mathbf{P}$—the true, second-order, version of Peano's Arithmetic, consisting of the eleven forms in **Q** plus

$$\forall\zeta.(\zeta\bar{0} \supset \forall x.(\zeta x \supset \zeta x') \supset \forall x.\zeta x)$$

—augmented by

$$\exists\zeta.\forall x.(\zeta x \equiv \Theta[\zeta, x]).$$

The appropriate rules for second-order regular tableaux are given in, e.g., *Takeuti* ch. 3.

Now if one takes *Tr* to be what Tarski suggests, viz.

$$x.\forall\zeta.(\forall x.(\zeta x \equiv \Theta[\zeta, x]) \supset \zeta x),$$

it is more or less immediate that the 'global *Tr*-equivalence' is formally deducible (in the sense of second-order logic) from $\forall x.(Tr[x] \equiv \Theta[Tr, x]$; however, the latter form itself is formally deducible from $^2\mathbf{P}^+$; consequently, reasoning as in Theorem VIII.8.1, the local *Tr*-equivalences for grounded forms are all formally deducible from $^2\mathbf{P}^+$: so it appears that *Tr* meets Tarski's "adequacy" requirement.

: (4) On defining truth. Finding even an "adequate" representation of a predicate doesn't establish its definability—unless by a definition one understands, not a statement, but a stipulation, of meaning; for example, to show that **Σpr** is an "adequate" representation of '*n.n* is the Gödel number of a Σ-form that is standardly assigned $\mathbb{T}$' is not to exhibit, even implicitly, another predicate with the *same meaning*—for '*n.n* is the Gödel number of a Σ-provable form' is *only* (though indeed necessarily) co-extensive.

Tarski's project of defining truth is not nearly as grand as it sounds because he uses the word 'definition' in an entirely extensional sense. There are certainly some remarks that point in the opposite direction, as when he says that the "desired definition does not aim to specify the meaning of a familiar word used to denote a novel notion; on the contrary, it aims to catch hold of the actual meaning of an old notion" (*1944*, p. 341); but when he glancingly recognizes the existence of indefinitely many materially adequate definitions of truth other than the one he picks out (pp. 353–4) he pays no attention at all to whatever differences may separate them—such as that some might better express the meaning of the truth-predicate than others do. His suspicion that to recognize significant differences between adequate truth-definitions is to involve oneself in primitive pre-scientific metaphysics is nowhere made explicit but is clear from the condescending brush-off he gives one group of objectors: "I have been informed ... that my definition, though it states necessary and sufficient conditions for a sentence to be true, does not really grasp the 'essence' of this concept. Since I have never been able to understand what the 'essence' of a concept is, I must be excused from discussing this point any longer" (p. 361: what is needed, of course, is not to understand what the essence of a concept is, but to understand what it is for one of the things that Tarski calls "definitions" to grasp the essence of the concept more closely than another does). And perhaps he thought, as many did at the time, that the meaning of a predicate is its extension, and that to state its meaning is to pick out that extension, no matter how or in what words (compare his use of "define" to mean "uniquely determine [a given object]": pp. 345, 373).

IX.3 In this section we establish some results closely related to Tarski's Theorem; their significance will be discussed in the next section.

To begin with, if we remember that Carnap's fixed-point for a Σ-form is itself a Σ-form, we can prove, using Church's Thesis and the reasoning of Tarski's Theorem,

THEOREM IX.3.1. *The predicate*

'X.X is a Σ-form that is standardly assigned $\mathbb{T}$'

is not effectively decidable.

(The predicate is related to Church's "unsolvable problem of elementary number theory"—cf. Theorem XIX of his *1936*—but not so closely as to Kleene's in Theorem XVI of his *1936*.)

Using Theorem III.1.2, we deduce as a corollary

THEOREM IX.3.2. *Consider an extension S of* **R**: *if it is sound, the predicate*

$$\ulcorner X.X \text{ is a } \Sigma\text{-form and } S \vdash X \urcorner$$

is not effectively decidable.

We shall need, furthermore, the following strengthening of this result:

THEOREM IX.3.3. *Consider an extension S of* **R**: *if it is consistent, the predicate*

$$\ulcorner X.X \text{ is a } \Sigma\text{-form and } S \vdash X \urcorner$$

is not effectively decidable.

—which we obtain by deducing it, using Church's Thesis, from

THEOREM IX.3.4. *Consider an extension S of* **R**: *if it is consistent, the extension of*

$$\ulcorner n.n \text{ is the Gödel number of a } \Sigma\text{-form } X \text{ such that } S \vdash X \urcorner$$

is not recursive.

—a refinement of a result in *Mostowski, Robinson & Tarski* (p. 60), itself a simple generalization of an earlier result in *Rosser* (Theorem III); Rosser's trick, mentioned in the preamble to Theorem VIII.4.2, is used again in the following essential

Lemma. For each recursive set there is a singulary Σ-predicate-form P such that, for any number n,

— $\mathbf{R} \vdash P[\bar{n}]$ if n is a member of the set;

— $\mathbf{R} \vdash \sim P[\bar{n}]$ if n is not a member of the set.

(P is said to *numeralwise express* what it represents *in* **R**: cf. *Kleene 1952*, pp. 195, 296.)

Proof. Given such a set there are Σ-representations Q, R of the predicates $\ulcorner n.n$ is a number that is a member of the set$\urcorner$ and $\ulcorner n.n$ is a number that is not a member of the set$\urcorner$ respectively; let

$$P_+ \text{ be } \mathrm{x}.\exists \mathrm{w}.(\exists \mathrm{y}<\mathrm{w}.S_1[{*Q*}, \mathrm{x}, \mathrm{y}] \wedge \sim\exists \mathrm{y}<\mathrm{w}.S_1[{*R*}, \mathrm{x}, \mathrm{y}])$$
$$P_- \text{ be } \mathrm{x}.\exists \mathrm{w}.(\exists \mathrm{y}<\mathrm{w}.S_1[{*R*}, \mathrm{x}, \mathrm{y}] \wedge \sim\exists \mathrm{y}<\mathrm{w}.S_1[{*Q*}, \mathrm{x}, \mathrm{y}])$$

where S_1 is $\mathrm{zxy}.(\mathbf{Cl\Sigma tb}[\mathrm{y}] \wedge \mathbf{ap}_1[\mathrm{z}, \mathbf{fn}[\mathrm{x}]] = \mathbf{tpfm}[\mathrm{y}])$ (a form mentioned earlier, at the end of VI.5).

Suppose n is a number that is a member of the set; then $Q[\bar{n}]$ is but $R[\bar{n}]$ is not standardly assigned $\mathbb{T}$; so $Q[\bar{n}]$ is but $R[\bar{n}]$ is not Σ-provable; so $P_+[\bar{n}]$ is standardly assigned $\mathbb{T}$ and thus, because it is a Σ-form, $\mathbf{R} \vdash P_+[\bar{n}]$.

Suppose n is a number that is not a member of the set; then, in the same way, **R** $\vdash P_-[\bar{n}]$; however it is more or less obvious that **R** $\vdash \sim\exists x.(P_+[x] \wedge P_-[x])$; so **R** $\vdash \sim P_+[\bar{n}]$.

We can now give a proof of the theorem, which should be compared carefully with that of Gödel's First Theorem:

PROOF. Suppose the extension of the predicate is recursive; then so is its complement—let U be the appropriate Σ-predicate-form supplied by the lemma, and let C be Carnap's fixed-point for U. Then we have:

1— for any Σ-form X, if X is formally deducible from S then $\sim U[{*X*}]$ is too;

2— if $\sim U[{*C*}]$ is formally deducible from S then $\sim C$ is too;

3— if $U[{*C*}]$ is formally deducible from S then C is too; and

4— for any Σ-form X, if X is not formally deducible from S then $U[{*X*}]$ is.

Since C is a Σ-form because U is, these four propositions are incompatible unless S is inconsistent.

Q.E.D.

It is an important fact that there is a uniform effective procedure for associating with any Σ-form Y a form X such that $\vdash X$ iff Y is standardly assigned $\mathbb{T}$: this was in essence known to Gödel (see Theorem X of *1931*) but he was unaware of Theorem IX.3.1 and so could not deduce

THEOREM IX.3.5. **CHURCH'S THEOREM.** *The predicate*

$$`X. \vdash X'$$

is not effectively decidable.

It was not by this route that Church showed that "the general case of the Entscheidungsproblem of the engere Funktionenkalkül is unsolvable" (*1936a*, p. 114); what he did was to define a non-recursive set A and show that there is a uniform effective procedure for associating with any number n a form X such that $\vdash X$ iff n is a member of A, but his set A is not itself of any great logical significance: for this reason we adopt the procedure in *Mostowski, Robinson & Tarski* (p. 62) to prove

THEOREM IX.3.6. *Consider a set S: if it is formally compatible with* **Q**, *the predicate*

$$\ulcorner X.X \text{ is a } \Sigma\text{-form and } S \vdash X \urcorner$$

is not effectively decidable

—one set being *formally compatible with* another just in case their union (the set whose members are those of both) is consistent.

PROOF. Consider our version **Q** of Robinson's Arithmetic (sections I.1 and II.4); replace the fourth and fifth of its members by $\sim\exists y.y<\bar{0}$ and $\forall x.(x<x' \wedge \sim\exists z.(x<z \wedge z<x'))$ respectively to obtain a new set **Q**′. Note that all members of **Q**′ are formally deducible from **Q** and conversely; we introduce **Q**′ simply because, for any Σ-sentence-form X, $(Q_1' \supset Q_2' \supset \ldots \supset Q_{11}' \supset X)$ is also a Σ-form ($Q_1', Q_2', \ldots, Q_{11}'$ being the eleven members of **Q**′).

Now if ⌜$X.X$ is a Σ-form and $S \vdash X$⌝ is effectively decidable then so is ⌜$X.X$ is a Σ-form and $S \vdash (Q_1' \supset Q_2' \supset \ldots \supset Q_{11}' \supset X)$⌝, and hence so is ⌜$X.X$ is a Σ-form and $S \cup$**Q**′ $\vdash X$⌝; but $S \cup$**Q**′ is an extension of **R**; so by Theorem IX.3.3 S is formally incompatible with **Q**′; so S is formally incompatible with **Q**.

Q.E.D.

(To revert to the remark made in the preamble to Church's Theorem, the procedure that associates with any Σ-form Υ the form $(Q_1' \supset Q_2' \supset \ldots \supset Q_{11}' \supset \Upsilon)$ is a uniform effective one and, by Theorem III.1.2 (and the fact that **Q** is a sound extension of **R**), $\vdash (Q_1' \supset Q_2' \supset \ldots \supset Q_{11}' \supset \Upsilon)$ iff Υ is standardly assigned $\mathbb{T}$.)

IX.4 It is an old dream of philosophy that truth, or mathematical truth, or at least logical truth, should be decidable. Leibniz spoke throughout his life of a *Lingua Philosophica* that was to make possible an *ars combinatoria* by which "all truths that can be demonstrated about things expressible in this language with the addition of new concepts not yet expressed in it ... can be demonstrated *solo calculo*, or solely by manipulation of characters according to a certain form, without any labour of the imagination or effort of the mind, just as occurs in arithmetic and algebra"—"if controversies were to arise, there would be no more need of disputation between two philosophers than between two accountants. For it would suffice to take their pencils in their hands, to sit down to their slates, and to say to each other ...: Let us calculate" (*Mates*, p. 185; *Russell 1900*, p. 170). This project clearly demands the *prior* completion of all the work of all science, to enable the dictionary for the new language to be constructed: and thus can be left comfortably vague until that moment. Wittgenstein was, characteristically, more definite: "The propositions of logic describe the scaffolding of the world .... It is possible ... to give in advance a description of all 'true' logical propositions. Hence there can *never* be surprises in logic .... Proof in logic is merely a mechanical expedient to facilitate the recognition of tautologies in complicated cases .... Our fundamental principle is that whenever a question can be decided by logic at all it must be possible to decide it without more ado" (*1921*, 6.124 ff., 5.551).

Hilbert, as a working mathematician and eulogist of the mathematical imagination, could not agree with Leibniz: "my proof theory cannot specify a general method for solving every mathematical problem; that does not exist" (*1925*, p. 384; cf. also von Neumann's expository article *1927*, p. 11). But, since he did not share the prevalent belief in the identity of mathematics and logic, he was at liberty not to disagree with Wittgenstein and was content to leave that issue as an open problem under the name of the *Entscheidungsproblem*: "*The following question now arises as a fundamental problem: Is it possible to determine whether or not a given statement pertaining to a field of knowledge is a consequence of the axioms?*"[1]

In view of Theorem IX.3.1, the facts are now seen to favour Hilbert rather than Leibniz on the issue of the decidability of mathematical truth; and in view of Church's Theorem, the facts are against Wittgenstein on the issue of logical truth.

Thus the *Entscheidungsproblem* has been settled, negatively. We must remember, however, that even had matters turned out the other way, we should have been not one whit better off: for it is clear in advance that the effort involved in finding an effective decision procedure for '*X.X* is standardly assigned $\mathbb{T}$' and of proving it to be one could be no less than the effort involved in proving that the predicate applies to this form or that—that is, in doing number-theory. If it is said that at least the application of the decision procedure in specific cases would satisfy Leibniz's conditions and involve only *mechanical* effort, not intellectual effort, one may legitimately wonder why this is deemed an advantage—given, what is surely true, that in all interesting cases it is only intellectual effort that can reach a decision in an acceptable time. A positive solution to the *Entscheidungsproblem* would not have made it any less *rational* for the mathematical community to continue its labours just as before, any more than the existence of a decision procedure for primality makes it less rational to seek answers to

[1] *Hilbert & Ackermann*, p. 108, his italics: by "determine" he means "give a general criterion for", as becomes clear on p. 113. It was of course to the first edition, which came out in 1928, that Gödel was responding; the section was entirely rewritten after the appearance of the incompleteness results.

questions of the form 'Is it prime?' in the old way (cf. IV.1 *ad fin*). The mathematical imagination would not *in fact* be put in jeopardy even if it could *in principle* be dispensed with.[1]

With the *Entscheidungsproblem* settled, the interest now lies in the following problem: For what θ (being a singulary effectively decidable predicate of sentence-forms) is the predicate

$$\ulcorner X. \vdash X \text{ and } \theta \text{ is true of } X\urcorner$$

effectively decidable? Two of the oldest and best known results are:
— '$X. \vdash X$ and all predicate- or descriptor-letters that occur in X are singulary' is effectively decidable;
— take any binary predicate-letter R: then $\ulcorner X. \vdash X$ and R is the only predicate- or descriptor-letter that occurs in $X\urcorner$ is not effectively decidable.

Hundreds of similar results are now known: the territory is mapped in *Dreben & Goldfarb* and *H. R. Lewis.*

There is a further corollary of Theorem IX.3.1 that it is appropriate to mention here. Let us say that a function is a *choice function for* a relation just in case it is a subset of the relation but they have the same domain—for example, the extension of

$$\text{'}mn.n \text{ is } (m+1)!\text{'}$$

is one amongst infinitely many choice functions for the extension of

$$\text{'}mn. \text{ all numbers from 1 to } (m+1) \text{ divide } n\text{'}.$$

The notorious Axiom of Choice is to the effect that *any relation has a choice function*; but, independently of it, it is clear that *any relation over the natural numbers has a choice function*—for we may take the domain of the function to be that of the relation, and stipulate its value for a given argument to be the least value of the relation for that argument; essentially the same reasoning establishes that *any recursive relation has a recursive choice function*—in, say, the binary case, given Σ-predicate-forms R and S such that $|S|$ is the complement of $|R|$, $|\mathrm{xy}.(R[\mathrm{x},\mathrm{y}] \wedge \forall \mathrm{z}<\mathrm{y}.S[\mathrm{x},\mathrm{z}])|$ is a recursive choice function for $|R|$. From this last it follows without difficulty that *any recursively enumerable relation has a recursive choice function.*

[1] *Pace* von Neumann (loc. cit.) and Hardy, who wrote: "Suppose, for example, that we could find a finite system of rules which enabled us to say whether any given formula was demonstrable or not. This system would embody a theorem of metamathematics. There is of course no such theorem, and this is very fortunate, since if there were we should have a mechanical set of rules for the solution of all mathematical problems, and our activities as mathematicians would come to an end" (p. 16).

But *not every relation over the natural numbers has a recursive choice function*—for instance, $|\mathrm{xy}.(\mathbf{\Sigma pr}[\mathrm{x}] \supset (\mathbf{Cl\Sigma tb}[\mathrm{y}] \wedge \mathrm{x} = \mathbf{tpfm}[\mathrm{y}]))|$ doesn't: for if there were a binary Σ-predicate-form F such that $|F|$ is a choice function for it, then

$$\forall \mathrm{x}.(\sim \mathbf{\Sigma pr}[\mathrm{x}] \equiv \exists \mathrm{y}.(F[\mathrm{x},\mathrm{y}] \wedge \sim(\mathbf{Cl\Sigma tb}[\mathrm{y}] \wedge \mathrm{x} = \mathbf{tpfm}[\mathrm{y}])))$$

would be standardly assigned $\mathbb{T}$, and thus, using Church's Thesis,

'*X.X* is a Σ-form that is standardly assigned $\mathbb{T}$'

would be effectively decidable (cf. IV.5, *ad fin*).

Now the significance of this is that most constructivists—certainly all intuitionists—insist that *any total relation over the natural numbers has a constructive choice function*—such a relation, say binary, being *total* just in case its arguments are the numbers, so that the relation has a value for each number: for, they reason, a proof of its totality must actually show how, for each number, to construct a value—that is, a proof must actually give (or at least give an effective procedure for determining) a constructive choice function. Intuitionists in particular are further committed to holding that *any total relation over the natural numbers has a recursive choice function* (*Kleene 1952*, pp. 508–10); it follows that they cannot prove that $|\mathrm{xy}.(\mathbf{\Sigma pr}[\mathrm{x}] \supset (\mathbf{Cl\Sigma tb}[\mathrm{y}] \wedge \mathrm{x} = \mathbf{tpfm}[\mathrm{y}]))|$ is total; so they cannot prove that *for any form there is a Σ-tableau that is closed if the form is Σ-provable*; and thus they cannot prove that *for any form, it either is or is not Σ-provable*. The point, of course, is that these propositions are what classical mathematicians would call logical truths: "It appears that there is a proposition provable classically for which no constructive proof is possible" (*Kleene 1943*, p. 255); but then this only means that there are sentences which, understood in the classical manner, express logical truths, but which, understood in the intuitionist manner, do not.

IX.5 Consider: a consistent extension *S* of **R** for which ⌜*X.X* is one of its members⌝ is effectively confirmable; and an extension *T* of **R** from which are formally deducible some forms that are not so from *S*.

In the abstract *1936*, Gödel announced a further result relevant to the matter of VIII.6: we know that *S* is incomplete, and so we may choose *T* to be "more complete" than *S*; then, Gödel said, passing from *S* to *T* has the effect, not only of making formally deducible certain forms that were not so before, but also of making it possible to shorten, by an arbitrary *pre-assigned* amount, infinitely many of the formal deductions already available (p. 397). Gödel's notion of one formal deduction's being shorter than another is that of there being fewer points on the former than on the latter, but we shall use a different-though-similar notion[1] to obtain a different-though-similar result: we say that one syntactic sequent σ is *shorter (in Mostowski's sense) than* another τ just in case σ's Gödel number is smaller than τ's; and, more generally, for any singulary recursive operation f, that σ is *shorter by degree f than* τ just in case the value of f for σ's Gödel number as argument is smaller than τ's Gödel number. Then we have (cf. *Mostowski 1952*, p. 112 f.; *Ehrenfeucht & Mycielski*; *Arbib*):

Theorem IX.5.1. **Mostowski's Speed-up Theorem.** *Suppose f is a singulary recursive operation: for each form that is formally deducible from T but not S, there is another that is so from both, although it has a formal deduction from T that is shorter by degree f than any it has from S.*

Proof. Let P be a Σ-representation of $\ulcorner n.n$ is the Gödel number of a member of $S\urcorner$, F be a binary Σ-predicate-form such that $|F|$ is f, X be a form that is formally deducible from T but not S, and d be a singulary Δ-descriptor-form such that, for any sentence-form Y, $|d[{*}Y{*}]|$ is the Gödel number of a formal deduction of $(X \vee Y)$ from T.

Arguing as in the penultimate paragraph of the previous section (relying on Theorem IX.3.3 rather than IX.3.1), we see that

$$|\mathrm{yz}.(\mathbf{Fmdbl}_P[\mathbf{dsjn}[{*}X{*},\mathrm{y}]] \supset \exists \mathrm{u}{<}\mathrm{z}'.\mathbf{Fmddn}_P[\mathrm{u},\mathbf{dsjn}[{*}X{*},\mathrm{y}]])|$$

has no recursive choice function and hence that, in particular, $|\mathrm{yz}.F[d[\mathrm{y}],\mathrm{z}]|$ is not one; so

$$\sim\forall \mathrm{y}.\forall \mathrm{z}.(F[d[\mathrm{y}],\mathrm{z}] \supset \mathbf{Fmdbl}_P[\mathbf{dsjn}[{*}X{*},\mathrm{y}]] \supset \exists \mathrm{u}{<}\mathrm{z}'.\mathbf{Fmddn}_P[\mathrm{u},\mathbf{dsjn}[{*}X{*},\mathrm{y}]])$$

is standardly assigned $\mathbb{T}$ and therefore, for some form Y, so is

$$(\mathbf{Fmdbl}_P[{*}(X \vee Y){*}] \wedge \forall \mathrm{u}.(\mathbf{Fmddn}_P[\mathrm{u},{*}(X \vee Y){*}] \supset \imath \mathrm{z}.F[d[{*}Y{*}],\mathrm{z}] < \mathrm{u}).$$

Q.E.D.

Although making for a theorem that is easily stated and proved, this notion of one formal deduction's being shorter than another is by no means a natural one, and for three separate reasons. In the first place, it provides one with a *measure* of shortness, so that we can sensibly say, not only that one formal deduction is shorter than

[1] cf. Theorem VIII.4.2.

another, but even *by how much* it is so: the un-naturalness of this is seen, e.g., by reflecting on Socrates' confidence that we can sensibly say, not only that one life is less worthwhile than another, but even by how much it is so—the tyrant's life is 729 times less worthwhile than the philosopher-king's (*Republic*, 587c). In the second place, according to this notion we can discriminate in point of shortness formal deductions that we would naturally be inclined to say were indiscriminable—e.g. $\langle\langle\bar{0}=\bar{0}\rangle\rangle$ and $\langle\langle\bar{1}=\bar{1}\rangle\rangle$ are two formal deductions the first of which, on Mostowski's account, is shorter than the second: this, too, is thoroughly counter-intuitive. Thirdly, damningly, the purely conventional nature of Gödel numbering ensures that for any pair of formal deductions one can devise numberings relative to which either term is shorter than the other. Unfortunately, however, more natural notions, even Gödel's, do not lead to easy proofs: see *Parikh 1986*, and the papers cited therein.

X
The Arithmetical Hierarchy

X.1 Up to this point in the book we have concentrated narrowly on the properties of Σ-forms, paying only glancing attention to other kinds of grounded form. In this last chapter it is appropriate to widen the gaze in order to see more clearly.

The grounded forms dispose themselves into a natural hierarchy, called the *arithmetical*—more precisely, after its independent discoverers, the *Kleene-Mostowski*—hierarchy (cf. *Kleene 1943*, *Mostowski 1947*). A grounded sentence-form is

— a Σ_0-*form* iff it is of type **B**;

— a Π_0-*form* iff it is of type **B**;

and, for any number *n*, is

— a Σ_{n+1}-*form* iff it has no descendant of type ∀ that is not a Π_n-form;

— a Π_{n+1}-*form* iff it has no descendant of type ∃ that is not a Σ_n-form;

— a Δ_n-*form* iff it is both a Σ_n-form and a Π_n-form.

For each number *n*, the Σ_n-, Π_n- and Δ_n-*predicate*-, *subject*- and *descriptor*-forms are defined as in the first paragraph of III.1.

Thus the sentence-forms

$$\exists x.(\exists x.x=x \supset x=x) \quad \forall x.(x=x \supset \exists x.x=x) \quad (\exists x.x=x \supset \exists x.x=x)$$

are respectively a Σ_2-, a Π_2- and a Δ_2-form.[1] The Σ_1-forms are the

[1] The hierarchy is usually imposed, not on the forms themselves, but on what they are standardly assigned. This leads to a possibility of confusion: for on such an account a relation is Δ_1 iff it is both Σ_1 and Π_1—that is, is assigned both to a Σ_1-form and to a Π_1-form; so a relation is Δ_1 if it is assigned to a form that is both Σ_1 and Π_1—i.e. is Δ_1; but the converse is *not* true (cf. Theorem X.2.2). Put another way: the Δ_1-relations are the recursive relations; the relations assigned to Δ_1-forms are the elementary relations (cf. V.5); and not all recursive relations are elementary.

Σ-forms, and the Δ_1-forms are the Δ-forms; for each number *n*, all the Σ_n-forms and all the Π_n-forms are Δ_{n+1}-forms; and the negations of Σ_n-forms are Π_n-forms and vice versa.

We now re-define the Σ-*tableaux*, as those tableaux that are obtained from (*any*, not necessarily Σ-) forms by successively applying the extension rules given in III.2; and symmetrically define the Π-*tableaux* as those obtained using the 'dual' extension rules, derived by reading '$\wedge$', '$\forall$' and '$\vee$' in place of '$\vee$', '$\exists$' and '$\wedge$' respectively. Then a form is
— Σ_0-*provable* iff it is a Σ_0-form that is standardly assigned $\mathbb{T}$;
— Π_0-*provable* iff it is a Π_0-form that is standardly assigned $\mathbb{T}$;
and, for any number *n*, is
— Σ_{n+1}-*provable* iff it is a Σ_{n+1}-form and some Σ-tableau for it is such that on every branch some Π_n-form of type **B** or $\forall$ is Π_n-provable;
— Π_{n+1}-*provable* iff it is a Π_{n+1}-form and every Π-tableau for it is such that on some branch every Σ_n-form of type **B** or $\exists$ is Σ_n-provable.[1]

For example, $\forall y.(\exists z.y=(\overline{2}\times z) \vee \exists z.y=(\overline{2}\times z)')$ is Π_2-provable: to see this, consider a Π-tableau for it, and imagine tracing a path down the tree, choosing, wherever there's a choice, the form that is standardly assigned $\mathbb{T}$ (there is one and only one, because the two choices are the disjuncts of an immediate descendant of the top-form); the result is a branch on which every Σ_1-form of type **B** or $\exists$ is Σ_1-provable.

Again, and consequently, $\exists x.\forall y.(\exists z.y=(x\times z) \vee \exists z.y=(x\times z)')$ is Σ_3-provable: because the Σ-tableau

$$\begin{array}{c}\exists x.\forall y.(\exists z.y=(x\times z) \vee \exists z.y=(x\times z)') \\ | \\ \forall y.(\exists z.y=(\overline{2}\times z) \vee \exists z.y=(\overline{2}\times z)')\end{array}$$

is such that on the only branch some Π_2-form of type **B** or $\forall$ is Π_2-provable.

In the same way, every one of the immediate descendants of the form $\forall w.(w=(w^w) \supset \exists x.\forall y.(\exists z.y=(x\times z) \vee \exists z.y=((x\times z)+w)))$ is Σ_3-provable, and therefore it itself is Π_4-provable. And so on.

[1] In its use in the phrase 'Π_n-provable' the adjective 'provable' is deprived of its ordinary connexion with the noun 'proof': a form's Π_n-provability is not a matter of there being anything that might reasonably be called a Π_n-proof of it, in the way that a closed Σ_1-tableau might reasonably be called a Σ_1-proof of its top-form. Anyone who finds this intolerable can of course operate with the dual notion of a form's Π_n-*refutability*.

Now by arguing as in the proof of Theorem III.2.1 we can deduce:

THEOREM X.1.1. *For each number $n>0$:*

(a) *a Σ_n-form*
— *of type* **B** *or* $\forall$ *is Σ_n-provable iff it is Π_{n-1}-provable;*
— *of type* **R** *is Σ_n-provable iff its immediate descendant is;*
— *of type* $\vee$ *or* $\exists$ *is Σ_n-provable iff at least one of its immediate descendants is;*
— *of type* $\wedge$ *is Σ_n-provable iff every one of its immediate descendants is;*
and

(b) *a Π_n-form*
— *of type* **B** *or* $\exists$ *is Π_n-provable iff it is Σ_{n-1}-provable;*
— *of type* **R** *is Π_n-provable iff its immediate descendant is;*
— *of type* $\wedge$ *or* $\forall$ *is Π_n-provable iff every one of its immediate descendants is;*
— *of type* $\vee$ *is Π_n-provable iff at least one of its immediate descendants is.*

Then, using *double* induction—that is, arguing as in the proof of Theorem III.2.2 to move from Σ_n to Π_{n+1} and simultaneously from Π_n to Σ_{n+1}—we have:

THEOREM X.1.2. *For each number n:*

(a) *the Σ_n-provable forms are those Σ_n-forms that are standardly assigned* $\mathbb{T}$*;*
and

(b) *the Π_n-provable forms are those Π_n-forms that are standardly assigned* $\mathbb{T}$.

It follows that, although all Σ_1-provable forms are Deducible—that is, formally deducible from **P**—, not all Π_1-provable forms are: Carnap's fixed-point G for x. $\sim$**Dbl**[x] is one that isn't, since it is standardly assigned $\mathbb{T}$ but is not Deducible.

X.2 Now, for any number $n>0$, we can—following the definitions of the predicates and using the techniques illustrated in VI.2—write down a pair $\boldsymbol{\Sigma_n}$**fm** and $\boldsymbol{\Pi_n}$**fm** such that
— $\boldsymbol{\Sigma_n}$**fm** is a Δ_1-representation of ⌜*m.m* is the Gödel number of a Σ_n-form⌝;
— $\boldsymbol{\Pi_n}$**fm** is a Δ_1-representation of ⌜*m.m* is the Gödel number of a Π_n-form⌝;
and, as in VI.5, write down a pair $\boldsymbol{\Sigma_n}$**pr** and $\boldsymbol{\Pi_n}$**pr** such that
— $\boldsymbol{\Sigma_n}$**pr** is a Σ_n-representation of ⌜*m.m* is the Gödel number of a

Σ_n-provable form⌝;[1]

— $\mathbf{\Pi_n pr}$ is a Π_n-representation of ⌜*m.m* is the Gödel number of a Π_n-provable form⌝.

From Theorem X.1.2 follows (as VI.5.3 does from III.1.2)

THEOREM X.2.1. *For each number* $n > 0$*:*

(a) *for any* Σ_n*-sentence-form* X, $(\mathbf{\Sigma_n pr}[{}^*X^*] \equiv X)$ *is standardly assigned* $\mathbb{T}$*;*

and

(b) *for any* Π_n*-sentence-form* X, $(\mathbf{\Pi_n pr}[{}^*X^*] \equiv X)$ *is standardly assigned* $\mathbb{T}$.

Also, using the reasoning of Theorem IX.3.1 and the fact that the negations of Σ_n-forms are Π_n-forms and *vice versa*, we have

THEOREM X.2.2. *For each number* $n > 0$*:*

— *the predicate* ⌜*m.m is the Gödel number of a* Δ_n*-form that is standardly assigned* $\mathbb{T}$⌝ *is both* Σ_n*- and* Π_n*- but not* Δ_n*-representable;*

— *the predicate* ⌜*m.m is the Gödel number of a* Σ_n*-form that is standardly assigned* $\mathbb{T}$⌝ *is* Σ_n*- but not* Π_n*-representable;*

— *the predicate* ⌜*m.m is the Gödel number of a* Π_n*-form that is standardly assigned* $\mathbb{T}$⌝ *is* Π_n*- but not* Σ_n*-representable;*

— *the predicate* ⌜*m.m is the Gödel number of a* Σ_n*- or* Π_n*-form that is standardly assigned* $\mathbb{T}$⌝ *is* Δ_{n+1}*- but neither* Σ_n*- nor* Π_n*-representable.*

We can now see that even so subtle a logician as A. N. Prior was incautious in concluding from Tarski's results that "No sentence in any language considered by Tarski can discuss ... the truth or falsehood of other sentences of its own language" (*1971*, p. 100: the exact significance of "discuss" is not relevant): that that is at least vague should have been clear from Theorem II of Tarski's paper (*1933*, p. 255). Even the more precise remark that "an assertion *about* the truth or falsehood of a sentence cannot itself be true or false in the language or level or stage of a language to which the sentence itself belongs" (*1962*, p. 134) is not sufficiently accurate to capture the facts as summarized in Theorems X.2.1 and X.2.2: the inaccuracy is located in the assumption that truth and falsehood are *symmetrical* in point of 'discussability'—that negation, as it were, *makes no difference*; but in the arithmetical hierarchy the

[1] But it is a corollary of the last theorem that the *binary* predicate '*mn.m* is the Gödel number of a Σ_n-provable form' is not representable—otherwise the predicate of Tarski's Theorem would be representable. By contrast, '*mn.m* is the Gödel number of a Σ_n-form' is Δ_1-representable.

difference negation makes is reflected in the oscillation between Σ and Π. (The point, buried in the—obscure and apparently technical—distinction between recursiveness and recursive enumerability, only became widely understood in the years after Prior wrote; but the incautious conclusion is still frequently drawn.)

Let us now justify a couple of earlier claims. First, in IV.4 it was said that not all decidable predicates are Δ-representable: the theorem provides an example. Secondly, in V.5 it was said that there is an operation that is elementary in Kalmár's relational sense but not in his operational sense: the proof of Theorem III.3.3 shows that

$$|\mathrm{xz}.((\mathbf{\Delta fm}[\mathrm{x}] \wedge \mathbf{\Sigma pr}[\mathrm{x}]) \supset \exists \mathrm{y}<\mathrm{z}'.(\mathbf{Cl\Sigma tb}[\mathrm{y}] \wedge \mathrm{x}=\mathbf{tpfm}[\mathrm{y}]))|$$

has a choice function that is elementary in the weaker sense, but—arguing as in the penultimate paragraph of IX.4 (relying on the first part of Theorem X.2.2 rather than IX.3.1)—it is clear that it doesn't have one that is so in the stronger sense (cf. IV.1, *ad fin*).

X.3 The ability to "discuss truth and falsehood within the language", in the limited way made available in the last section, was exploited by Mostowski and Montague (*1952a*, *1961*) to solve the following problem: The set **P** is infinite—but is it necessarily so? Could its formal deductive powers be exercised by a finite set? Might not a judicious selection of Deducible forms amount to a *finite* version of it? Freely adapting their methods, we shall see that it is *necessarily* infinite.

We need a couple of preliminary results; first, proceeding as we did in Theorem VIII.8.1 (relying on Theorem X.1.1 rather than III.2.1) we have:

THEOREM X.3.1. *For each number n and any Σ_n-sentence-form X,*

$$(\mathbf{\Sigma}_n\mathbf{pr}[{}^*X^*] \equiv X)$$

is Deducible.

(Throughout this section we restrict attention to the Σ-side of the hierarchy; but analogous things are true for the Π-side, too.)

Next we state, without its somewhat complicated proof,

THEOREM X.3.2. *For each number n,*

$$\forall \mathrm{x}.(\mathbf{Fmdbl}_{\mathbf{\Sigma}_n\mathbf{pr}}[\mathrm{x}] \supset \mathbf{\Sigma}_n\mathbf{fm}[\mathrm{x}] \supset \mathbf{\Sigma}_n\mathbf{pr}[\mathrm{x}])$$

is Deducible.

By Gödel's Second Theorem we know that there is an *infinite* set of Deducible grounded forms—viz. **P**—such that there is a representation P of ⌜$n.n$ is the Gödel number of one of its members⌝ for which $\sim\exists$x.(**Fmdbl**$_P$[x] $\wedge$ **Fmdbl**$_P$[**ngn**[x]]) is not Deducible.[1] By contrast, in the paper mentioned Mostowski showed that for any *finite* set of Deducible grounded forms there is a representation P of ⌜$n.n$ is the Gödel number of one of its members⌝ for which $\sim\exists$x.(**Fmdbl**$_P$[x] $\wedge$ **Fmdbl**$_P$[**ngn**[x]]) *is* Deducible.

To see this, suppose $X_1, \ldots, X_k$ are Deducible grounded forms. Then, for some number n, each is a Σ_n-form and so, by Theorem X.3.1, $\mathbf{\Sigma}_n$**pr**[*it*] is Deducible. If P is x.(x = *X_1* $\vee \ldots \vee$ x = *X_k*), it follows that $\forall$x.(P[x] $\supset$ $\mathbf{\Sigma}_n$**pr**[x]) is Deducible, whence, obviously, so is $\forall$x.(**Fmdbl**$_P$[x] $\supset$ **Fmdbl**$_{\mathbf{\Sigma}_n\mathbf{pr}}$[x]) and thus, by Theorem X.3.2, $\forall$x.(**Fmdbl**$_P$[x] $\supset$ $\mathbf{\Sigma}_n$**fm**[x] $\supset$ $\mathbf{\Sigma}_n$**pr**[x]). Consequently, as $\bar{0} = \bar{1}$ is a Σ_n-form and so $\mathbf{\Sigma}_n$**fm**[*$\bar{0} = \bar{1}$*] is Deducible, $\sim$**Fmdbl**$_P$[*$\bar{0} = \bar{1}$*] is Deducible. Thence the result.

It follows that there is no pair $\langle S, P\rangle$ such that S is a finite set of Deducible grounded forms and P a representation of the appropriate predicate for which $\forall$x.(**Dbl**[x] $\supset$ **Fmdbl**$_P$[x]) is Deducible; and Mostowski managed to show, by an ingenious manoeuvre, that in fact there is no such pair for which $\forall$x.(**Dbl**[x] $\supset$ **Fmdbl**$_P$[x]) is even standardly assigned $\mathbb{T}$—i.e. that no finite set of Deducible grounded forms is an extension of **P**.

Mostowski's manoeuvre need not detain us, however, for there is a still more general result in the offing, which is more easily proved. Let us say that one set S of sentence-forms is *reducible to* another T just in case there is a singulary descriptor-form r such that, for each grounded form X, there is a grounded form $\check{X}$ for which

(1) $S \vdash r$[*X*] = *$\check{X}$*;

(2) $S \vdash (\check{X} \supset X)$;

(3) $T \vdash \check{X}$ if $S \vdash X$.

Obviously an extension S of **R** is reducible to T if T is an extension of S or S is a finite extension of T: **R** itself is reducible to **Q**, and **Q** is reducible to the empty set as in the proof of Theorem IX.3.6—but note that it doesn't follow that **R** is reducible to the empty set (which perhaps makes the choice of term rather poor: the notion is

[1] Feferman observed (*1960*, Theorem 5.10) that there is another representation Q of the same predicate for which $\sim\exists$x.(**Fmdbl**$_Q$[x] $\wedge$ **Fmdbl**$_Q$[**ngn**[x]]) *is* Deducible—namely w.(**P**[w] $\wedge$ $\sim\exists$v<w.$\exists$x.(**Dbl**′[v,x] $\wedge$ **Dbl**′[v,**ngn**[x]])), **Dbl**′ being the binary predicate-form with prefix vx whose matrix is just like that of **Dbl** except for having (**P**[pt[w,z]] $\wedge$ pt[w,z] < v) where the other has **P**[pt[w,z]].

closely connected with that of eliminability described in *Kleene 1952*, §74). More interestingly, **P** is reducible to $\mathbf{P}^{a,m}$, the set consisting of just those members of **P** in which the descriptor-letter e doesn't occur: for there is a ternary Δ-predicate-form E, in which e doesn't occur, such that $\forall x.\forall y.\forall z.(E[x,y,z] \equiv (x^y)=z)$ is Deducible (cf. *Pudlák*).

Our main result is based on Theorem 19 of *Kreisel & Levy*:

THEOREM X.3.3. *For each number n: no extension of* **P** *is reducible to any set of Σ_n-forms with which it is formally compatible.*

PROOF. Let S be an extension of **P**, and suppose it reducible to a set T of Σ_n-forms; we shall show that S is then formally incompatible with T.

Let P be $\mathbf{\Sigma_n pr}$, r be the 'reducer' and C be Carnap's fixed-point for $x.\sim\mathbf{Fmdbl}_P[r[x]]$. Then, by condition (1) of the definition,

$$S \vdash (\mathbf{Fmdbl}_P[r[{}^*C^*]] \supset \mathbf{Fmdbl}_P[{}^*\check{C}^*]).$$

Now $\check{C}$ is a grounded form and so there is a number m greater than n such that it is a Σ_m-form; letting Q be $\mathbf{\Sigma_m pr}$, we know from Theorems X.3.1 and X.3.2 that $(\mathbf{Fmdbl}_Q[{}^*\check{C}^*] \supset \check{C})$ is Deducible; hence, as $\forall x.(P[x] \supset Q[x])$ is Deducible, $(\mathbf{Fmdbl}_P[{}^*\check{C}^*] \supset \check{C})$ is Deducible; thus

$$S \vdash (\mathbf{Fmdbl}_P[r[{}^*C^*]] \supset \check{C}).$$

Consequently, by condition (2) of the definition,

$$S \vdash (\mathbf{Fmdbl}_P[r[{}^*C^*]] \supset C).$$

However, by Carnap's Lemma,

$$S \vdash (\sim\mathbf{Fmdbl}_P[r[{}^*C^*]] \supset C).$$

Hence

$$S \vdash C$$

and so, by condition (3) of the definition,

$$T \vdash \check{C}.$$

Now, for each member X of T, $S \cup T \vdash \mathbf{Fmdbl}_P[{}^*X^*]$—$S \cup T$ being the union of S and T: for X is a Σ_n-form and so, by Theorem X.3.1, $(X \supset P[{}^*X^*])$ is Deducible, whence trivially so is $(X \supset \mathbf{Fmdbl}_P[{}^*X^*])$; however, $S \cup T$ is an extension of **P** and so $S \cup T \vdash (X \supset \mathbf{Fmdbl}_P[{}^*X^*])$; and $S \cup T \vdash X$.

Consequently, by the following Lemma, for each form X that is formally deducible from T, $S \cup T \vdash \mathbf{Fmdbl}_P[{}^*X^*]$—in particular,

$$S \cup T \vdash \mathbf{Fmdbl}_P[{}^*\check{C}^*].$$

Hence, by condition (1) of the definition,

$$S \cup T \vdash \mathbf{Fmdbl}_P[r[{}^*C^*]]$$

and so, by Carnap's Lemma,

$$S \cup T \vdash \sim C.$$

Thus $S \vdash C$ and $S \cup T \vdash \sim C$, and so $S \cup T$ is inconsistent.

Lemma. If X is formally deducible from $Y_1, \ldots, Y_k$, then

$$(\mathbf{Fmdbl}_P[{}^*Y_1{}^*] \supset \ldots \supset \mathbf{Fmdbl}_P[{}^*Y_k{}^*] \supset \mathbf{Fmdbl}_P[{}^*X^*])$$

is Deducible for any singulary predicate-form P.

Proof. For then $\vdash (Y_1 \supset \ldots \supset Y_k \supset X)$ and so, letting Λ be $\mathrm{x.x} \neq \mathrm{x}$, $\mathbf{Fmdbl}_\Lambda[{}^*(Y_1 \supset \ldots \supset Y_k \supset X)^*]$ is standardly assigned $\mathbb{T}$ and thus, as a Σ-form, Deducible. But now $\forall \mathrm{x}.(\Lambda[\mathrm{x}] \supset P[\mathrm{x}])$ is Deducible and hence so is $\forall \mathrm{x}.(\mathbf{Fmdbl}_\Lambda[\mathrm{x}] \supset \mathbf{Fmdbl}_P[\mathrm{x}])$. Thus $\mathbf{Fmdbl}_P[{}^*(Y_1 \supset \ldots \supset Y_k \supset X)^*]$ is Deducible. Finally, we know that $\forall \mathrm{x}.\forall \mathrm{y}.(\mathbf{Fmdbl}_P[\mathbf{hk}[\mathrm{x},\mathrm{y}]] \supset \mathbf{Fmdbl}_P[\mathrm{x}] \supset \mathbf{Fmdbl}_P[\mathrm{y}])$ is Deducible from VIII.8. The result follows.

Q.E.D.

Corollary X.3.4. **Rabin's Theorem.** *For each number n: no consistent set of Σ_n-forms is an extension of* **P**.

Corollary X.3.5. **Ryll-Nardjewski's Theorem.** *No finite set of Deducible forms is an extension of* **P**.

The arguments used in *Rabin* and *Ryll-Nardjewski* to establish their corollaries were quite different from the present one, relying as they did on complex model-theoretic considerations.

X.4 For a final illustration of the uses to which the restricted 'truth-predicates' may be put, we discuss a certain improvement of the Correctness and Adequacy Theorems for Regular Tableaux. These, we recall—cf. A.10—amount to this: *for any sentence-form X, $\vdash X$ iff every assignment assigns $\mathbb{T}$ to X.* The result was progressively improved by Bernays, Kleene and Putnam to obtain: *for any sentence-form X, $\vdash X$ iff every* Putnam *assignment assigns $\mathbb{T}$ to X*— where a *Putnam* assignment is an assignment A for which there is a singulary Δ_2-predicate-form U such that $|U|$ is the universe of A and, for each l that is $*$ or a non-logical letter, there is a Δ_2-form $\underline{l}$ of the appropriate kind such that A assigns $|\underline{l}|$ to l (*Hilbert & Bernays* II, pp. 202–53; *Kleene 1952*, Theorem 35; *Putnam*).

Given a Putnam assignment A we can easily write down, for

each sentence-form, *grounded* sentence-forms that are standardly assigned $\mathbb{T}$ just in case A assigns $\mathbb{T}$ to the original: we shall call them its *Putnam instances*—they are just what it is translated into by the formal translations associated, in the obvious way, with A. So the refined version of the result can be put like this: *for any sentence-form X, $\vdash X$ iff every Putnam instance of X is standardly assigned* $\mathbb{T}$.

Next, note that there is a uniform effective procedure for associating, with any sentence-form, a least number n such that either all its Putnam instances are Σ_n-forms or all its Putnam instances are Π_n-forms: in the first case we shall call it a $\Sigma_n^\bullet$-form and in the second case a $\Pi_n^\bullet$-form—e.g., $\forall y.\exists x.(Pxy \supset \forall x.Pxy)$ is a $\Pi_4^\bullet$-form, as you can see by testing a few cases (for example,

take U to be $\quad x.(\forall z.V[x,z] \vee \exists z.W[x,z])$
and $\underline{P}$ to be $\quad xy.(\forall z.R[x,y,z] \wedge \exists z.S[x,y,z])$

where V, W, R and S are Δ_1-forms).

So we have

THEOREM X.4.1. *For each number n:*

(a) *for any $\Sigma_n^\bullet$-sentence-form X, $\vdash X$ iff every Putnam instance of X is Σ_n-provable;*

and

(b) *for any $\Pi_n^\bullet$-sentence-form X, $\vdash X$ iff every Putnam instance of X is Π_n-provable.*

In fact, given appropriately selected representations of the various predicates involved, we have that, *for each number n,*

$$\forall x.(\boldsymbol{\Sigma_n^\bullet}\mathbf{fm}[x] \supset (\mathbf{Fmdbl}_\Lambda[x] \equiv \forall y.(\mathbf{Pminst}[y,x] \supset \boldsymbol{\Sigma}_n\mathbf{pr}[y])))$$

and

$$\forall x.(\boldsymbol{\Pi_n^\bullet}\mathbf{fm}[x] \supset (\mathbf{Fmdbl}_\Lambda[x] \equiv \forall y.(\mathbf{Pminst}[y,x] \supset \boldsymbol{\Pi}_n\mathbf{pr}[y])))$$

are Deducible, Λ being $x.x \neq x$.

Envoi

... a very intricate theorem and can be worked out with algebra but you would want to take it by degrees with rulers and cosines and familiar other instruments and then at the wind-up not believe what you had proved at all. If that happened you would have to go back over it till you got a place where you could believe your own facts and figures as exactly delineated from Hall and Knight's Algebra and then go on again from that particular place till you had the whole pancake properly believed and not have bits of it half-believed or a doubt in your head hurting you like when you lose the stud of your shirt in the middle of the bed.

The Dalkey Archive

Appendix: Terminological Matters

A.1 The discussion of formal arithmetic in this book is carried out in terms of a large number of concepts drawn from linguistics, logic, semantics, set-theory, and arithmetic itself; all of these are familiar but are known under different names in the work of different authors. It is the purpose of this appendix to fix the necessary terminology, to which reference may be made as required.

A.2 A *sentence* is an ordinary grammatical sentence of (logico-mathematical) English, such as 'The product of two and three is less than six' and 'Every even number is the sum of two primes'. *Subjects* are noun-phrases occurring in sentences, though not all such noun-phrases are subjects—'every even number' is not: an attempt to make it plausible that the notion of a subject "is in principle capable of being supplied with precise criteria which are formal and linguistic" is made in *Dummett 1973*, ch. 4.

A *predicate* is the result of prefixing variables and a full point to what results from substituting the variables for subjects in a sentence: e.g. '*m*. The product of *m* and three is less than six', '*n*. The product of two and three is less than *n*', '*mn*. The product of *m* and three is less than *n*', '*mn*.*m* is less than *n*'.[1] Predicates are *singulary*, *binary*, *ternary*, *quaternary*, etc., according as the number of prefixed variables is one, two, three, four, etc. The result of *applying* a predicate *to* a sequence of expressions (of appropriate length) is what results from substituting the expressions for the variables: e.g.

[1] Russell writes '$\hat{x}$(x is mortal)', meaning that which "we are justified in treating ... as the class defined by" the propositional function '$\hat{x}$ is mortal' (*1908*, VII).

the result of applying '*mn.m* is less than *n*' to $\langle$'three','two'$\rangle$ is 'Three is less than two'; the result of applying it to $\langle$'the product of two and three', 'six'$\rangle$ is 'The product of two and three is less than six'.

Descriptors are to subjects as predicates are to sentences: thus '*n.* the product of two and *n*' and '*mn.* the product of *m* and *n*' are descriptors, and the result of applying the latter to $\langle$'six', 'the sum of two and three'$\rangle$ is 'the product of six and the sum of two and three'.

A.3 A predicate is *true of* a sequence of things (of appropriate length) just in case the result of applying it to a corresponding sequence of subjects that denote those things is true: e.g. '*mn.m* is less than *n*' is true of $\langle 2,3\rangle$ but not of $\langle 3,2\rangle$. Note that the only predicates we have to do with are those that are extensional, in the sense that the results of applying them to different sequences of co-denoting subjects are either all true or all false.

The sequences of objects of which a predicate is true *satisfy* it, and are *members of*, or are *in*, its *extension*. *Sets* are the extensions of singulary predicates; *relations* the extensions of non-singulary predicates. Thus relations are binary, ternary, quaternary, etc. Two predicates are *co-extensive* just in case each is true of what the other is true of; in such a case, the extension of one is the *same relation as* that of the other. We sometimes write, e.g. in the binary case, ⌜$\{mn. \ldots m \ldots n \ldots\}$⌝ in place of ⌜the extension of ⌜$mn. \ldots m \ldots n \ldots$⌝⌝; so $\{mn.m$ is less than or equal to $n\}$ is the same relation as $\{mn.m$ is no greater than $n\}$. A relation is *over* a set iff all the terms of its members are members of the set.

Let k be a positive natural number. The *complement of* a k-ary relation *in* a set is that one whose members are those k-tuples of members of the set that are not members of the relation: e.g. in the set of natural numbers, the complement of $\{mn.m$ is greater than $n\}$ is $\{mn.m$ is less than or equal to $n\}$. The *union of* a pair of k-ary relations is that one whose members are members either of one or of the other.

Given a $k+1$-ary relation, its *values for* a k-tuple $\langle m_1, \ldots, m_k\rangle$ are those things n for which $\langle m_1, \ldots, m_k, n\rangle$ is a member of the relation; and its *arguments* are those k-tuples for which there are values; its *domain* is the relation whose members are its arguments; and its *range* is the set whose members are its values. Thus the arguments of $\{mn.\ 9m=n^2$ or $9m=(n+1)^2\}$ are the square numbers, and it has two values for each non-zero argument. A k-ary *function* is a $k+1$-ary relation that has only one value for each argument, such as $\{mn.\ 9m=n^2\}$. A k-ary *operation on* a set is a k-ary function whose arguments are the k-tuples of members of the set, and all of whose values are members of the set: thus $\{mn.\ 9m^2=n^2\}$ is an operation on the set of natural numbers, but $\{mn.\ 9m=n^2\}$ is not.

A.4 *Finite sequences*, which entered so largely into the definitions in A.2 and A.3, are mathematical objects, each of a certain *length* (a positive natural number) and having certain *terms*, one and only one for each number between 1 and its length: its *first*, *second*, *third*, *fourth*, etc. terms. Finite sequences of length n are n-tuples; *pairs*, *triples*, *quadruples*, etc. are 2-, 3-, 4-tuples. For any pair of finite sequences, the first is the *same sequence as* the second just in case they are of the same length, and have the same terms in the same order.

We write $\ulcorner\langle\sigma_1,\sigma_2,\ldots,\sigma_l\rangle\urcorner$ in place of $\ulcorner$the finite sequence of length l whose first, second, ..., l^{th} terms are respectively $\sigma_1,\sigma_2,\ldots,\sigma_l\urcorner$; so $\langle 7,3^2,4-1\rangle$ is the same sequence as $\langle 6+1,9,\sqrt{9}\rangle$.

The concept of a sequence is sometimes explained as that of a certain kind of relation—viz. of a function whose domain is an initial segment of the series of natural numbers. But notice that relations themselves are only understood insofar as the idea of a predicate's being true of a finite sequence is understood.

Given a finite sequence σ whose terms are themselves finite sequences, the *concatenation of* σ is that finite sequence whose terms are, in order, those of the terms of σ: thus the concatenation of $\langle\langle 2,3,0\rangle,\langle 1,\langle 21,7\rangle\rangle,\langle\langle 9\rangle\rangle\rangle$ is $\langle 2,3,0,1,\langle 21,7\rangle,\langle 9\rangle\rangle$.

A.5 One, and only one, *formal language* is considered in this book; its simple signs, called *letters*, fall exhaustively and exclusively into classes as follows:

— denumerably many *subject-letters*
— denumerably many n-ary *descriptor-letters*, for each number $n>0$
— denumerably many *sentence-letters*
— denumerably many n-ary *predicate-letters*, for each number $n>0$
— denumerably many *variables*
— the *null* letter $*$ and the *identity* letter $=$
— three *connectives* $\sim$, $\wedge$ and $\vee$
— two *quantifiers* $\forall$ and $\exists$, and the *description operator* ι
— three *punctuation marks* (,), .

(In two allusive discussions, those of the Recursion Theorem and of Tarski's 'definition of arithmetical truth', we suppose the formal language to contain denumerably many variables of a further kind: then we distinguish the ordinary variables as *subject* variables and the others as *singulary predicate* variables.) The subject-, descriptor-, sentence- and predicate-letters are collectively known as the *non-logical* letters.

Since there are denumerably many classes, each containing countably many letters, there are denumerably many letters, and we stipulate that they are given according to some fixed and standard well-ordering, so that we may refer to the *first*, *second*, *third*, ... letter. In particular, we take u, v, w, x, y, z, p, t to be the first eight variables, L to be the first binary predicate-letter, and a, m, e to be the first three binary descriptor-letters. The well-ordering of the letters induces, in any of a number of familiar ways, well-orderings of the *expressions*, which are finite sequences of letters; again, we fix one of these well-orderings as standard, so that we may refer to the *first*, *second*, *third*, ... expression.

In mentioning expressions we adopt the ordinary convention of suppressing the symbols '⟨', '⟩' and ',' from their descriptions. For example, ⟨∀, x, ., x, =, x⟩ is an expression, which we refer to under the description '∀x.x=x'. In similar fashion, given a finite sequence $\langle e_1, e_2, \ldots, e_n \rangle$ of expressions, we refer to its concatenation, abbreviatedly, as $\ulcorner e_1 e_2 \ldots e_n \urcorner$ rather than, long-windedly, as ⌜the concatenation of $\langle e_1, e_2, \ldots, e_n \rangle$⌝; hence ∀x.x=x is the concatenation of ⟨∀x., x=x⟩. These conventions lead to no confusion in elementary discussion and the gain in perspicuity makes them well worth adopting.

In the writings of some logicians—indeed, some of the best of them—expressions are *linguistic* objects of the same order of being as sentences, subjects and predicates, and so quotation marks are used in displaying or 'mentioning' them. We however take expressions to be *mathematical* objects of the same order of being as numbers, Hilbert spaces and polygons, and so quotation marks are *not* used in displaying them. It is, on this view, as improper to write "The expression '∀x.x=x' has three identical terms" as it is to write "The sequence '⟨7, 2, 3, 2, 1, 2⟩' has three identical terms"; and as proper to write "For any sentence-forms X, Y, Z: $(X \vee Y)$ is formally deducible from Z if either X or Y is" as to write "For any natural numbers k, l, m: $(k+l)$ is greater than m if either k or l is".

Certain expressions are distinguished as 'well-formed', the most important of them being the *subject-forms* and the *sentence-forms*,

which are given by the following recursive definition:
— $*$ is a *subject-form*;
— if b is a subject-letter, then b is a *subject-form*;
— if d is an n-ary descriptor-letter ($n>0$) and $s_1,\ldots,s_n$ are *subject-forms*, then $ds_1\ldots s_n$ is a *subject-form*;
— if p is a sentence-letter, then p is a *sentence-form*;
— if s_1 and s_2 are *subject-forms*, then $s_1=s_2$ is a *sentence-form*;
— if Q is an n-ary predicate-letter ($n>0$) and $s_1,\ldots,s_n$ are *subject-forms*, then $Qs_1\ldots s_n$ is a *sentence-form*;
— if X and Y are *sentence-forms*, so are $\sim X$, $(X \vee Y)$ and $(X \wedge Y)$;
— if α is a variable, and M is the result of substituting it for a subject-letter in a *sentence-form*, then $\exists\alpha.M$ and $\forall\alpha.M$ are *sentence-forms* and $\iota\alpha.M$ is a *subject-form*.

Thus, for example, by the first and fifth clauses, $*=*$ is a sentence-form; if b is a subject-letter, by the first, second and fifth clauses, $b=*$ and $b=b$ are sentence-forms; hence, by the eighth clause, $\exists\mathrm{x}.\mathrm{x}=*$ and $\forall\mathrm{x}.\mathrm{x}=\mathrm{x}$ are sentence-forms and $\iota\mathrm{x}.\mathrm{x}=*$ is a subject-form, remembering that x is the fourth variable. Again, $\exists\mathrm{x}.\mathrm{Lx}*$ and $\forall\mathrm{x}.\mathrm{Lxx}$ are sentence-forms and $\iota\mathrm{x}.\mathrm{Lx}*$ is a subject-form, remembering that L is the first binary predicate-variable. Further, by the fifth clause, $\iota\mathrm{x}.\mathrm{Lx}*=b$ is a sentence-form and, by the sixth, $\mathrm{L}\iota\mathrm{x}.\mathrm{Lx}*b$ is a sentence-form. And so on.

Where no confusion can arise, we write

$$\ulcorner s_1\neq s_2\urcorner \text{ in place of } \ulcorner \sim s_1=s_2\urcorner$$
$$\ulcorner (X\supset Y)\urcorner \text{ in place of } \ulcorner (\sim X\vee Y)\urcorner$$
$$\ulcorner (X\equiv Y)\urcorner \text{ in place of } \ulcorner ((Y\supset X)\wedge(X\supset Y))\urcorner$$
$$\ulcorner (Z_1\wedge Z_2\wedge\ldots\wedge Z_n)\urcorner \text{ in place of } \ulcorner (Z_1\wedge(Z_2\wedge(\ldots\wedge Z_n)\ldots))\urcorner$$
$$\ulcorner (Z_1\vee Z_2\vee\ldots\vee Z_n)\urcorner \text{ in place of } \ulcorner (Z_1\vee(Z_2\vee(\ldots\vee Z_n)\ldots))\urcorner$$
$$\ulcorner (Z_1\supset Z_2\supset\ldots\supset Z_n)\urcorner \text{ in place of } \ulcorner (Z_1\supset(Z_2\supset(\ldots\supset Z_n)\ldots))\urcorner$$
$$\ulcorner \exists_0\alpha.M\urcorner \text{ in place of } \ulcorner \sim\exists\alpha.M\urcorner$$
$$\ulcorner \exists_{n+1}\alpha.M\urcorner \text{ in place of } \ulcorner \exists\beta.(M^{\alpha}_{\beta}\wedge\exists_n\alpha.(M\wedge\alpha\neq\beta))\urcorner$$

n being a number, $s_1, s_2, X, Y, Z_1, Z_2, \ldots, Z_n, M$ being any expressions at all, α being a variable, β being the first variable different from α that does not occur in M, and M^{α}_{β} being the result of substituting β for α in M.

One expression is *congruent to* another just in case they differ at most as to variables—that is, there is a one-to-one correlation between the variables of one and those of the other such that each is the result of substituting its own variables for the correlated ones in the other; hence

$$\exists x.\forall y.(Lxy \supset \exists z.Lx\iota z.(z=x \wedge Lxz))$$
$$\exists y.\forall x.(Lyx \supset \exists u.Ly\iota u.(u=y \wedge Lyu))$$

are congruent.

A *singular predicate-form* is an expression $\alpha.M$, where α is a variable and M is the result of substituting it for a subject-letter in a sentence-form; then α is its *prefix* and M its *matrix*. It is *applicable to* an expression s just in case s is free for α in M at the free occurrences of α, and then the *result of applying* it *to* s is the result of substituting s for α in M at the free occurrences of α (on 'free', etc., see *Kleene 1952*, §18). If the predicate-form is inapplicable to s, then the *result of applying* it *to* s is the result of applying to s the first form applicable to s to which it is congruent. For example, because $(b=* \supset \exists y.y=b)$ is a sentence-form,

$$x.(x=* \supset \exists y.y=x) \qquad y.(y=* \supset \exists y.y=y)$$

are both singular predicate-forms; the former is applicable to x but not y, the latter to both; and the results of applying them

— to x are $(x=* \supset \exists y.y=x)$ $\qquad$ $(x=* \supset \exists y.y=y)$
— to y are $(y=* \supset \exists \alpha.\alpha=y)$ $\qquad$ $(y=* \supset \exists y.y=y)$

(α being some variable other than y).

The advantage of so arranging matters is that we can say: *if P is a singular predicate-form, then $\exists P$ and $\forall P$ are sentence-forms and ιP a subject-form*; and *the result of applying P to a subject-form is a sentence-form. Binary, ternary, quaternary ... predicate-forms* are defined analogously, with prefixes of two, three, four ... variables. And *descriptor-forms* are so defined that they are to subject-forms as predicate-forms are to sentence-forms. If f is a k-ary predicate- or descriptor-form $(k>0)$ and $e_1,\ldots,e_k$ are expressions, we write

$$\ulcorner f[e_1,\ldots,e_k]\urcorner$$

for

$$\ulcorner \text{the result of applying } f \text{ to } e_1,\ldots,e_k\urcorner.$$

A.6 The direct way to 'interpret' the formal language is to give readings for its well-formed expressions; this is done by providing a universal-predicate and associating with $*$ and each non-logical letter a grammatical expression of the appropriate category—predicates with predicate-letters, etc. Subject to certain conditions, and given the usual conventions for reading the connectives and quantifiers etc., this *dictionary* allows each sentence-form to be read as a sentence. For example, the *standard* dictionaries that feature in the text are those that provide '*m.m* is a (natural) number' as universal predicate, and associate as follows:

L : '*mn*. *m* is less than *n*'
a : '*mn*. the sum of *m* and *n*'
m : '*mn*. the product of *m* and *n*'
e : '*mn*. the nth power of *m*'

so that

$$\forall x.\exists y.\text{Laxxy}$$

is read as

'Every number *m* is such that some number *n* is such that the sum of *m* and *m* is less than *n*'.

In the general case, we say that the sentence *fits* the sentence-form *under* the dictionary; in the particular case, that the sentence *standardly fits* the sentence-form.

For many metalogical purposes, however, it is at least useful to have to hand the notion of a (set-theoretical) *assignment*, which distils from the notion of a dictionary what are taken to be its essential features. We select two set-theoretical objects, 𝕋 and 𝔽—it doesn't matter what they are, just that they are two: then an assignment provides a *universal-set*, the *universe of* the assignment, and associates with ∗ and each non-logical letter a set-theoretical object of the appropriate category—relations with predicate-letters, etc.; in more detail, it associates
— with ∗, and each subject-letter, a member of the universe;
— with each *n*-ary descriptor-letter ($n>0$), an *n*-ary operation on the universe;
— with each sentence-letter, one or the other of 𝕋 and 𝔽;
— with each *n*-ary predicate-letter ($n>0$), an *n*-ary relation over the universe.

Given such an assignment *A* and such a letter *l*, we write $\ulcorner|l|_A\urcorner$ for $\ulcorner$what *A* associates with $l\urcorner$.

For any subject-letter *b*, a *b-variant of* an assignment is one that has the same universe and associates the same objects with all letters except perhaps *b* (thus each assignment is a *b*-variant of itself); for a given assignment *A* and member *m* of the universe, we write $\ulcorner A_m^b\urcorner$ in place of $\ulcorner$the *b*-variant of *A* that associates *m* with $b\urcorner$.

Now an assignment *assigns to* each subject- and sentence-form an object of the appropriate category and, for any such assignment *A* and such form *f*, we write $\ulcorner|f|_A\urcorner$ for $\ulcorner$what *A* assigns to $f\urcorner$. If the length of *f*, qua expression, is 1, then $|f|_A$ is what *A* associates with the single letter that occurs in f. For longer forms, the notion is introduced by the following recursive definition (in which $n>0$, d is an n-ary descriptor-letter, Q is an n-ary predicate-letter, $s_1, s_2, \ldots, s_n$ are subject-forms, X and Y are sentence-forms, P is a singulary predicate-form, and b is the first subject-letter that doesn't occur in P):

— $|ds_1 \ldots s_n|_A$ is the value of $|d|_A$ for the argument $\langle |s_1|_A, \ldots, |s_n|_A \rangle$;

— $|s_1 = s_2|_A$ is $\mathbb{T}$ if $|s_1|_A$ is the same member of the universe as $|s_2|_A$; but $\mathbb{F}$ otherwise;

— $|Qs_1 \ldots s_n|_A$ is $\mathbb{T}$ if $\langle |s_1|_A, \ldots, |s_n|_A \rangle$ is a member of $|Q|_A$; but $\mathbb{F}$ otherwise;

— $|{\sim} X|_A$ is $\mathbb{T}$ if $|X|_A$ is not $\mathbb{T}$; but $\mathbb{F}$ otherwise;

— $|(X \vee Y)|_A$ is $\mathbb{T}$ if either $|X|_A$ or $|Y|_A$ is $\mathbb{T}$; but $\mathbb{F}$ otherwise;

— $|(X \wedge Y)|_A$ is $\mathbb{T}$ if both $|X|_A$ and $|Y|_A$ are $\mathbb{T}$; but $\mathbb{F}$ otherwise;

— $|\exists P|_A$ is $\mathbb{T}$ if some member m of the universe is such that $|P[b]|_{A^b_m}$ is $\mathbb{T}$; but $\mathbb{F}$ otherwise;

— $|\forall P|_A$ is $\mathbb{T}$ if every member m of the universe is such that $|P[b]|_{A^b_m}$ is $\mathbb{T}$; but $\mathbb{F}$ otherwise;

— $|\iota P|_A$ is the unique member m of the universe such that $|P[b]|_{A^b_m}$ is $\mathbb{T}$, if there is one and only one such member; but $|{*}|_A$ otherwise.

Assignments also *assign to* predicate- and descriptor-forms appropriate relations and operations: thus, to a singulary predicate-form P, an assignment A assigns the set whose members are those members m of the universe such that $|P[b]|_{A^b_m}$ is $\mathbb{T}$, b being the first subject-letter that doesn't occur in P; to a binary descriptor-form d, it assigns the binary operation on the universe whose values for an argument $\langle m, n \rangle$ is $|d[b,c]|_{A^{bc}_{mn}}$, b and c being the first two subject-letters that don't occur in d; and so forth. Again, we write $\ulcorner |\ldots|_A \urcorner$ for $\ulcorner$what A assigns to $\ldots\urcorner$, and we can easily establish

THEOREM A.6.1. *For any assignment A and singulary predicate-form P,*

— $|\exists P|_A$ *is* $\mathbb{T}$ *iff some member of A's universe is a member of* $|P|_A$*;*

— $|\forall P|_A$ *is* $\mathbb{T}$ *iff every member of A's universe is a member of* $|P|_A$*;*

— $|\iota P|_A$ *is the unique member of A's universe that is a member of* $|P|_A$*, if there is one and only one such member; but* $|{*}|_A$ *otherwise.*

This High Fregean theory of definite descriptions avoids that "imperfection of language", the occurrence of "apparent proper names without any meaning", by a device invented by Carnap and worked out in *Scott*, the significant feature of which is that, for any singulary predicate-forms P and Q,

$$(Q[\imath P] \equiv \begin{pmatrix} (\exists_1 \alpha.P[\alpha] \wedge \forall \alpha.(P[\alpha] \supset Q[\alpha])) \\ \vee (\sim \exists_1 \alpha.P[\alpha] \wedge Q[*]) \end{pmatrix})$$

is assigned $\mathbb{T}$ in every assignment (α being any variable).

Also easily proved are the following two principles:

THEOREM A.6.2. **THE APPLICATION PRINCIPLE.** *For any assignment A and subject-forms $s_1, \ldots, s_n$ ($n>0$),*

— $|d[s_1, \ldots, s_n]|_A$ is the value of $|d|_A$ for the argument $\langle |s_1|_A, \ldots, |s_n|_A \rangle$, if d is an n-ary descriptor-form;

— $|Q[s_1, \ldots, s_n]|_A$ is $\mathbb{T}$ iff $\langle |s_1|_A, \ldots, |s_n|_A \rangle$ is a member of $|Q|_A$, if Q is an n-ary predicate-form.

THEOREM A.6.3. **THE RELEVANCE PRINCIPLE.** *What an assignment assigns to a form is entirely determined by what its universe is and what it assigns to the non-logical letters that occur in the form (and what it assigns to $*$, if either $*$ or $\imath$ occurs in the form): nothing else is relevant.*

In the body of the book our interest is confined to forms in which occur no non-logical letters other than L, a, m, e. With such forms in mind we distinguish the class of *standard* assignments, which have as universe the set of natural numbers and associate with L, a, m, e respectively the extensions of '*mn.m* is less than *n*', '*mn.* the sum of *m* and *n*', '*mn.* the product of *m* and *n*' and '*mn.* the nth power of *m*'. By the Relevance Principle, standard assignments agree on all forms of the specified kind in which neither $*$ nor $\imath$ occur; but they agree on some, such as $\imath$x.$\sim\exists$y.Lyx, and disagree on some, such as $\imath$x.$\exists$y.Lyx, in which either $*$ or $\imath$ occurs: where they agree, we write ⌜what ... is standardly assigned⌝ or, more briefly still, ⌜|...|⌝, in place of ⌜what standard assignments assign to ...⌝—thus $\imath$x.$\sim\exists$y.Lyx is standardly assigned 0 but $\imath$x.$\exists$y.Lyx is not standardly assigned anything (the difference being that $\exists_1$x.$\sim\exists$y.Lyx is standardly assigned $\mathbb{T}$ but $\exists_1$x.$\exists$y.Lyx is standardly assigned $\mathbb{F}$). A consequence of deciding to use this abbreviation is the constant use of the rebarbative phrase 'is standardly assigned $\mathbb{T}$': it would have been pleasant to have been able to avoid it, but the only more attractive expression that suggests itself is 'is true', whose use would have led to immediate confusion of sentence-forms with sentences—a confusion even worse that that with which Frege charged Hilbert, of confusing pseudo-axioms with axioms: "This would seem to constitute a considerable fallacy" (*1906*, p. 402).

Finally, an assignment is a *model of* a set of sentence-forms just in case what it assigns to each member of the set is $\mathbb{T}$.

A.7 We adopt, as 'proof-theory' for the formal language, the elegant technique of the New York school under R. M. Smullyan based upon one-sided semantic tableaux. It is explained in *Smullyan 1968* and *Jeffrey*, but we adapt it slightly.

A *tableau* is a finite sequence of finite sequences of sentence-forms; the terms of the tableau are its *branches*; and the terms of its branches are its *points*. A *regular* tableau is one that is obtained from a one-point tableau by successively applying the following tableau-rules; its branches then all have a common first, or *top*, point and the tableau is *for* that point. Regular tableaux are displayed as inverted trees.

Using Smullyan's notation for displaying his rules (op. cit., pp. 17, 22, 53) we can list ours as follows:

$$\begin{array}{c} \sim X \\ | \\ \bar{X} \end{array}$$

$$\begin{array}{c} (X \vee Y) \\ | \\ Z \end{array} \qquad\qquad \begin{array}{c} (X \wedge Y) \\ \overline{\;\;|\;\;} \\ X \qquad Y \end{array}$$

$$\begin{array}{c} \exists P \\ | \\ P[s] \end{array} \qquad\qquad \begin{array}{c} \forall P \\ | \\ P[b] \end{array}$$

$$\begin{array}{c} s_1 \neq s_2, P[s_i] \\ | \\ P[s_j] \end{array} \qquad \begin{array}{c} Q[\imath P] \\ | \\ \left(\begin{array}{c} (\exists_1 a.P[a] \wedge \forall a.(P[a] \supset Q[a])) \\ \vee (\sim \exists_1 a.P[a] \wedge Q[*]) \end{array} \right) \end{array}$$

$$\begin{array}{c} X \\ \overline{\;\;|\;\;} \\ Y \qquad \sim Y \end{array}$$

where X and Y are sentence-forms and Z is one of them, P and Q are singulary predicate-forms, s is a subject-form, b is a subject-letter that occurs in no form on the branch, s_1 and s_2 are subject-forms and s_i, s_j are each one of them, and a is a variable. We refer to them as the *∼-Rule*, *∨-Rule*, *∧-Rule*, *∃-Rule*, *∀-Rule*, *≠-Rule*, *ɿ-Rule* and *Cut Rule*. For the ∼-Rule we need the notion of the *conjugate*, $\bar{X}$, *of* a sentence-form X:

— if X is $\sim \Upsilon$, for some form Υ, then $\bar{X}$ is Υ;
— if X is $(\Upsilon \vee Z)$ or $(\Upsilon \wedge Z)$, for some forms Υ and Z, then $\bar{X}$ is respectively $(\sim \Upsilon \wedge \sim Z)$ or $(\sim \Upsilon \vee \sim Z)$;
— if X is $\exists P$ or $\forall P$, for some singulary predicate-form P with prefix α, then $\bar{X}$ is respectively $\forall \alpha. \sim P[\alpha]$ or $\exists \alpha. \sim P[\alpha]$;
— in any other case, $\bar{X}$ is $\sim X$.

We may follow Smullyan and further explain that the $\sim$-Rule allows one to subjoin the conjugate of X to any branch passing through $\sim X$; the $\vee$-Rule allows one to subjoin either X or Υ to any branch passing through $(X \vee \Upsilon)$; the $\wedge$-Rule allows one to subjoin both X and Υ to any branch passing through $(X \wedge \Upsilon)$—that is, to 'split the branch'; the $\neq$-Rule allows one to subjoin $P[s_j]$ to any branch passing through *both* $s_1 \neq s_2$ *and* $P[s_i]$.

By way of illustration,

	$\iota x.x=x=*$	1
ι-Rule, 1	$\left(\begin{array}{c}(\exists_1 x.x=x \wedge \forall x.(x=x \supset x=*)) \\ \vee (\sim\exists_1 x.x=x \wedge *=*)\end{array}\right)$	2
$\vee$-Rule, 2	$(\sim\exists_1 x.x=x \wedge *=*)$	3
$\wedge$-Rule, 3	$\sim\exists_1 x.x=x \qquad *=*$	4
$\sim$-Rule, 4	$\forall u.\sim(u=u \wedge \sim\exists x.(x=x \wedge x\neq u))$	5
$\forall$-Rule, 5	$\sim(b=b \wedge \sim\exists x.(x=x \wedge x\neq b))$	6
$\sim$-Rule, 6	$(b\neq b \vee \sim\sim\exists x.(x=x \wedge x\neq b))$	7
$\vee$-Rule, 7	$\sim\sim\exists x.(x=x \wedge x\neq b)$	8
$\sim$-Rule, 8	$\exists x.(x=x \wedge x\neq b)$	9
$\exists$-Rule, 9	$(*=* \wedge *\neq b)$	10
$\wedge$-Rule, 10	$*=* \qquad *\neq b$	11
$\vee$-Rule, 2	$(\exists_1 x.x=x \wedge \forall x.(x=x \supset x=*))$	12
$\wedge$-Rule, 12	$\exists_1 x.x=x \qquad \forall x.(x=x \supset x=*)$	13
$\forall$-Rule, 13	$(c=c \supset c=*)$	14
$\vee$-Rule, 14	$c=*$	15
$\neq$-Rule, 11, 15	$c=b$	16
$\exists$-Rule, 9	$(c=c \wedge c\neq b)$	17
$\wedge$-Rule, 17	$c=c \qquad c\neq b$	18

is a regular tableau with five branches; the annotation at left and right shows the process of application of the rules; b and c are any two subject-letters.

A branch of a regular tableau is *closed* just in case either, for some subject-form s, it passes through $s = s$ or, for some sentence-form X, it passes through both X and $\sim X$. A regular tableau is *closed* just in case all its branches are closed: so the illustration is closed.

A regular tableau is *Cut-free* just in case no application of the Cut Rule need be made in constructing it. There is in fact a uniform effective procedure for associating with any closed regular tableau a Cut-free one for the same form, and so the rule is theoretically dispensable; however, since we have it we can prove the following result, which is very difficult to establish without it:

THEOREM A.7.1. *If there is a closed regular tableau for* $(X \supset Y)$ *then there is one for* Y *if there is one for* X.

PROOF. If σ and τ are closed regular tableaux for $(X \supset Y)$ and X respectively, then

$$
\begin{array}{c}
Y \\
\hline
\sigma \qquad\qquad\qquad \sim(X \supset Y) \\
\mid \\
(\sim \sim X \wedge \sim Y) \\
\hline
\sim \sim X \qquad\qquad\qquad \sim Y \\
\mid \\
\tau
\end{array}
$$

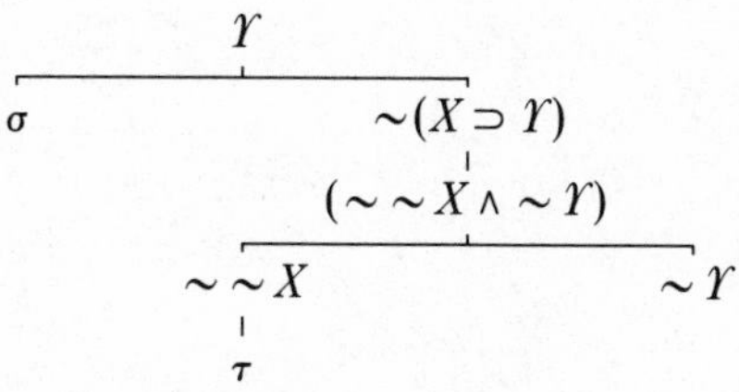

is one for Y: the first rule applied is the Cut Rule.

Q.E.D.

A.8 The sentence-form $(X_1 \supset \ldots \supset X_n)$ is the *hook-up of* the finite sequence $\langle X_1, \ldots, X_n \rangle$ of sentence-forms.[1] Now a *formal deduction of* a sentence-form X *from* a set is a closed regular tableau for the hook-up of a finite sequence whose last term is X and whose other terms (if any) are all members of the set; if there is such a formal deduction, we say that X is *formally deducible from* the set.

For any set S and sentence-forms X and Y, we write

⌜$\vdash X$⌝ in place of ⌜X is formally deducible from $\emptyset$⌝

⌜$S \vdash X$⌝ in place of ⌜X is formally deducible from S⌝

⌜$S, Y \vdash X$⌝ in place of ⌜X is formally deducible from $S \cup \{Y\}$⌝

($\emptyset$ is the empty set; $\{Y\}$ is the set whose only member is Y; $S \cup \{Y\}$ is the union of S and $\{Y\}$).

---

[1] I pronounce '$(X \supset Y)$' as 'ex hooks wy'.

Where S is a set, X, Y and Z are sentence-forms, P is a singulary predicate-form, s is a subject-form, and b is a subject-letter that doesn't occur in P, Z or any member of S:

$S \vdash {\sim}X$ if $S \vdash \bar{X}$	$S \vdash {\sim}X$ only if $S \vdash \bar{X}$
$S \vdash (X \vee Y)$ if $S \vdash X$ or $S \vdash Y$	
$S \vdash (X \wedge Y)$ if $S \vdash X$ and $S \vdash Y$	$S \vdash (X \wedge Y)$ only if $S \vdash X$ and $S \vdash Y$
$S \vdash \exists P$ if $S \vdash P[s]$	
$S \vdash \forall P$ if $S \vdash P[b]$	$S \vdash \forall P$ only if $S \vdash P[s]$
$S, {\sim}X \vdash Z$ if $S, \bar{X} \vdash Z$	$S, {\sim}X \vdash Z$ only if $S, \bar{X} \vdash Z$
$S, (X \vee Y) \vdash Z$ if $S, X \vdash Z$ and $S, Y \vdash Z$	$S, (X \vee Y) \vdash Z$ only if $S, X \vdash Z$ and $S, Y \vdash Z$
$S, (X \wedge Y) \vdash Z$ if $S, X \vdash Z$ or $S, Y \vdash Z$	
$S, \exists P \vdash Z$ if $S, P[b] \vdash Z$	$S, \exists P \vdash Z$ only if $S, P[s] \vdash Z$
$S, \forall P \vdash Z$ if $S, P[s] \vdash Z$	

Fig. 4: some familiar properties of formal deducibility

All the familiar properties of formal deducibility are easily derivable; for example, the 'introduction principles' in the left-hand column and 'elimination principles' in the right-hand column of Fig. 4 (q.v.). Three other very useful principles are that
— if $S \vdash Y$ and $S \vdash \sim Y$ then $S \vdash X$,
— if $S, Y \vdash X$ and $S, \sim Y \vdash X$ then $S \vdash X$, and
— $S \vdash (Y \supset X)$ iff $S, Y \vdash X$,
for any set S and sentence-forms X and Y.

One set is an *extension of* another just in case everything formally deducible from the second is formally deducible from the first: so any set is an extension of each of its subsets. (This use of the word 'extension' has absolutely nothing to do with that in A.3.) A set is *consistent* just in case there is no form X such that both X and $\sim X$ are formally deducible from it. It is easy to show that X is formally deducible from S iff $S \cup \{\sim X\}$ is not consistent.

A.9 Just as a dictionary provides a universal-predicate and associates with $*$ and each non-logical letter a grammatical expression of the appropriate category; and just as an assignment provides a universal-set and associates with $*$ and each non-logical letter a set-theoretical object of the appropriate category; so a *formal translation* provides a *universal-form* and associates with $*$ and each non-logical letter a form of the appropriate category—predicate-forms with predicate-letters, etc.

Then just as a dictionary gives each sentence-form a reading; and just as an assignment assigns to each sentence-form one of $\mathbb{T}$ and $\mathbb{F}$; so also a formal translation *translates* each sentence-form *into* another: for example, if it provides U as universal-form (necessarily a singulary predicate-form) and associates $\underline{\mathrm{L}}$ and $\underline{\mathrm{a}}$ with L and a respectively (necessarily a binary predicate-form and a singulary descriptor-form), then it translates

$$\forall \mathrm{x}.\exists \mathrm{y}.\mathrm{Laxxy}$$

into

$$\forall \mathrm{x}.(U[\mathrm{x}] \supset \exists \mathrm{y}.(U[\mathrm{y}] \wedge \underline{\mathrm{L}}[\underline{\mathrm{a}}[\mathrm{x},\mathrm{x}],\mathrm{y}])).$$

Now consider a formal translation τ and a letter l, other than a sentence- or predicate-letter, with which it associates an appropriate form $\underline{l}$: the *closure-condition on* τ *for* l is the sentence-form
— $U[\underline{l}]$, if l is $*$ or a subject-letter;
— $\forall a_1.\ldots\forall a_n.(U[a_1] \supset \ldots \supset U[a_n] \supset U[\underline{l}[a_1,\ldots,a_n]])$, if l is an n-ary descriptor-letter ($n>0$), where $a_1,\ldots,a_n$ are the first n

variables. (The closure-condition for l corresponds to the requirement, in the theory of assignments, that what is assigned to l be a *member of*, or an *operation on*, the universe.)

The following can now be established (cf. e.g. *Tarski 1956*, pp. 20–26; *Shoenfield*, pp. 61–63):

THEOREM A.9.1. *Given a formal translation, let C be the set of closure-conditions on it: if it translates X into* $\underline{X}$, *and* $\vdash X$ *then* $C \vdash \underline{X}$.

In fact, there is a uniform effective procedure for turning any closed regular tableau for X into one for $(C_1 \supset \ldots \supset C_n \supset \underline{X})$, where $C_1, \ldots, C_n$ are the closure conditions for the non-logical letters that occur in X (and $*$, if either $*$ or $\imath$ occurs in X).

A.10 Two famous results connect the theory of assignments in A.6 with the theory of tableaux in A.7. First we have

THEOREM A.10.1. **THE CORRECTNESS THEOREM FOR REGULAR TABLEAUX.** *If* $\vdash X$ *then every assignment assigns* $\mathbb{T}$ *to X.*

The proof is by mathematical induction—see *Smullyan 1968*, p. 55. We also have the converse:

THEOREM A.10.2. **THE ADEQUACY THEOREM FOR REGULAR TABLEAUX.** *If every assignment assigns* $\mathbb{T}$ *to X, then* $\vdash X$.

A proof is obtainable by making simple modifications to that of Theorem III.3.6, so that, for any sentence-form to which every assignment assigns $\mathbb{T}$, there is a systematically generated regular tableau that is closed and Cut-free (for help with the details, consult op. cit., V §3). Incidentally, while the Cut-Rule is dispensable it is perfectly obvious that none of the others is.

A further modification to the proof just outlined gives

THEOREM A.10.3. *For any set S and sentence-form X:* $S \vdash X$ *iff every model of S is one of X.*

THEOREM A.10.4. *For any set S: S is consistent iff there is a model of S.*

Consider a set of sentence-forms; the forms *relevant to* it are those in which occur no non-logical letters that occur in no member of it: we say that it is *sound* just in case every relevant form that is formally deducible from it is standardly assigned $\mathbb{T}$; and that it is *complete* just in case every relevant form that is standardly assigned $\mathbb{T}$ is formally deducible from it.

These conditions can be weakened slightly, by replacing 'relevant form' by 'relevant form in which ι does not occur': this is because there is a uniform effective procedure for associating with any sentence-form X another Y such that (a) ι doesn't occur in Y; (b) the same non-logical letters occur in both; (c) $\vdash (X \equiv Y)$—thus X and Y are relevant to the same sets, are formally deducible from the same sets, and are each standardly assigned $\mathbb{T}$ if the other is. (These things follow from the fact that, for any singulary predicate-forms P and Q,

$$\vdash (Q[\iota P] \equiv \begin{pmatrix} (\exists_1 \alpha.P[\alpha] \wedge \forall \alpha.(P[\alpha] \supset Q[\alpha])) \\ \vee (\sim \exists_1 \alpha.P[\alpha] \wedge Q[*]) \end{pmatrix})$$

(α being any variable).)

The completeness condition can be further weakened, by replacing 'relevant form' by 'relevant form in which neither ι nor $*$ occurs': this is because there is a uniform effective procedure for associating with any sentence-form X in which ι does not occur another Y such that (a) $*$ doesn't occur in Y; (b) the same non-logical letters occur in both; (c) Y is standardly assigned $\mathbb{T}$ if X is; (d) $\vdash (Y \supset X)$—thus Y is relevant to any set X is and Y is formally deducible from any set X is. (These things follow from the fact that, for any such form X, there is a singulary predicate-form Q in which neither ι nor $*$ occurs such that $Q[*]$ is X; by the Application and Relevance Principles, $\forall Q$ is standardly assigned $\mathbb{T}$ if $Q[*]$ is; and $\vdash (\forall Q \supset Q[*])$.)

The soundness condition, however, *cannot* be weakened in similar fashion: for a counter-example, consider the set whose only member is $\exists$x.Lx$*$, which is unsound although every relevant form in which neither ι nor $*$ occurs that is formally deducible from it is standardly assigned $\mathbb{T}$. (The first thing is true because $\exists$x.Lx$*$ is itself a relevant form that is formally deducible from it but not standardly assigned $\mathbb{T}$; the second is true because, by Theorem A.9.1, any $*$-free form that is formally deducible from $\exists$x.Lx$*$ is also formally deducible from $\exists$y.$\exists$x.Lxy and so, by Theorem A.10.3, is standardly assigned $\mathbb{T}$.)

Notice that any sound set is consistent, for there is no sentence-form X such that both X and $\sim X$ are standardly assigned $\mathbb{T}$. However, {$\exists$x.Lxx} is unsound although consistent.

References

All references are to works listed below; they are ordinarily made by giving the name of the author or editor and the year of the first printed publication in whatever language, both in italics; a further reference to the exact translation or edition used is then added if necessary: but such of this information as is well-known or obvious from the context of the reference may be omitted.

Titles of journals are abbreviated according to the styles of *Lineback* and *Brown & Stratton.*

ANON, 1961: **Infinitistic methods**

ARBIB, M. A., 1966: 'Speed-up theorems and incompleteness theorems', in *Caianiello*

BAR-HILLEL, Y. ET AL., 1966: **Essays on the foundations of mathematics** (edd.)

BARWISE, J., 1977: **Handbook of mathematical logic** (ed.)

BENACERRAF, P., 1965: 'What numbers could not be', *Phil Rev* 74

——— & PUTNAM, H., 1964: **Philosophy of mathematics: selected readings** (edd.)

BETH, E. W., 1959: **The foundations of mathematics**

BROUWER, L. E. J., 1927: 'On the domains of definitions of functions', in *van Heijenoort 1967*

BROWN, P. & STRATTON, G. B., 1963: **World list of scientific periodicals** (edd.)

BURIDAN, J., 1489: **Sophisms on meaning and truth** (tr. 1966)

BURKS, A. W., 1961: **Theory of self-reproducing automata**

CAIANIELLO, E. R., 1966: **Automata theory** (ed.)

CANTOR, G., 1895: 'Contributions to the founding of the theory of transfinite set-theory (first paper)', in *Cantor 1915*

———, 1897: 'Contributions to the founding of the theory of transfinite set-theory (second paper)', in *Cantor 1915*

———, 1915: **Contributions to the founding of the theory of transfinite numbers**

CARGILE, J., 1979: **Paradoxes**

CARNAP, R., 1937: **The logical syntax of language** (enlarged ed.)

CHURCH, A., 1936: 'An unsolvable problem of elementary number theory', in *Davis*
———, 1936a: 'A note on the Entscheidungsproblem', in *Davis*
———, 1956: **Introduction to mathematical logic**
CICHON, E. A., 1983: 'A short proof of two recently discovered independence results using recursion theoretic methods', *Pro. Am. math. Soc.* 87
COHEN, L. J., 1957: 'Can the logic of indirect discourse be formalized?', *J Sym Log* 22
CURRY, H. B., 1942: 'The inconsistency of certain formal logics', *J Sym Log* 7
DAVIDSON, D., 1965: 'Theories of meaning and learnable languages', in *Davidson 1985*
———, 1979: 'Quotation', in *Davidson 1985*
———, 1980: 'Towards a unified theory of meaning and action', *Grazer Phil Stud* 11
———, 1985: **Inquiries into truth and interpretation**
DAVIS, M., 1965: **The undecidable** (ed.)
DEDEKIND, R., 1888: **The nature and meaning of numbers**, in *Dedekind 1905*
———, 1905: **Essays on the theory of numbers**
DREBEN, B. & GOLDFARB, W., 1979: **The decision problem**
DUMMETT, M. A. E., 1963: 'The philosophical significance of Gödel's theorem', in *Dummett 1978*
———, 1973: **Frege—the philosophy of language**
———, 1975: 'Wang's paradox', in *Dummett 1978*
———, 1977: **The elements of intuitionism**
———, 1978: **Truth and other enigmas**
EDWARDS, H., 1977: **Fermat's last theorem**
———, 1988: 'Kronecker's place in history', *Minn Stud Phil Sci* 11
EHRENFEUCHT, A. & MYCIELSKI, J., 1971: 'Abbreviating proofs by adding new axioms', *Bull. Am. math. Soc.* 77
ENDERTON, H. B., 1972: **A mathematical introduction to logic**
ENGELER, E., LÄUCHLI, H. & STRASSEN, V., 1982: **Logic and algorithmic: an international symposium in honour of E. Specker**
ETCHEMENDY, J., 1988: 'Tarski on truth and logical consequence', *J Sym Log* 53
FEFERMAN, S., 1960: 'Arithmetization of mathematics in a general setting', *Fundam. Math.* 49
———, 1962: 'Transfinite recursive progressions of axiomatic theories', *J Sym Log* 27
FREGE, F. L. G., 1879: **Conceptual notation** (tr. 1972)
———, 1884: **The foundations of arithmetic** (tr. 1959)
———, 1893: **The basic laws of arithmetic** (tr. 1964)
———, 1895: 'A critical elucidation of some points ...', in *Frege 1984*
———, 1903: 'On the foundations of geometry: 1st series', in *Frege 1984*
———, 1906: 'On the foundations of geometry: 2nd series', in *Frege 1984*
———, 1918–19: 'Thoughts', in *Frege 1984*
———, 1984: **Collected papers on mathematics, logic, and philosophy**

Friedman, H. & Sheard, M., 1987: 'An axiomatic approach to self-referential truth', *Annals Pure Applied Log* 33

Geach, P. T., 1954: 'On insolubilia', *Analysis* 15

———, 1980: **Reference and generality** (3rd ed.)

Gödel, K., 1931: 'On formally undecidable propositions of *Principia mathematica* and related systems I', in *Gödel 1986*

———, 1931a: letter to Zermelo, 12 October 1931, in *Grattan-Guinness*

———, 1932: 'On completeness and consistency', in *Gödel 1986*

———, 1934: 'On undecidable propositions of formal mathematical systems', in *Gödel 1986*

———, 1936: 'On the length of proofs', in *Gödel 1986*

———, 1947: 'What is Cantor's continuum problem?', in *Benacerraf & Putnam*

———, 1958: 'On a hitherto unexploited extension of the finitary standpoint' (tr. *J Phil Log* 9 (1980))

———, 1961: letter to Burks, 7 November 1961, in *Burks*

———, 1967: letter to Wang, 7 December 1967, in *Wang 1974*

———, 1970: draft letter to Balas, 27 May 1970, in *Wang 1987*

———, 1986: **Collected works, I**

Grattan-Guinness, I., 1976: 'In memoriam Kurt Gödel ...', *Historia Mathematica* 6

Grzegorczyk, A., 1953: 'Some classes of recursive functions', *Rozpr. mat.* 4

Hallett, M., 1984: **Cantorean set theory and limitation of size**

Hardy, G. H., 1929: 'Mathematical proof', *Mind* 38

Harrington, L. A., Morley, M. D., Šćedrov, A. & Simpson, S. G., 1985: **Harvey Friedman's research on the foundations of mathematics** (edd.)

Haugeland, J., 1981: 'Analog and analog', *Phil Topics* 1

Herbrand, J., 1930: **Investigations in proof theory**, ch. 5, in *van Heijenoort 1967*

Hilbert, D., 1899: **The foundations of geometry** (tr. 1902)

———, 1904: 'On the foundations of logic and arithmetic', in *van Heijenoort 1967*

———, 1925: 'On the infinite', in *van Heijenoort 1967*

———, 1927: 'The foundations of mathematics', in *van Heijenoort 1967*

——— & Ackermann, W., 1938: **Principles of mathematical logic** (2nd ed., tr. 1950)

——— & Bernays, P., 1939: **Grundlagen der Mathematik**, vol. 2

Isaacson, D., 1987: 'Arithmetical truth and hidden higher-order concepts', in *Paris Logic Group*

Jeffrey, R. C., 1981: **Formal logic: its scope and limits** (2nd ed.)

Jeroslow, R. G., 1973: 'Redundancies in the Hilbert–Bernays derivability conditions for Gödel's second incompleteness theorem', *J Sym Log* 38

Jones, J. P. & Shepherdson, J. C., 1983: 'Variants of Robinson's essentially undecidable theory **Q**', *Arch. math. Logik GrundlForsch.* 23

Kaplan, D. & Montague, R., 1960: 'A paradox regained', *Notre Dame J Form Log* 1

KIRBY, L. & PARIS, J., 1982: 'Accessible independence results for Peano arithmetic', *Bull. Lond. Math. Soc.* 14

KLEENE, S. C., 1936: 'General recursive functions of natural numbers', in *Davis*

———, 1943: 'Recursive predicates and quantifiers', in *Davis*

———, 1952: **Introduction to metamathematics**

KNEALE, W., 1971: 'Russell's paradox and some others', *Brit J Phil Sci* 22

———, 1972: 'Propositions and truth in natural languages', *Mind* 81

KNEEBONE, G. T., 1963: **Mathematical logic and the foundations of mathematics**

KOCHEN, S. & KRIPKE, S., 1982: 'Non-standard models of Peano arithmetic', in *Engeler et al.*

KÖNIG, J., 1905: 'On the foundations of set theory and the continuum problem', in *van Heijenoort 1967*

KREISEL, G., 1965: 'Mathematical logic', in *Saaty*

———, 1980: 'Kurt Gödel', *Biogr. Mem. Fellows R. Soc.* 26

——— & LÉVY, A., 1968: 'Reflection principles and their use for establishing the complexity of axiomatic systems', *Z. math. Logik* 14

——— & TAKEUTI, G., 1974: 'Formally self-referential propositions for cut-free classical analysis and related systems', *Dissnes math.* 118

LANGFORD, C. H., 1927: 'Theorems on deducibility (second paper)', *Ann. Math.* II, 28

LEVEQUE, W. J., 1956: **Topics in number theory**, vol. 2

LEWIS, D., 1971: 'Analog and digital', *Noûs* 5

LEWIS, H. R., 1979: **Unsolvable classes of quantificational formulas**

——— & PAPADIMITRIOU, C. H., 1975: 'The efficiency of algorithms', *Scient. Am.* 238

LINEBACK, R. H., 1988: **The philosopher's index** (ed.)

LÖB, M. H., 1955: 'Solution of a problem of Leon Henkin', *J Sym Log* 20

MARTIN, R. L., 1984: **Recent essays on truth and the liar paradox** (ed.)

MATES, B., 1986: **The philosophy of Leibniz**

MENDELSON, E., 1964: **Introduction to mathematical logic**

MONTAGUE, R. L., 1961: 'Semantical closure and non-finite axiomatizability I', in *Anon*

———, 1962: 'Theories incomparable with respect to relative interpretability', *J Sym Log* 27

MOSTOWSKI, A., 1947: 'On definable sets of positive integers', *Trans. Am. math. Soc.* 53

———, 1952: **Sentences undecidable in formalized arithmetic: an exposition of the theory of Kurt Gödel**

———, 1952a: 'On models of axiomatic systems', *Fundam. Math.* 39

———, ROBINSON, R. M. & TARSKI, A., 1953: 'Undecidability and essential undecidability in arithmetic', in *Tarski, Mostowski & Robinson*

NELSON, E., 1986: **Predicative arithmetic**

PARIKH, R. J., 1971: 'Existence and feasibility in arithmetic', *J Sym Log* 36

———, 1973: 'Some results on the lengths of proofs', *Trans. Am. math. Soc.* 177

———, 1986: Introduction to *Gödel 1936*

PARIS, J. & HARRINGTON, L., 1977: 'A mathematical incompleteness in Peano arithmetic', in *Barwise*
PARIS LOGIC GROUP, 1987: **Logic colloquium '85** (ed.)
PARSONS, C., 1967: Introduction to *Brouwer*
PEANO, G., 1889: **The principles of arithmetic, presented by a new method**, in *van Heijenoort 1967*
POINCARÉ, J. H., 1902: **Science and hypothesis** (tr. 1952)
———, 1912: **Mathematics and science: last essays** (tr. 1963)
POST, E. L., 1941: 'Absolutely unsolvable problems and relatively undecidable propositions: account of an anticipation', in *Davis*
———, 1947: 'Recursive unsolvability of a problem of Thue', in *Davis*
PRIOR, A. N., 1958: 'Epimenides the Cretan', *J Sym Log* 23
———, 1962: 'Some problems of self-reference in John Buridan', in *Prior 1976*
———, 1971: **Objects of thought**
———, 1976: **Papers in logic and ethics**
PUDLÁK, P., 1983: 'A definition of exponentiation by a bounded arithmetical formula', *Comm. math. Univ. Carol.* 24
PUTNAM, H., 1965: 'Trial and error predicates and the solution to a problem of Mostowski', *J Sym Log* 30
QUINE, W. V. O., 1951: **Mathematical logic** (rev. ed.)
———, 1969: **Set theory and its logic** (rev. ed.)
RABIN, M. O., 1966: 'Non-standard models and independence of the induction axiom', in *Bar-Hillel et al.*
RICHARD, J., 1905: 'The principles of mathematics and the problem of sets', in *van Heijenoort 1967*
RITCHIE, R. W., 1963: 'Classes of predictably computable functions', *Trans. Am. math. Soc.* 106
ROGERS, H., 1967: **Theory of recursive functions and effective computability**
ROSSER, J. B., 1936: 'Extensions of some theorems of Gödel and Church', in *Davis*
RUSSELL, B. A. W., 1900: **The philosophy of Leibniz**
———, 1903: **The principles of mathematics**
———, 1908: 'Mathematical logic as based on the theory of types', in *Russell 1956*
———, 1956: **Logic and knowledge**
RYLE, G., 1949: **The concept of mind**
———, 1951: 'Heterologicality', *Analysis* 10
RYLL-NARDJEWSKI, C., 1952: 'The role of the axiom of induction in elementary arithmetic', *Fundam. Math.* 39
SAATY, T. L., 1965: **Lectures on modern mathematics**, vol. 3
SCHOENMAN, R., 1967: **Bertrand Russell, philosopher of the century** (ed.)
SCHWABHÄUSER, W., SZMIELEW, W. & TARSKI, A., 1983: **Metamathematische Methoden in der Geometrie**
SCOTT, D., 1967: 'Existence and description in formal logic', in *Schoenman*
SHOENFIELD, J. R., 1967: **Mathematical logic**
SMULLYAN, R. M., 1961: **Theory of formal systems**
———, 1968: **First-order logic**

STOCKMEYER, L. J. & CHANDRA, A. K., 1979: 'Intrinsically difficult problems', *Scient. Am.* 240

TAKEUTI, G., 1975: **Proof theory** (1st ed.)

TARSKI, A., 1933: 'The concept of truth in formalized languages', in *Tarski 1956*

———, 1936: 'The establishment of scientific semantics', in *Tarski 1956*

———, 1936a: 'Foundations of the calculus of systems, second part', in *Tarski 1956*

———, 1944: 'The semantic conception of truth and the foundations of semantics', *Phil Phenomenol Res* 4

———, 1953: 'A general method in proofs of undecidability', in *Tarski, Mostowski & Robinson*

———, 1956: **Logic, semantics, metamathematics**

———, MOSTOWSKI, A. & ROBINSON, R. M., 1953: **Undecidable theories**

TURING, A. M., 1936: 'On computable numbers, with an application to the *Entscheidungsproblem*', in *Davis*

VAN HEIJENOORT, J., 1967: **From Frege to Gödel: a source book in mathematical logic 1879–1931** (ed.)

———, 1967a: 'Logic as calculus and logic as language', in *van Heijenoort 1985*

———, 1985: **Selected essays**

———, 1987: 'Système et métasystème chez Russell', in *Paris Logic Group*

VON NEUMANN, J., 1927: 'Zur Hilbertschen Beweistheorie', *Math. Z.* 26

WAISMANN, F., 1936: **Introduction to mathematical thinking** (tr. 1959)

WANG, H., 1974: **From mathematics to philosophy**

———, 1987: **Reflections on Kurt Gödel**

WITTGENSTEIN, L., 1921: **Tractatus logico-philosophicus** (tr. 1961)

———, 1953: **Philosophical investigations**

———, 1967: **Zettel**

———, 1969: **Philosophical grammar** (tr. 1974)

———, 1978: **Remarks on the foundations of mathematics** (rev. ed.)

WRIGHT, C., 1982: 'Strict finitism', *Synthese* 51

———, 1986: **Realism, meaning and truth**

Index

Important passages are indicated by italics